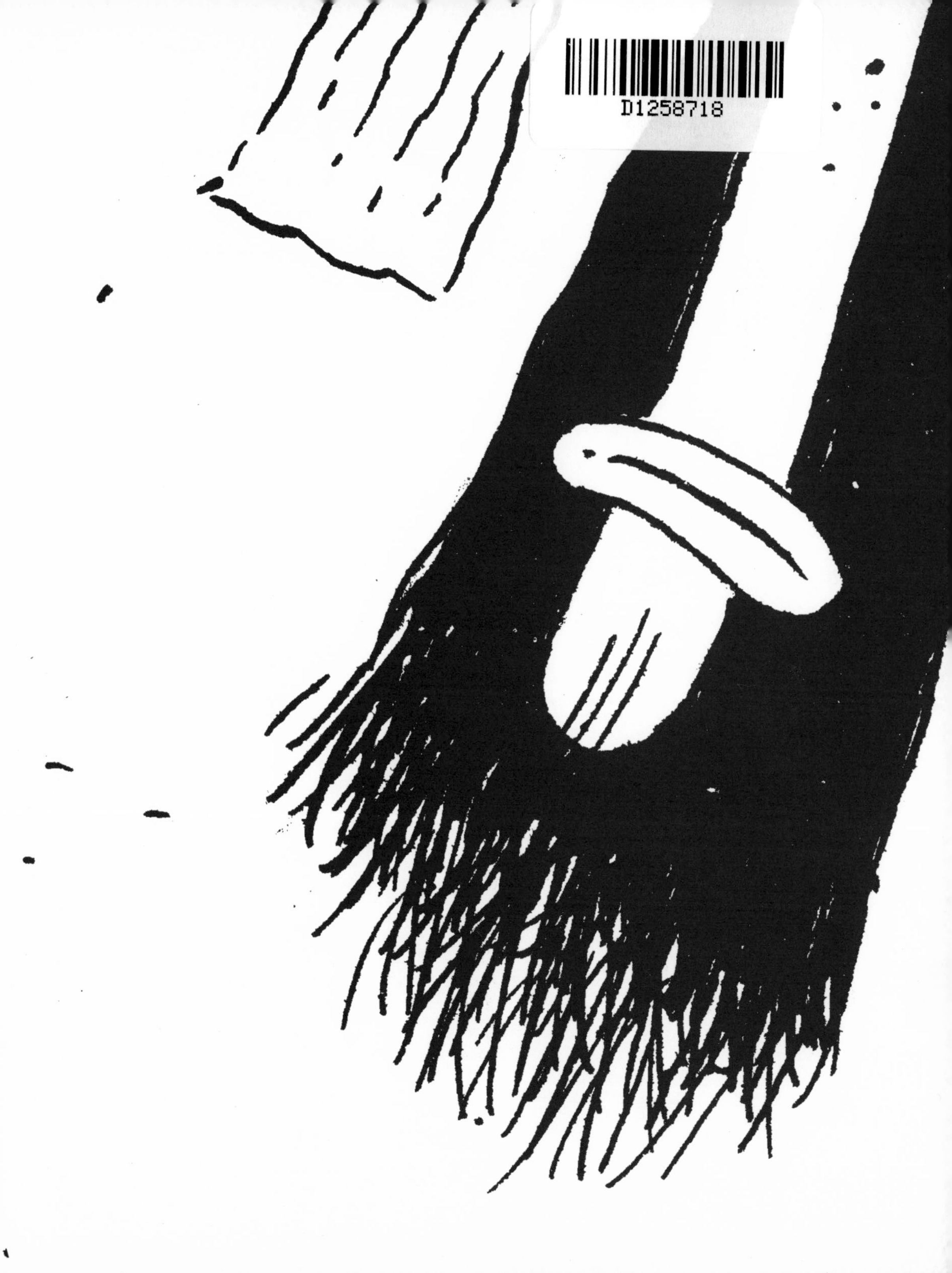

...INKWEED...

Some
Collected
Comics
By

Chris Wright

·2008·
Sparkplug Comic Books
Portland, Oregon

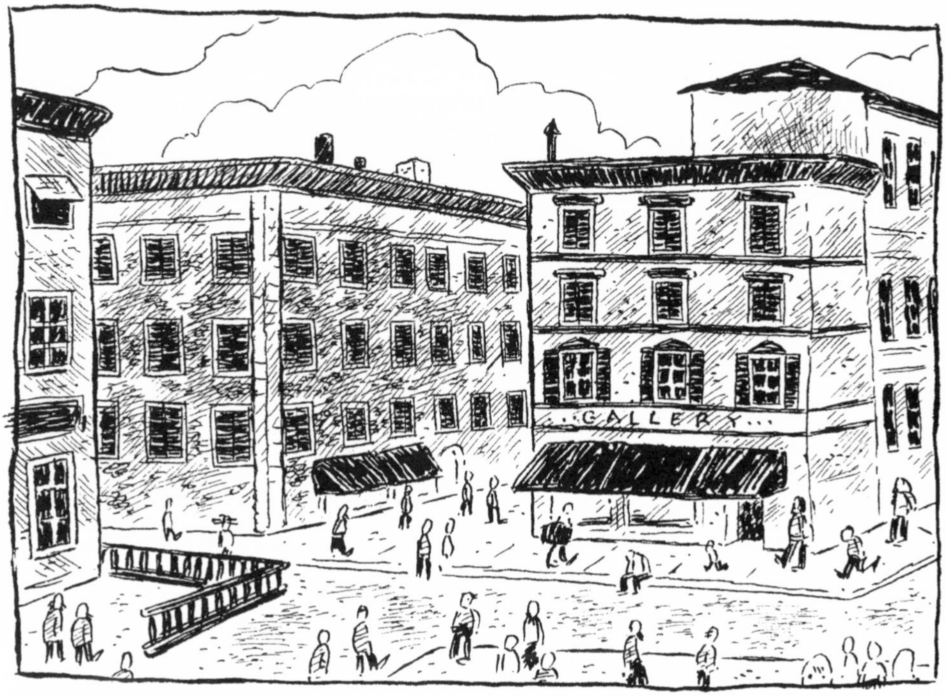
GALLERY

Special thanks to the Savannah crew
for their support and their example

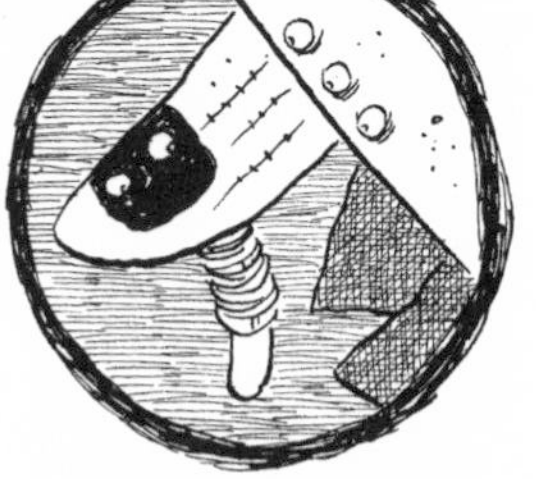

sparkplugcomicbooks.com

Printed in Canada at Westcan Printing Group

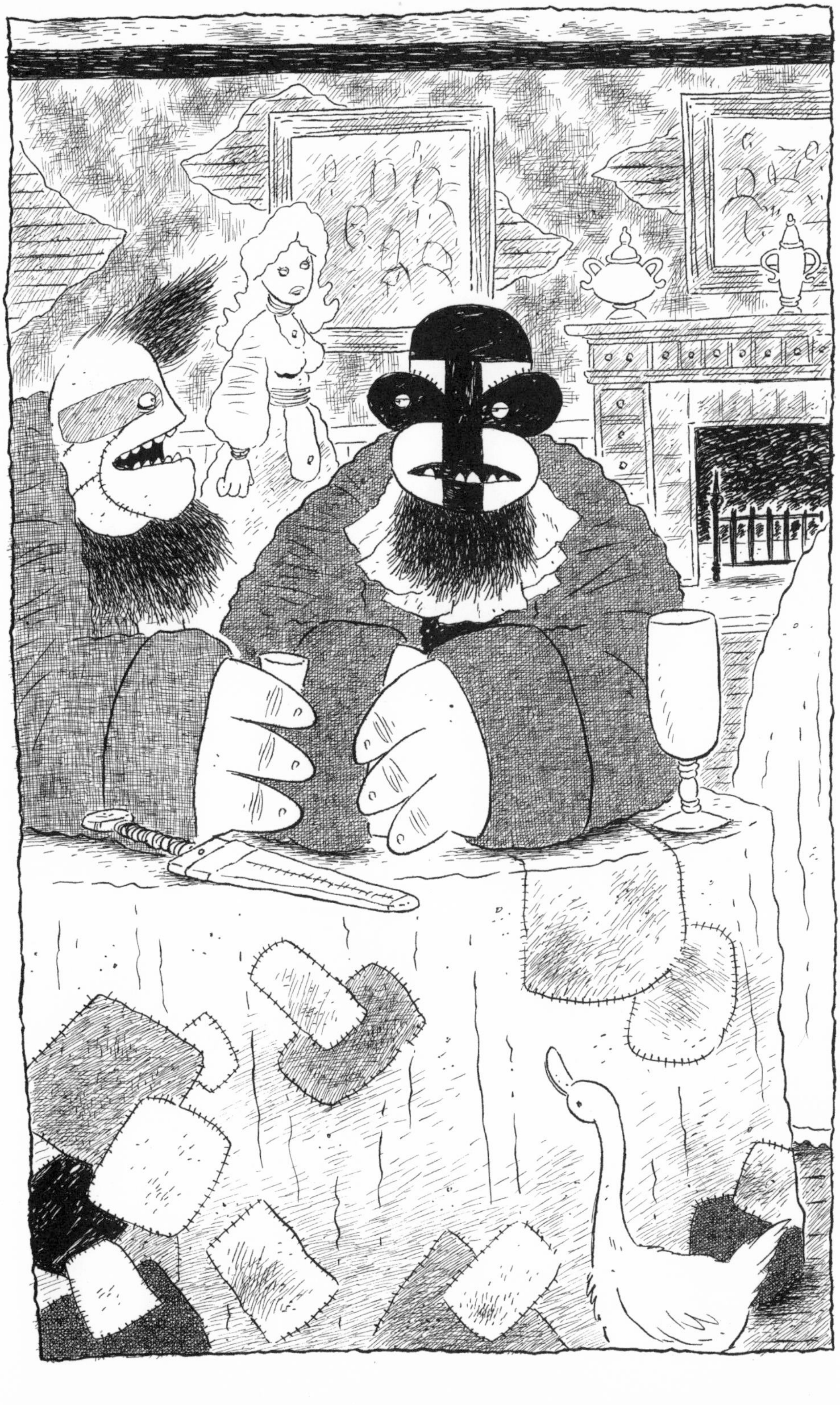

···~~ INKWEED ~~·

···Contents···

PREFACE

F. Scott Fitzgerald syndrome. The awareness that things will never again be as they once were, and that they were never that way to begin with.

My knack for letting go is deficient. I am an emotional packrat. When I look at the original pages contained in this book I am carried back to my old apartments. The sounds, the smells, the food eaten, the movies watched. It is a sense-memory experience... Method comics.

When I look at these old pages I usually pretend that I am pained by my poor perspective, my weak lettering, my too thin lines. But focus on such details only serves to mask the memories of who I was and where I was when I made those lines. I hope this volume will send those memories off. It is their viking funeral.

So! goodbye to those old apartments, goodbye to summer adventures with Matt, and early morning adventures with Doug and David, goodbye to Tybee island at night, goodbye to singing along to "Graceland" at the top of my voice when all my neighbors were gone, goodbye to drinking vodka and playing PS2 until my skills failed me, goodbye to discovering Townes Van Zandt, and Fellini, and Tarkovsky, and Stravinsky, and Yuri Norstein, goodbye to being on the balcony with friends in the old Savannah night, goodbye to the bars and the Spanish moss, goodbye to drinking too much with impunity, goodbye to the girl from Utah whose beauty oppressed and teased me every moment I put pen to paper, and goodbye finally to the pages themselves, I hope they will be at peace. 2002-2007

—Chris Wright
2008

Dedicated to Matt and Doug

The Unmerciful Gift

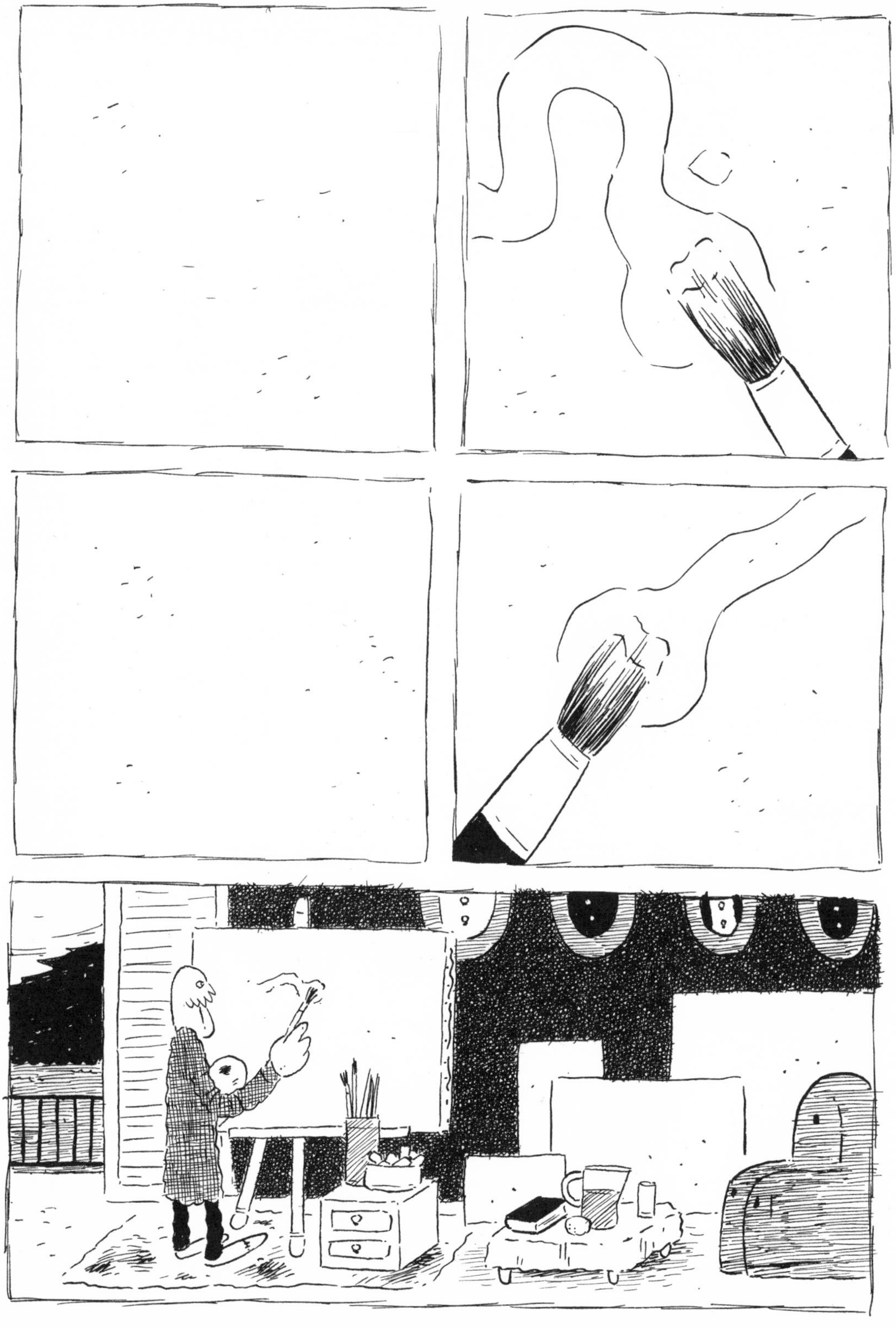

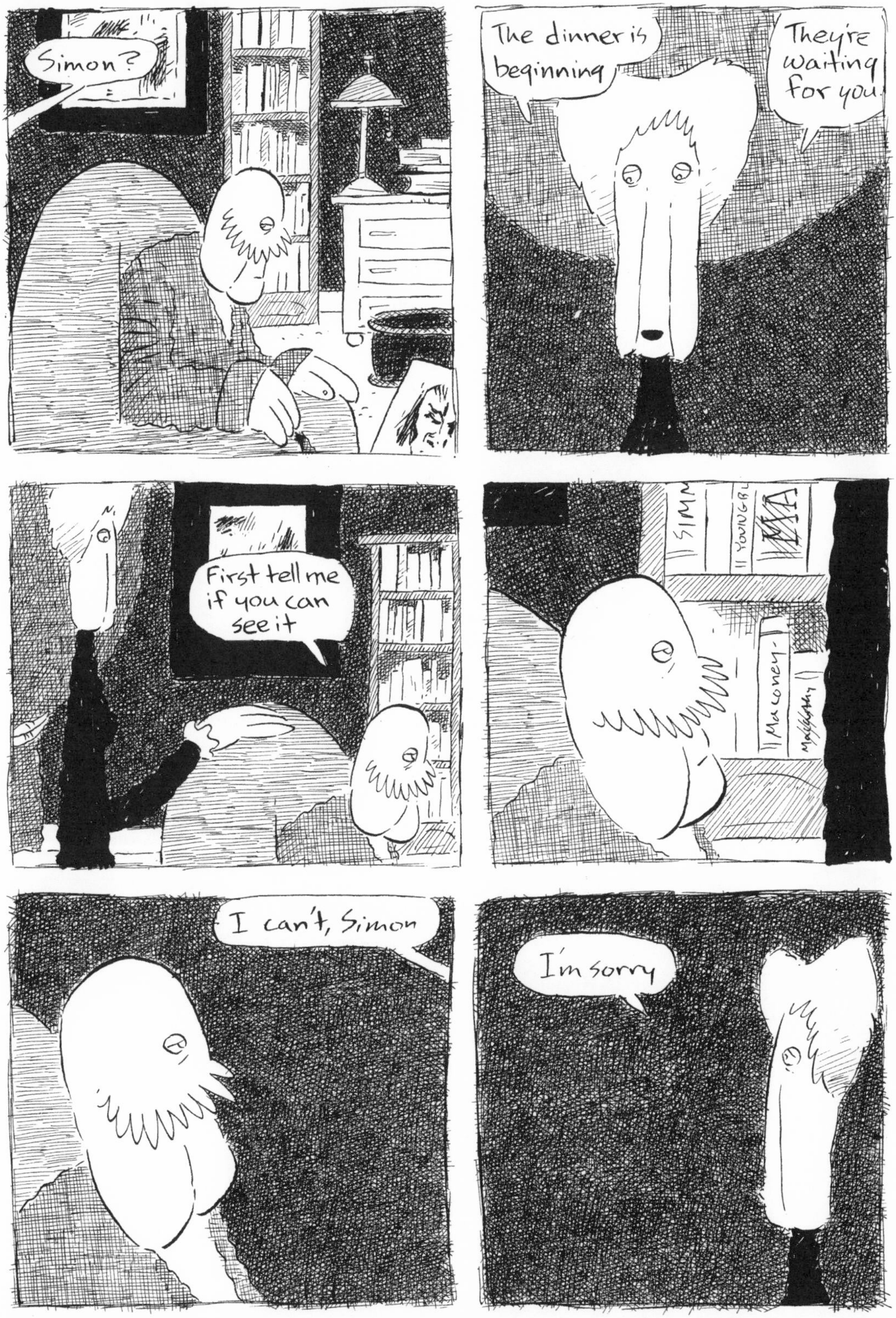
Simon?
The dinner is beginning
They're waiting for you
First tell me if you can see it
I can't, Simon
I'm sorry

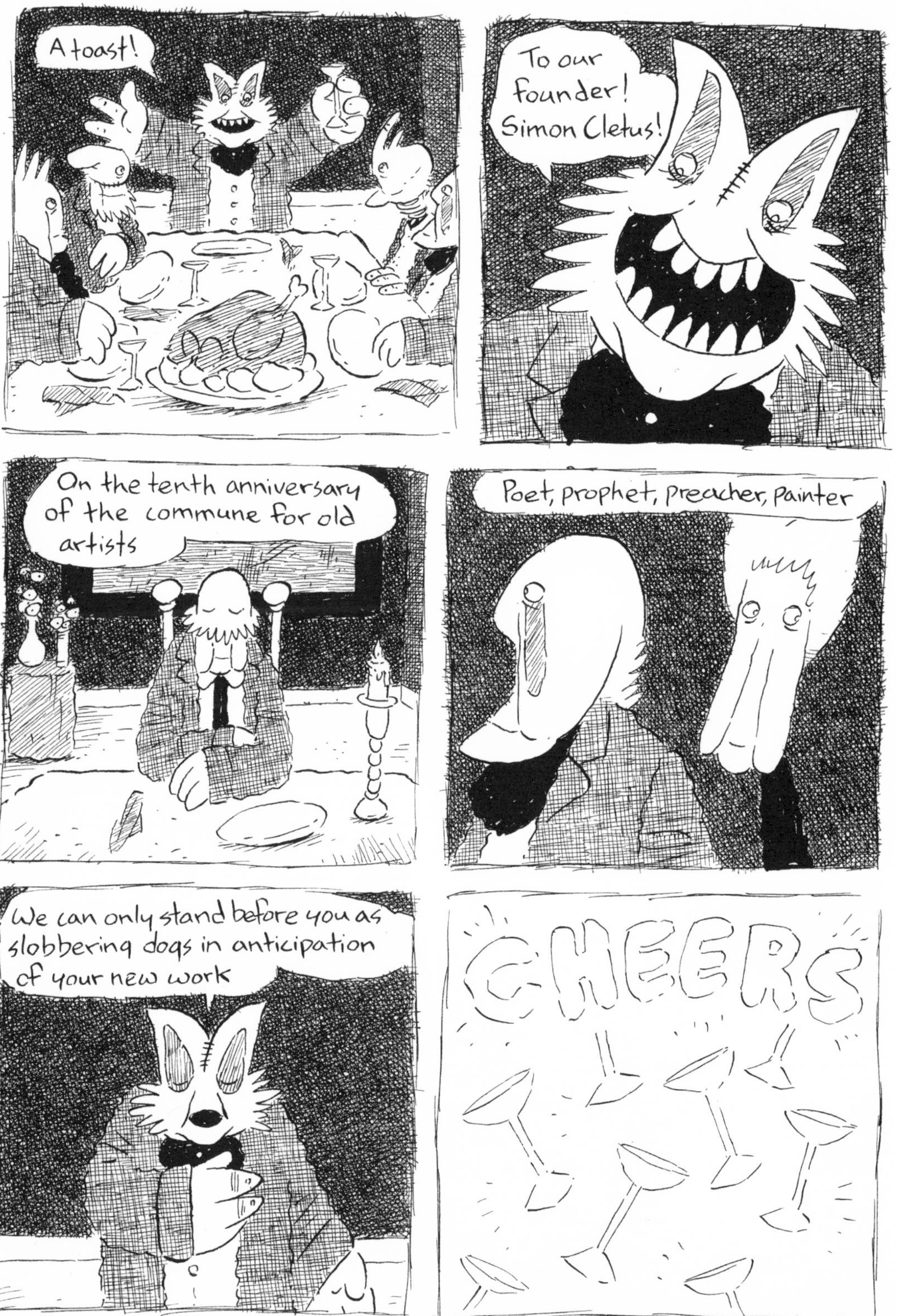
A toast!
To our founder! Simon Cletus!
On the tenth anniversary of the commune for old artists
Poet, prophet, preacher, painter
We can only stand before you as slobbering dogs in anticipation of your new work
CHEERS

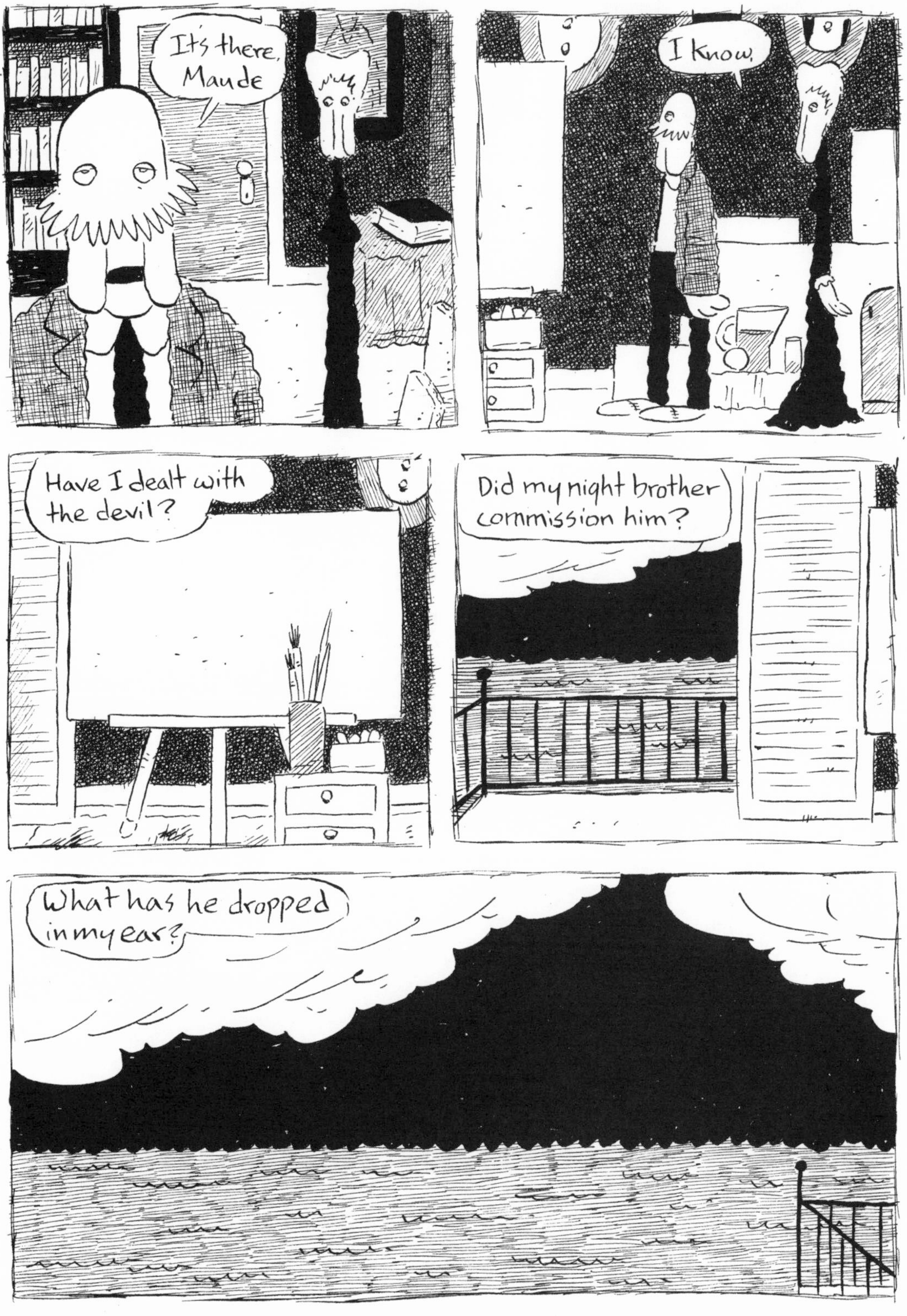
It's there, Maude
I know.
Have I dealt with the devil?
Did my night brother commission him?
What has he dropped in my ear?

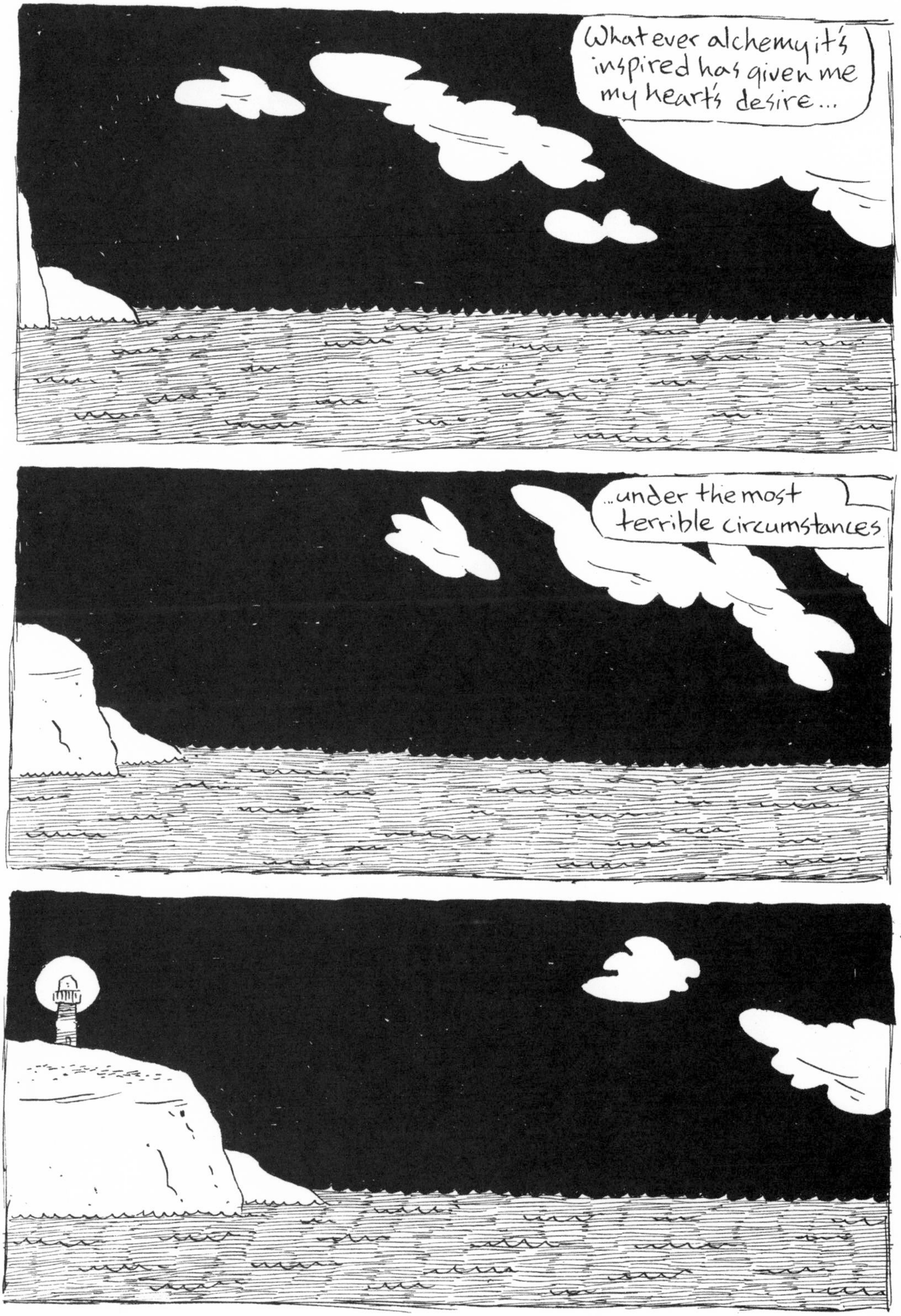
What ever alchemy it's inspired has given me my heart's desire...
...under the most terrible circumstances

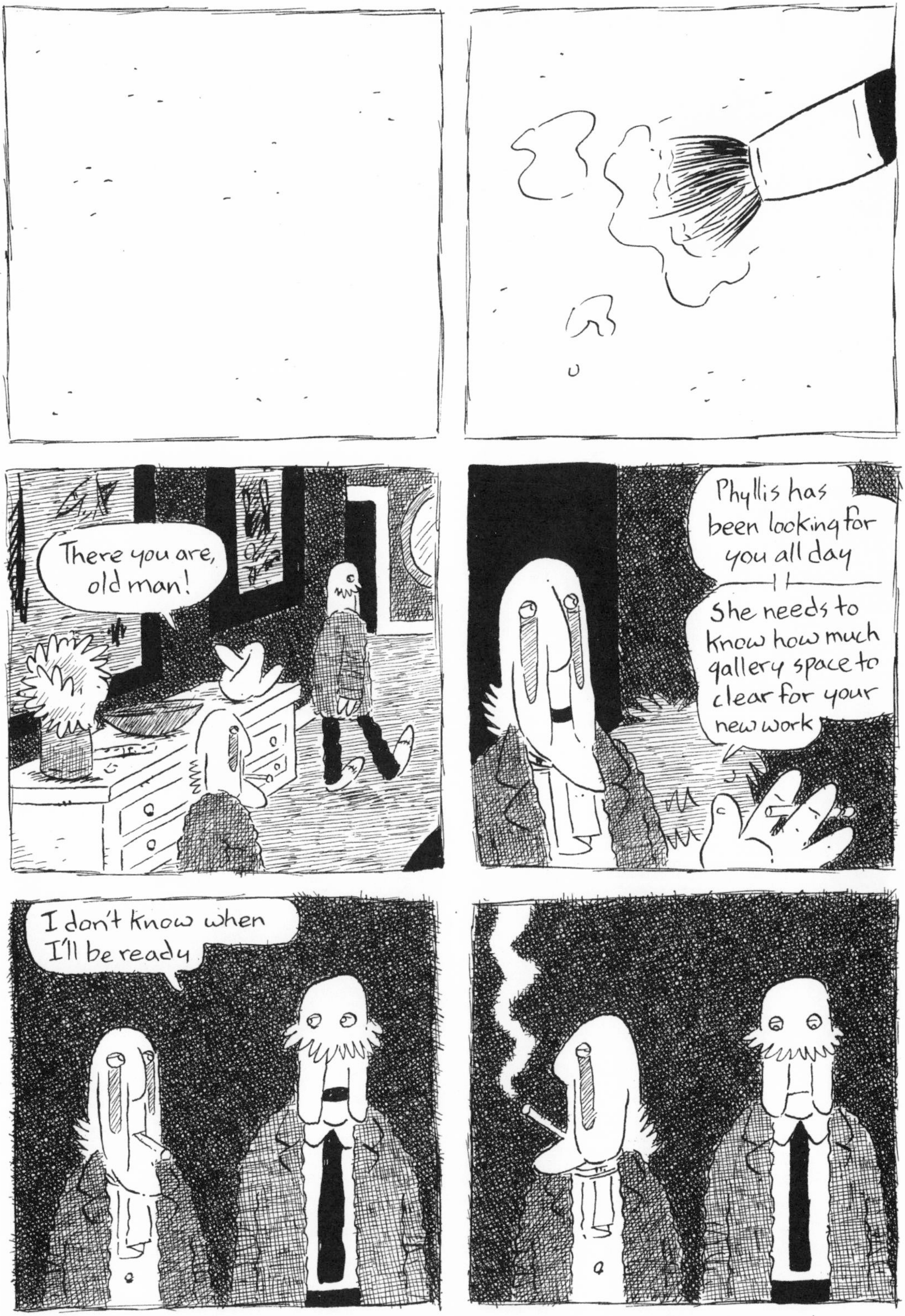
There you are, old man!
Phyllis has been looking for you all day
She needs to know how much gallery space to clear for your new work
I don't know when I'll be ready

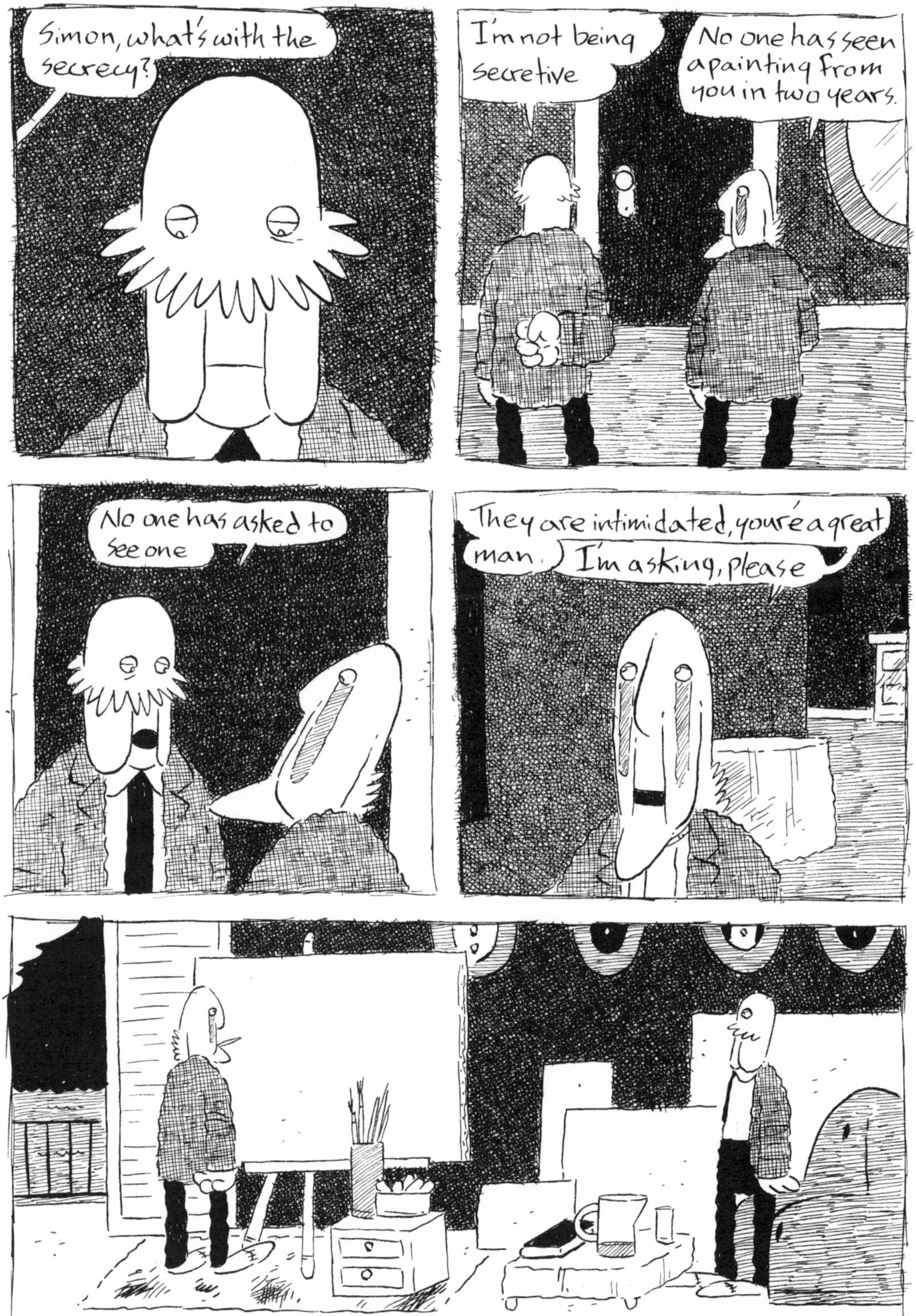
Simon, what's with the secrecy?
I'm not being secretive
No one has seen a painting from you in two years.
No one has asked to see one
They are intimidated, you're a great man.
I'm asking, please

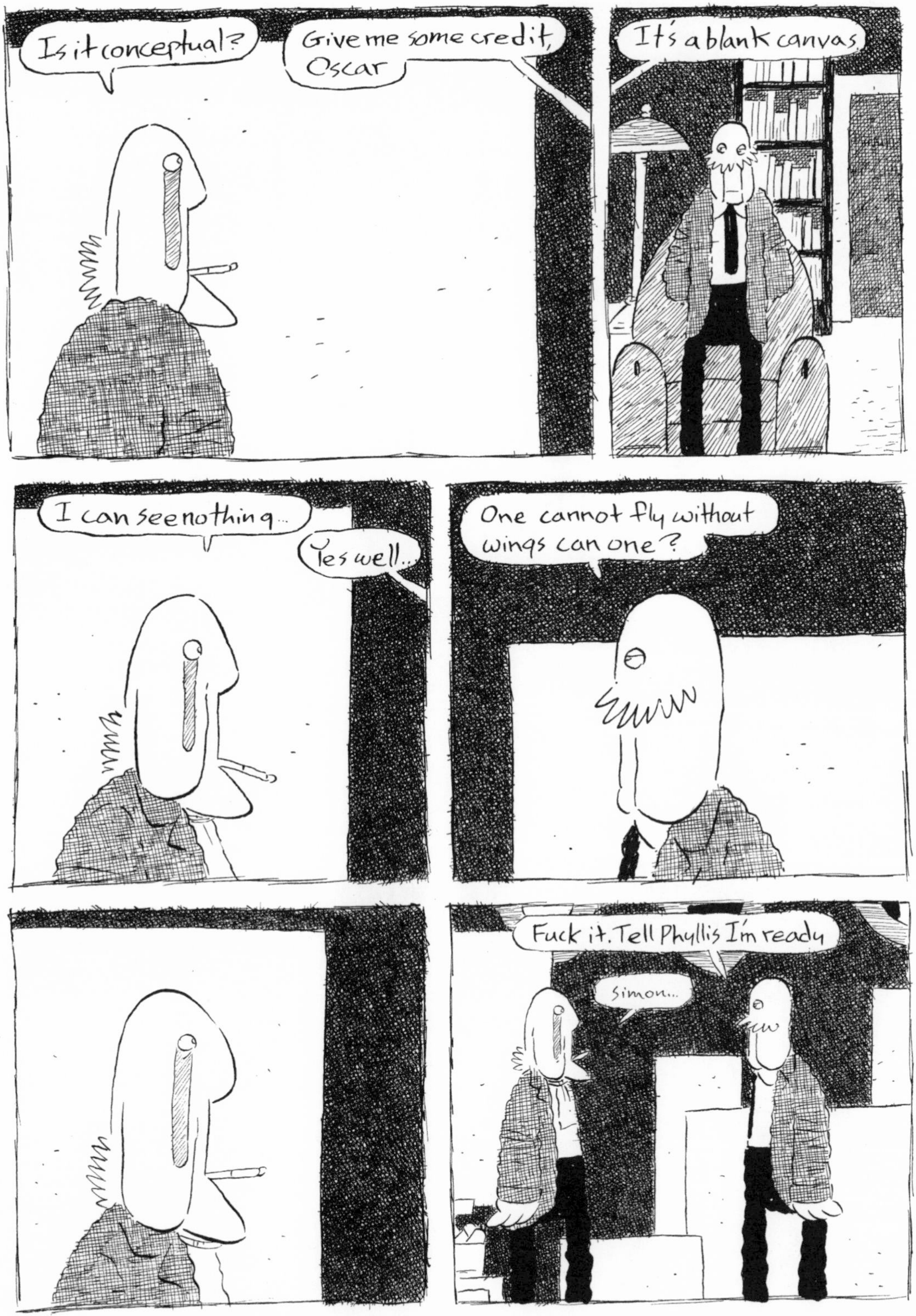

Is it conceptual?
Give me some credit, Oscar
It's a blank canvas.
I can see nothing...
Yes well...
One cannot fly without wings can one?
Fuck it. Tell Phyllis I'm ready
Simon...

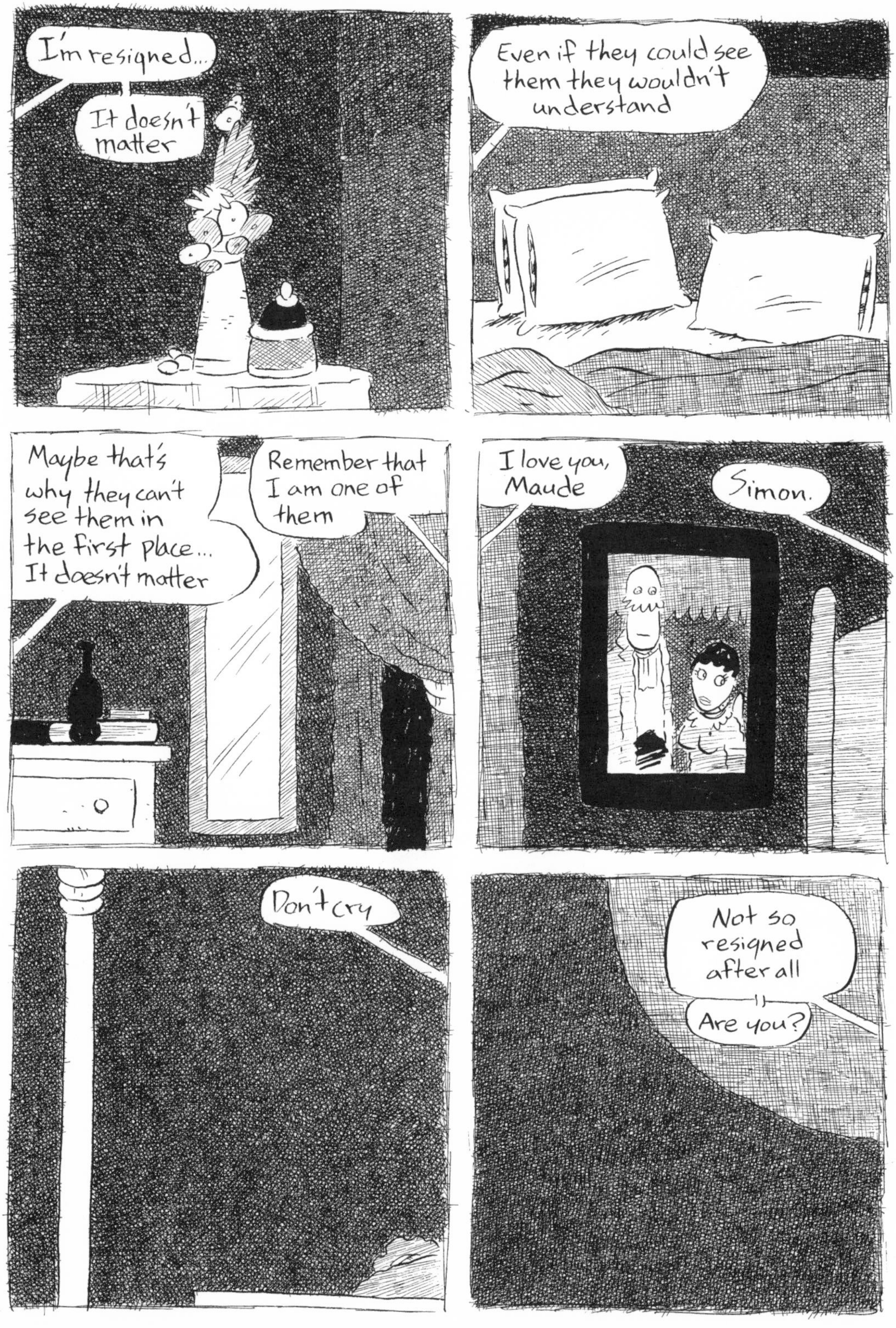
I'm resigned...
It doesn't matter
Even if they could see them they wouldn't understand
Maybe that's why they can't see them in the first place... It doesn't matter
Remember that I am one of them
I love you, Maude
Simon.
Don't cry
Not so resigned after all
Are you?

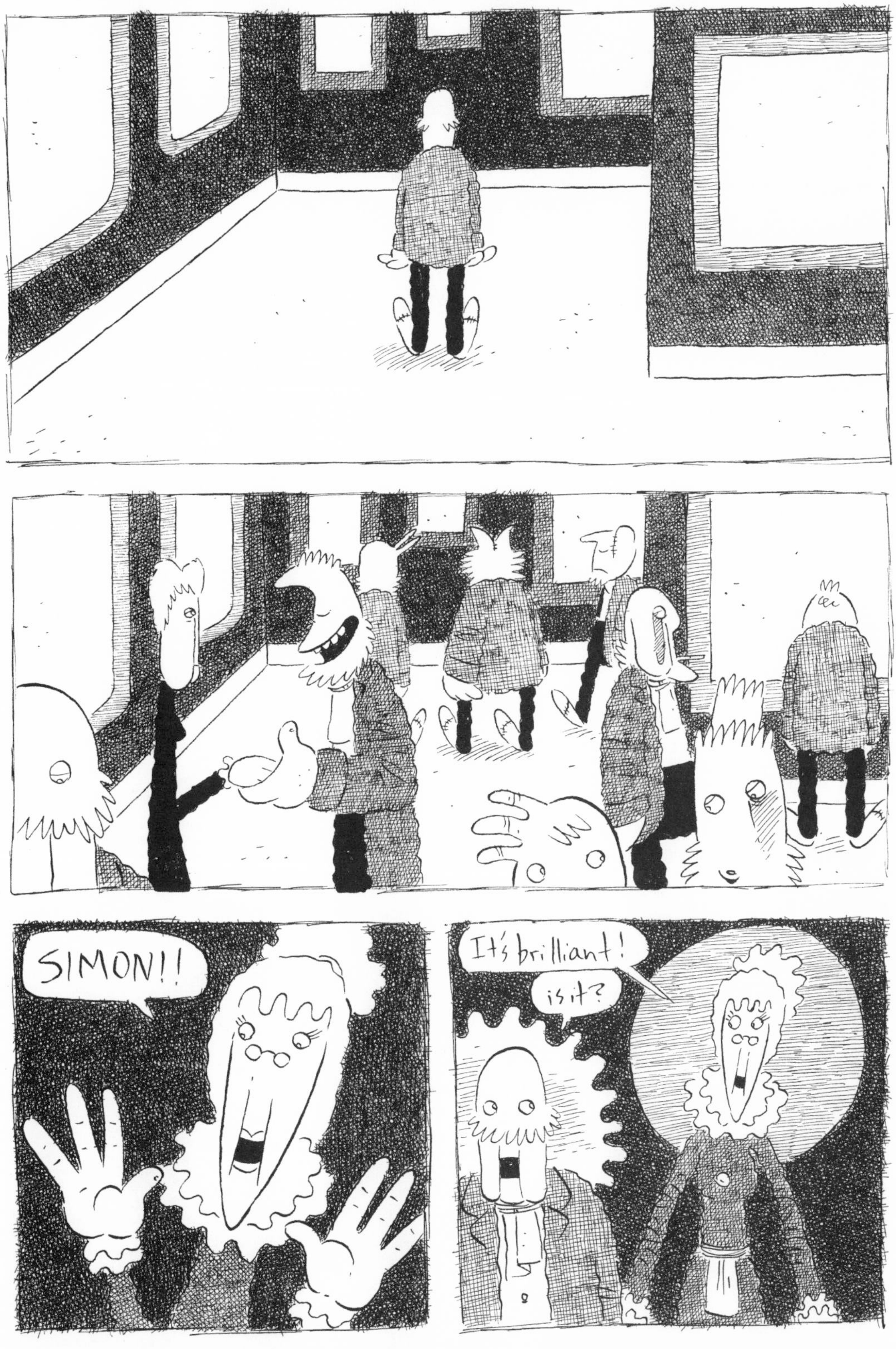
SIMON!!
It's brilliant!
is it?

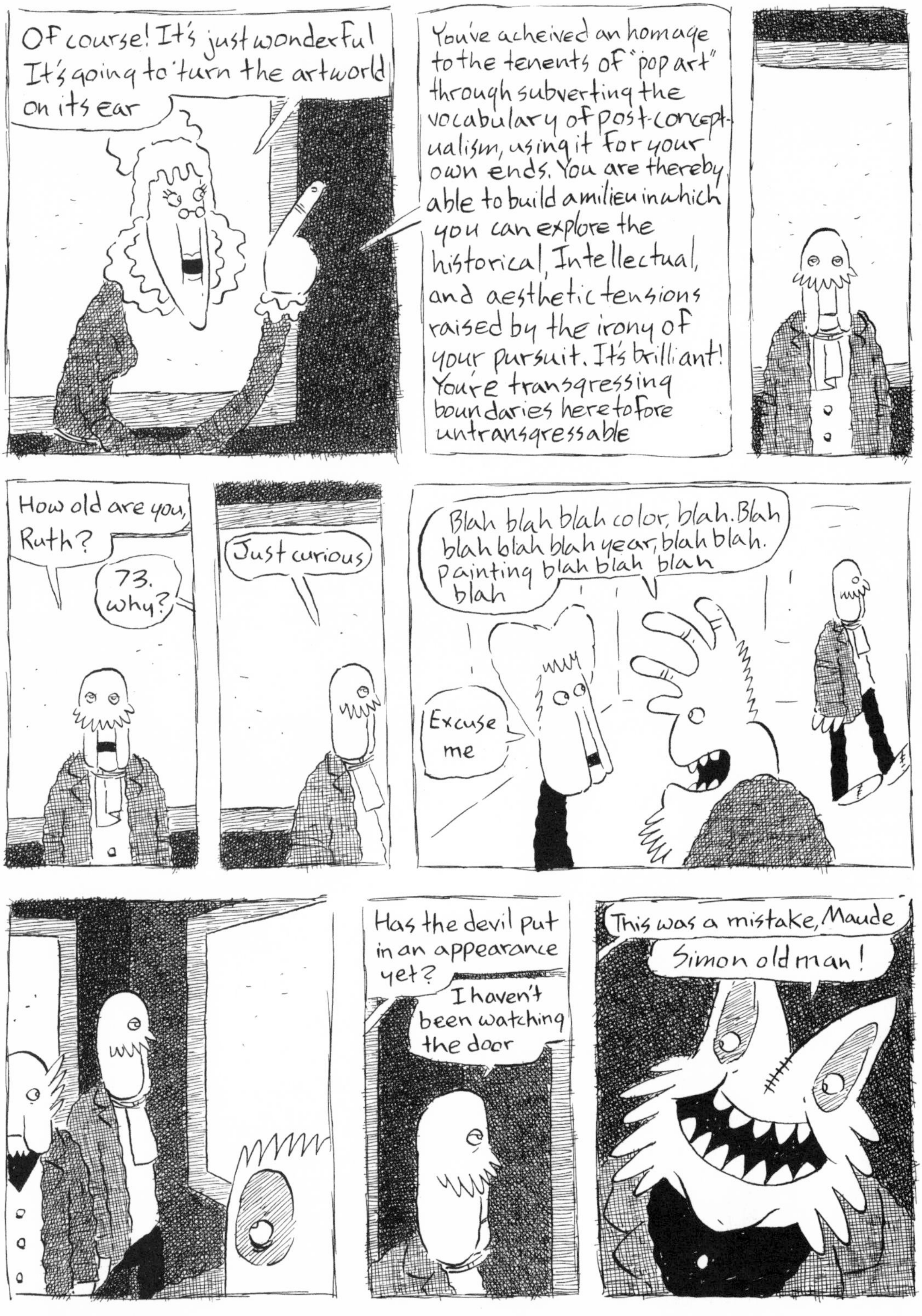
Of course! It's just wonderful It's going to turn the artworld on its ear
You've acheived an homage to the tenents of "pop art" through subverting the vocabulary of post-conceptualism, using it for your own ends. You are thereby able to build amilieu in which you can explore the historical, Intellectual, and aesthetic tensions raised by the irony of your pursuit. It's brilliant! You're transgressing boundaries heretofore untransgressable
How old are you, Ruth?
73. why?
Just curious
Blah blah blah color, blah. Blah blah blah blah year, blah blah. painting blah blah blah blah
Excuse me
Has the devil put in an appearance yet?
I haven't been watching the door
This was a mistake, Maude
Simon old man!

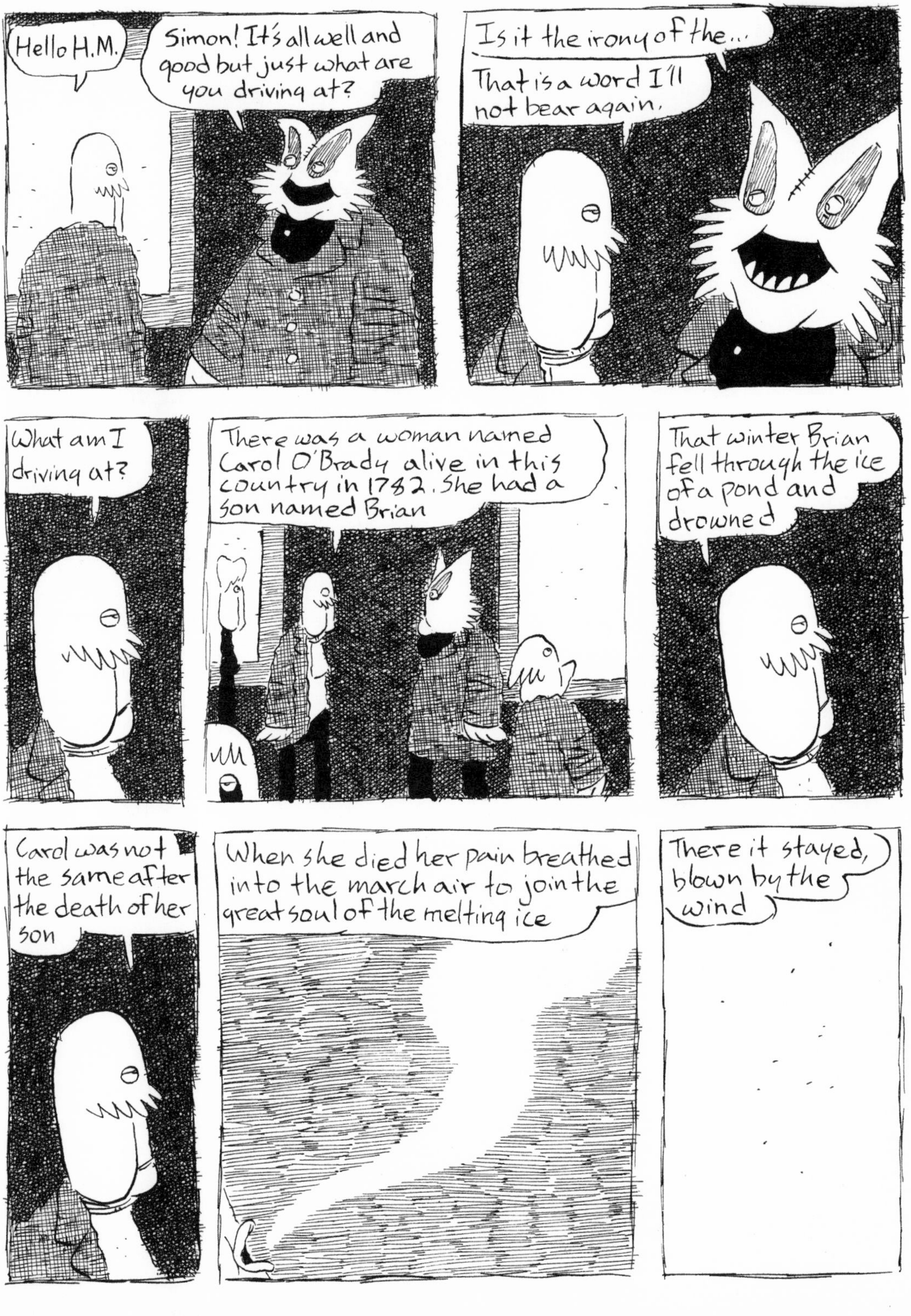
Hello H.M.
Simon! It's all well and good but just what are you driving at?
Is it the irony of the...
That is a word I'll not bear again.
What am I driving at?
There was a woman named Carol O'Brady alive in this country in 1782. She had a son named Brian
That winter Brian fell through the ice of a pond and drowned
Carol was not the same after the death of her son
When she died her pain breathed into the march air to join the great soul of the melting ice
There it stayed, blown by the wind

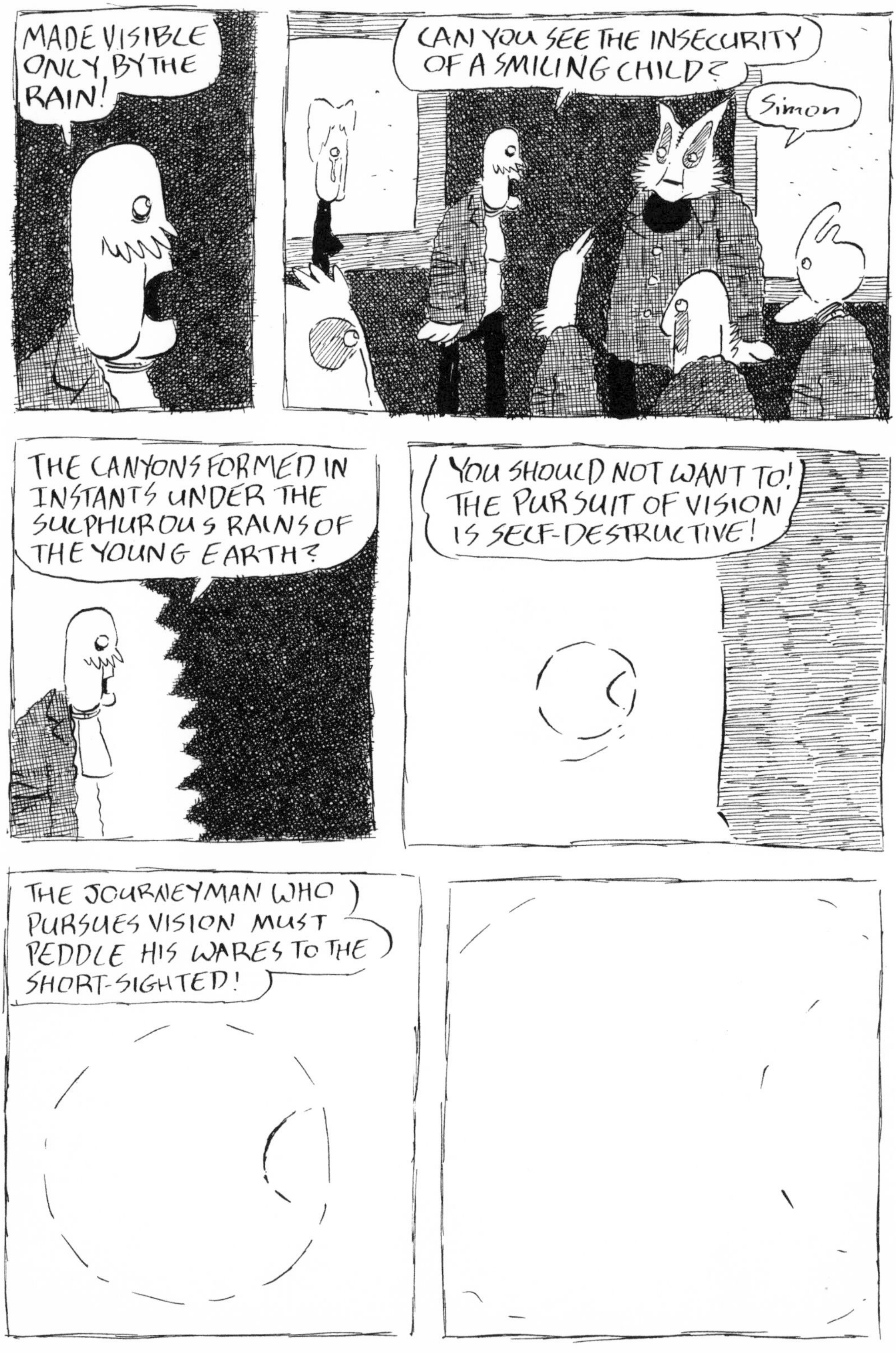
MADE VISIBLE ONLY BY THE RAIN!
CAN YOU SEE THE INSECURITY OF A SMILING CHILD?
Simon
THE CANYONS FORMED IN INSTANTS UNDER THE SULPHUROUS RAINS OF THE YOUNG EARTH?
YOU SHOULD NOT WANT TO! THE PURSUIT OF VISION IS SELF-DESTRUCTIVE!
THE JOURNEYMAN WHO PURSUES VISION MUST PEDDLE HIS WARES TO THE SHORT-SIGHTED!

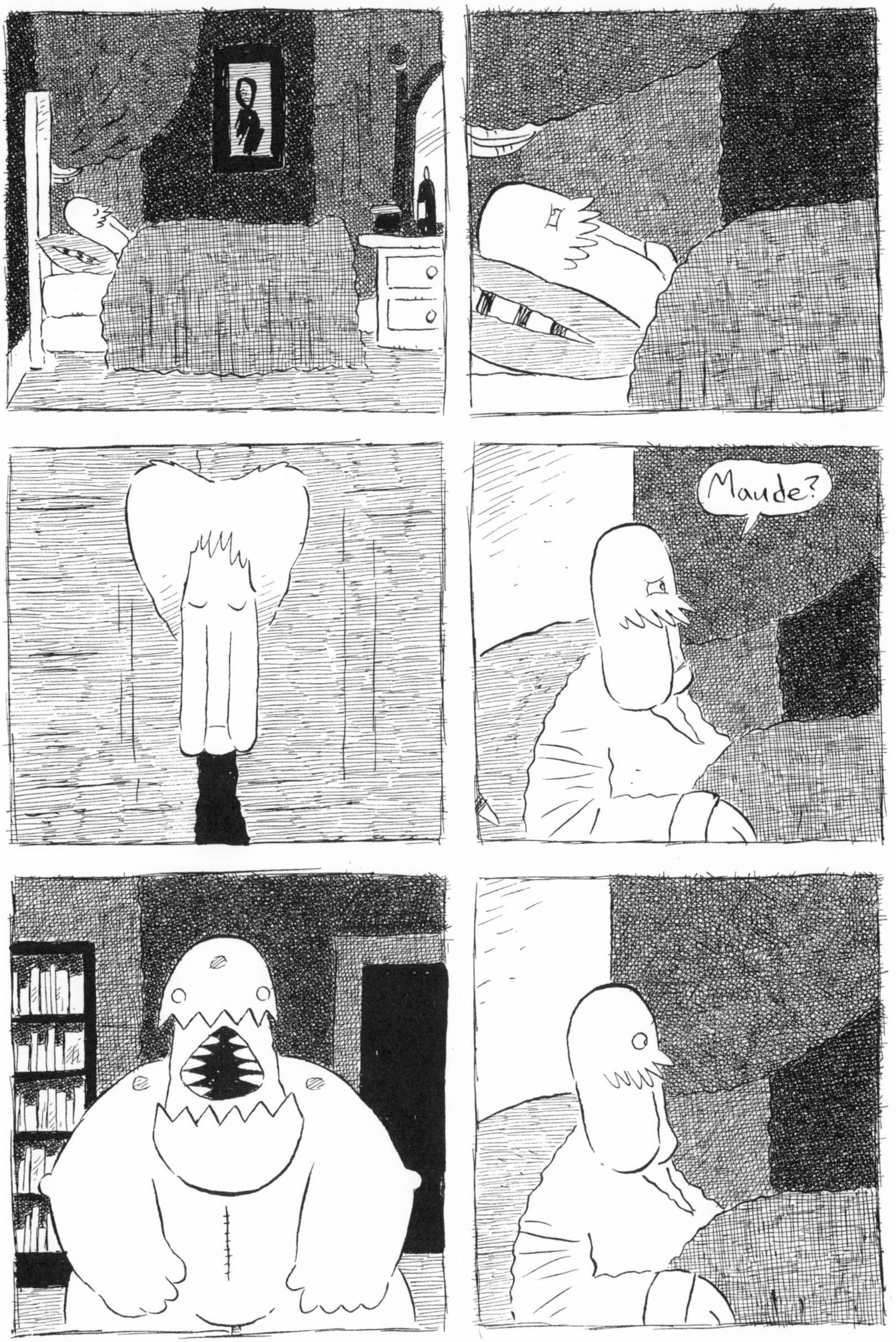
Maude?

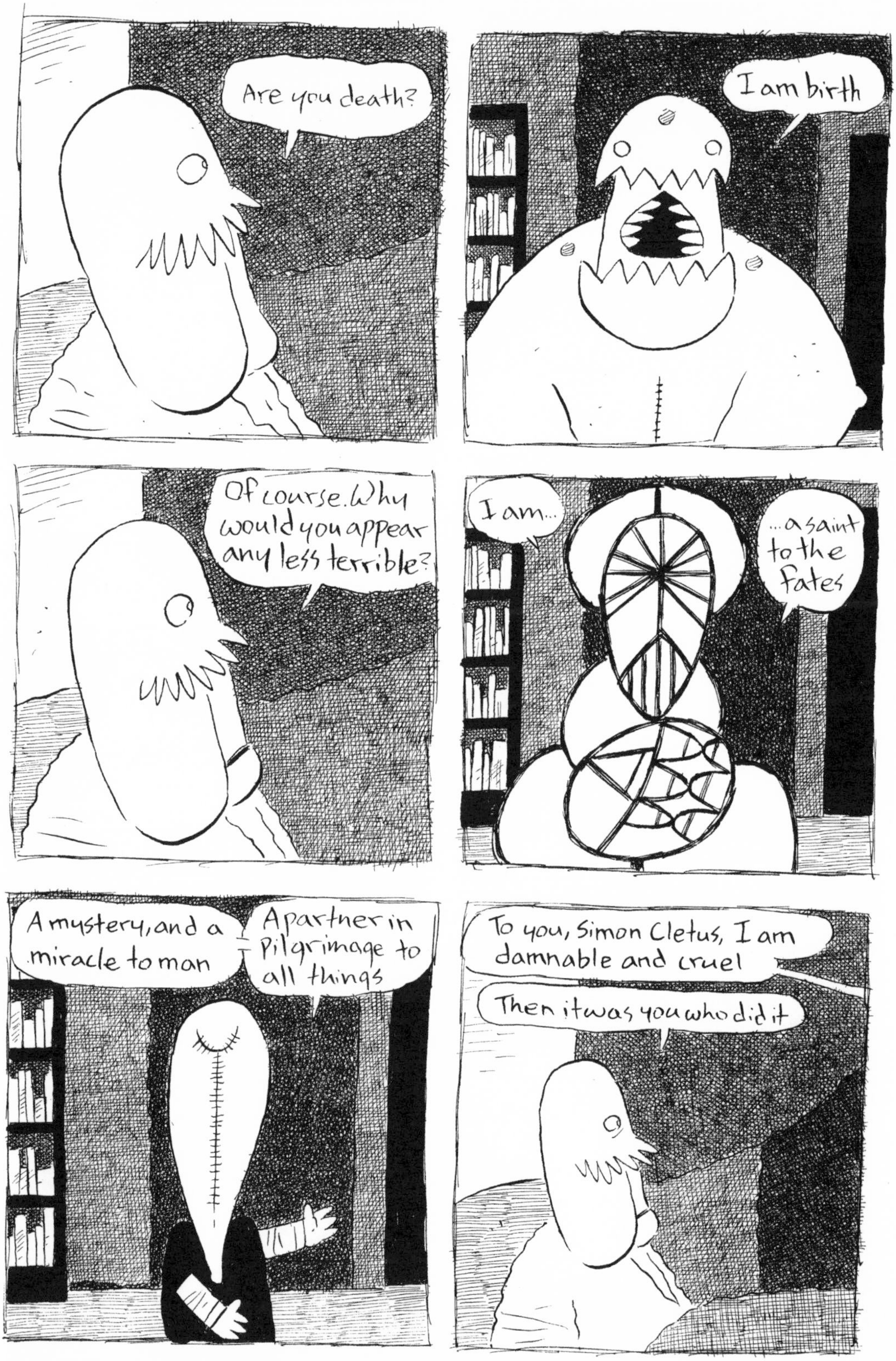
Are you death?
I am birth
Of course. Why would you appear any less terrible?
I am...
...a saint to the fates
A mystery, and a miracle to man
A partner in Pilgrimage to all things
To you, Simon Cletus, I am damnable and cruel
Then it was you who did it

I was an accomplice
That is all

I served you in guiding you to your new hand

As I guide all that breathe to be born, and reborn

Until I must bear them into the fold of care-taking death

I ferried your genius into tragedy

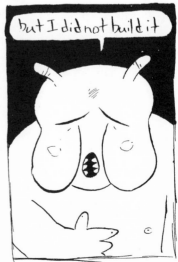

but I did not build it

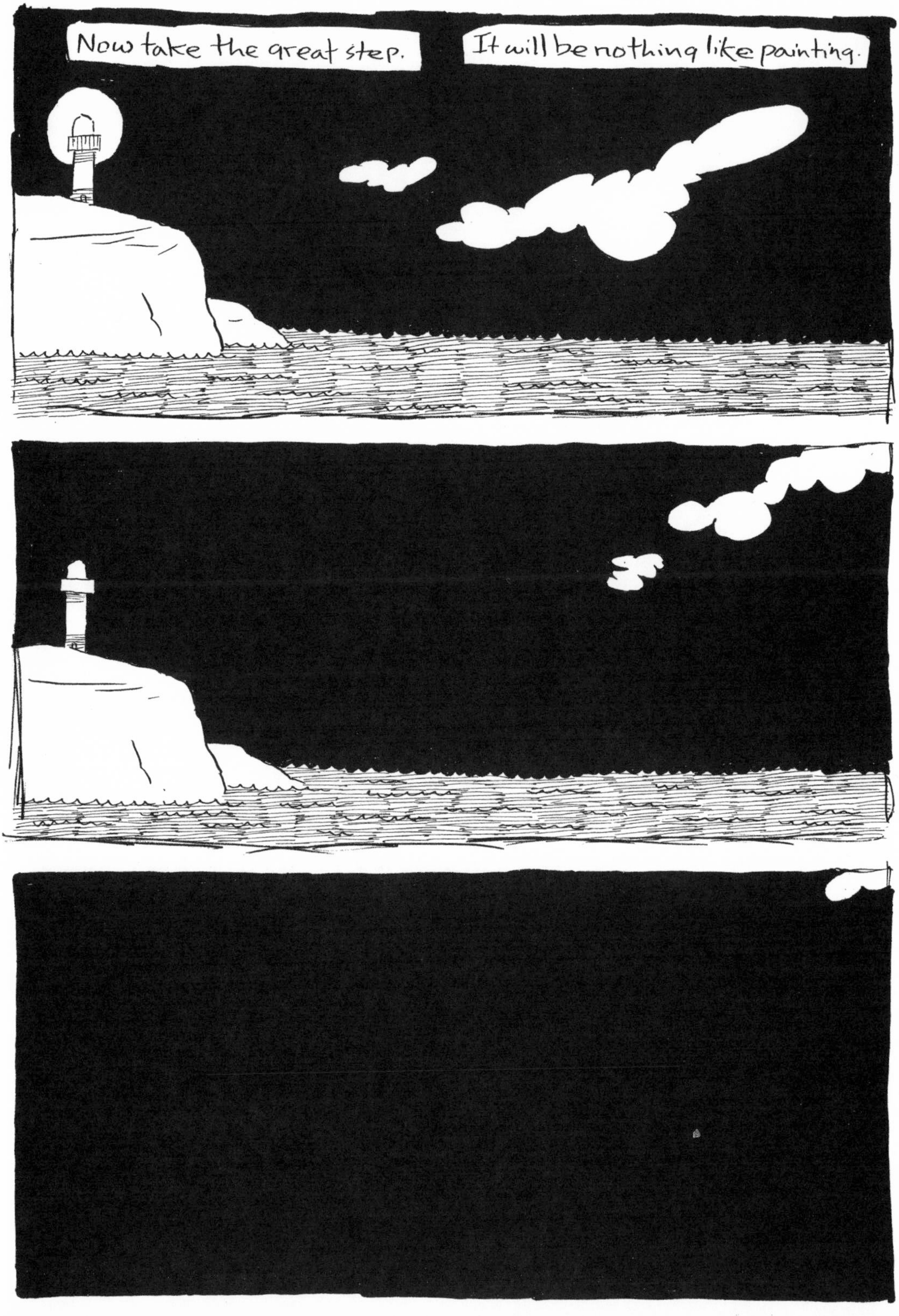
Now take the great step.
It will be nothing like painting.

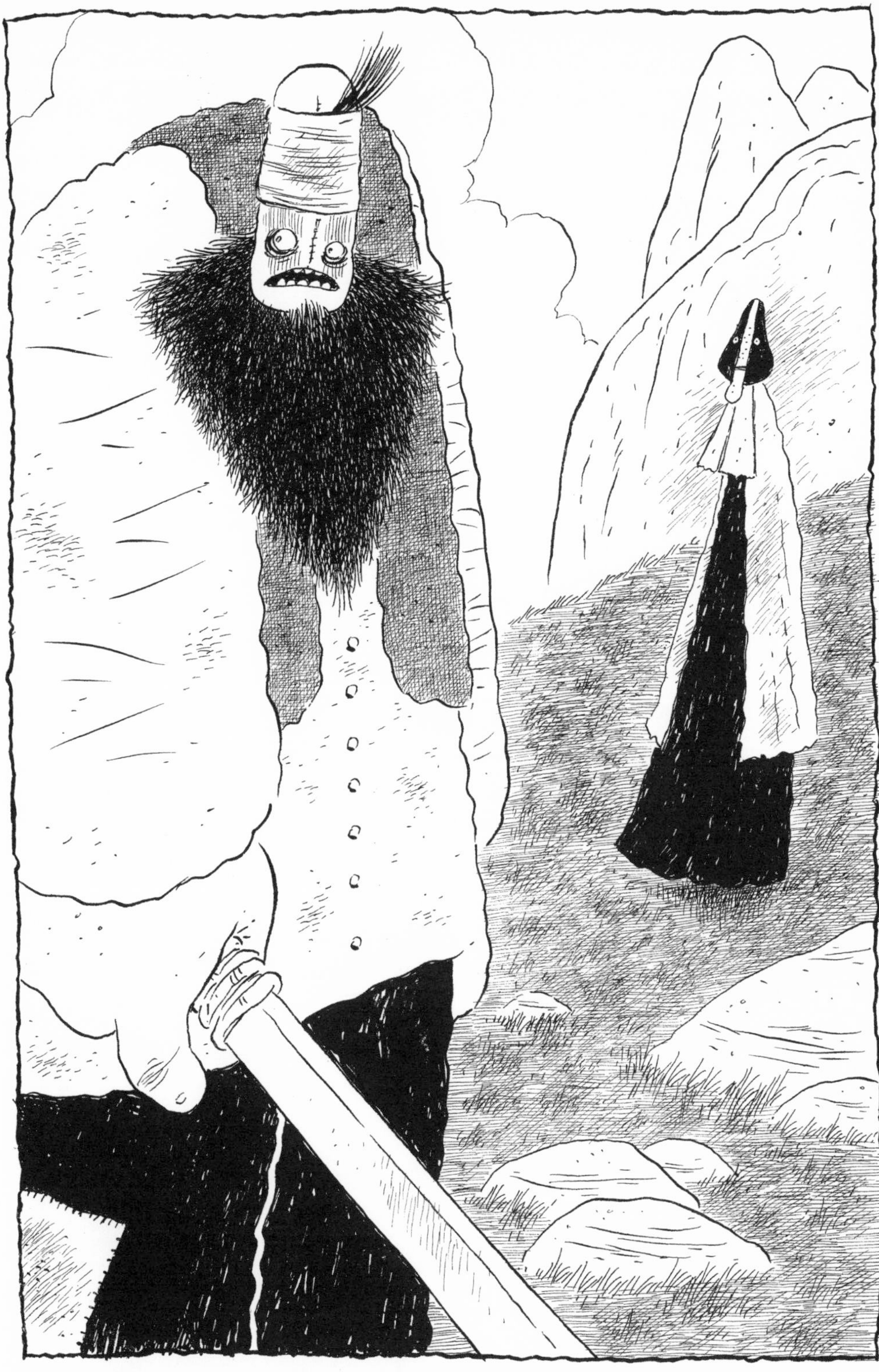

Tapestry

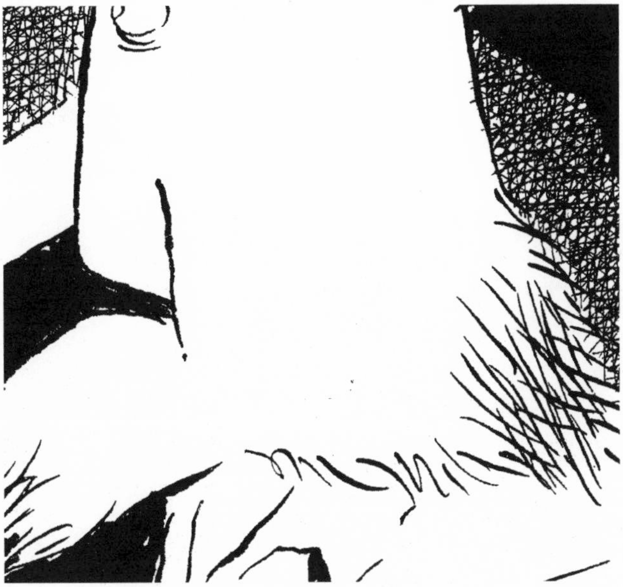

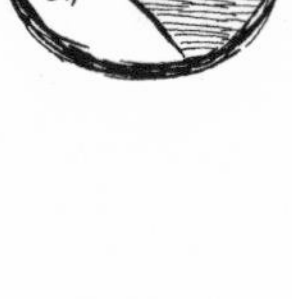

Claire?

Yes sir Kiril?

Grow wise without aging

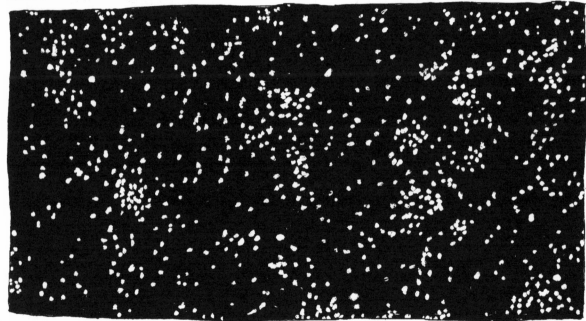

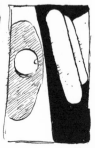

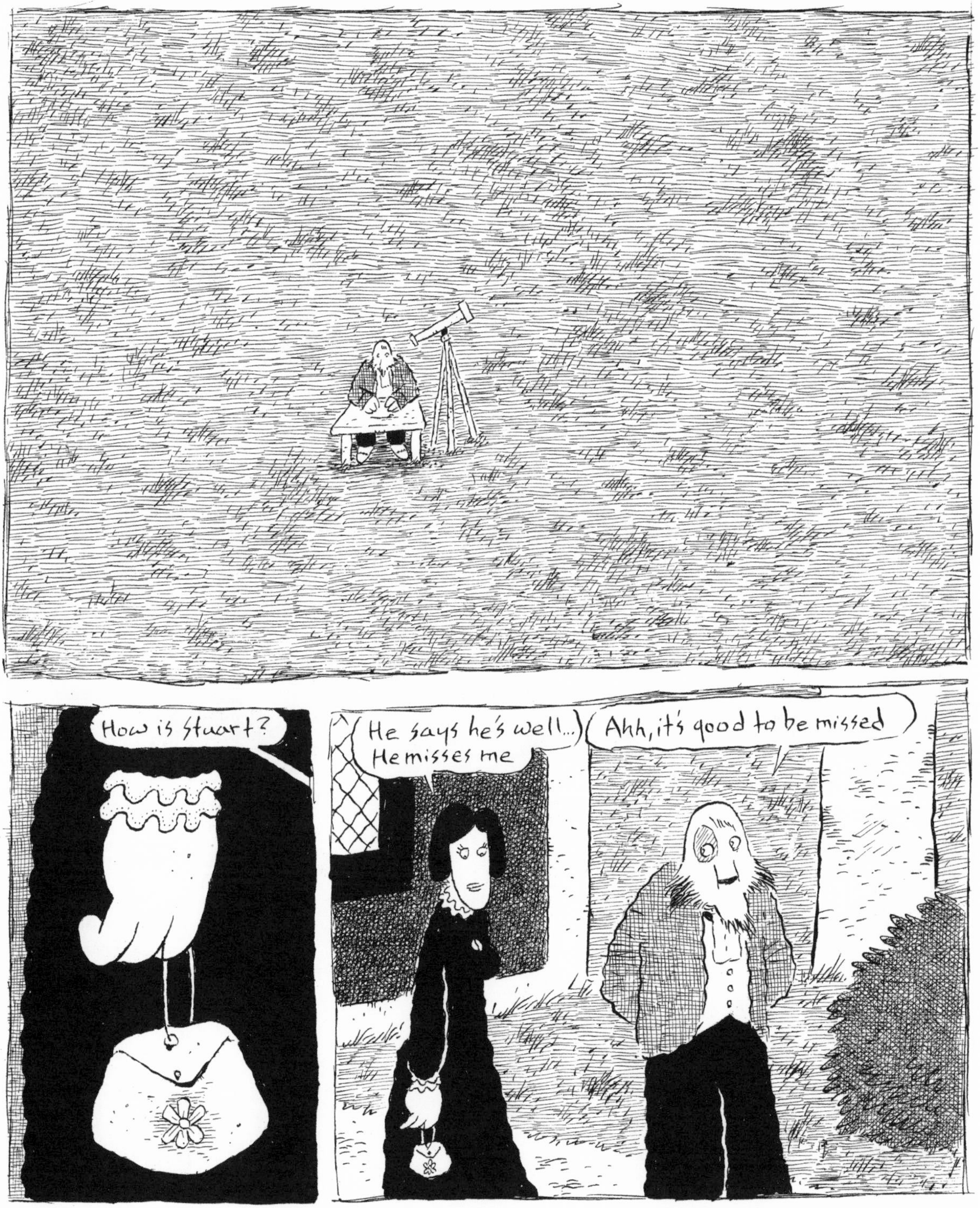
How is Stuart?
He says he's well... He misses me
Ahh, it's good to be missed

Yes, I'm worried that I'm beginning to enjoy it too much

Heh, so that's why you stay on with me

Ha ha

No, Stuart misses me but he understands that you need me for this

My dear nursemaid

And how are your studies?

Sigh Difficult but rewarding

It's so satisfying to know I'm beginning to understand the systems that make the world

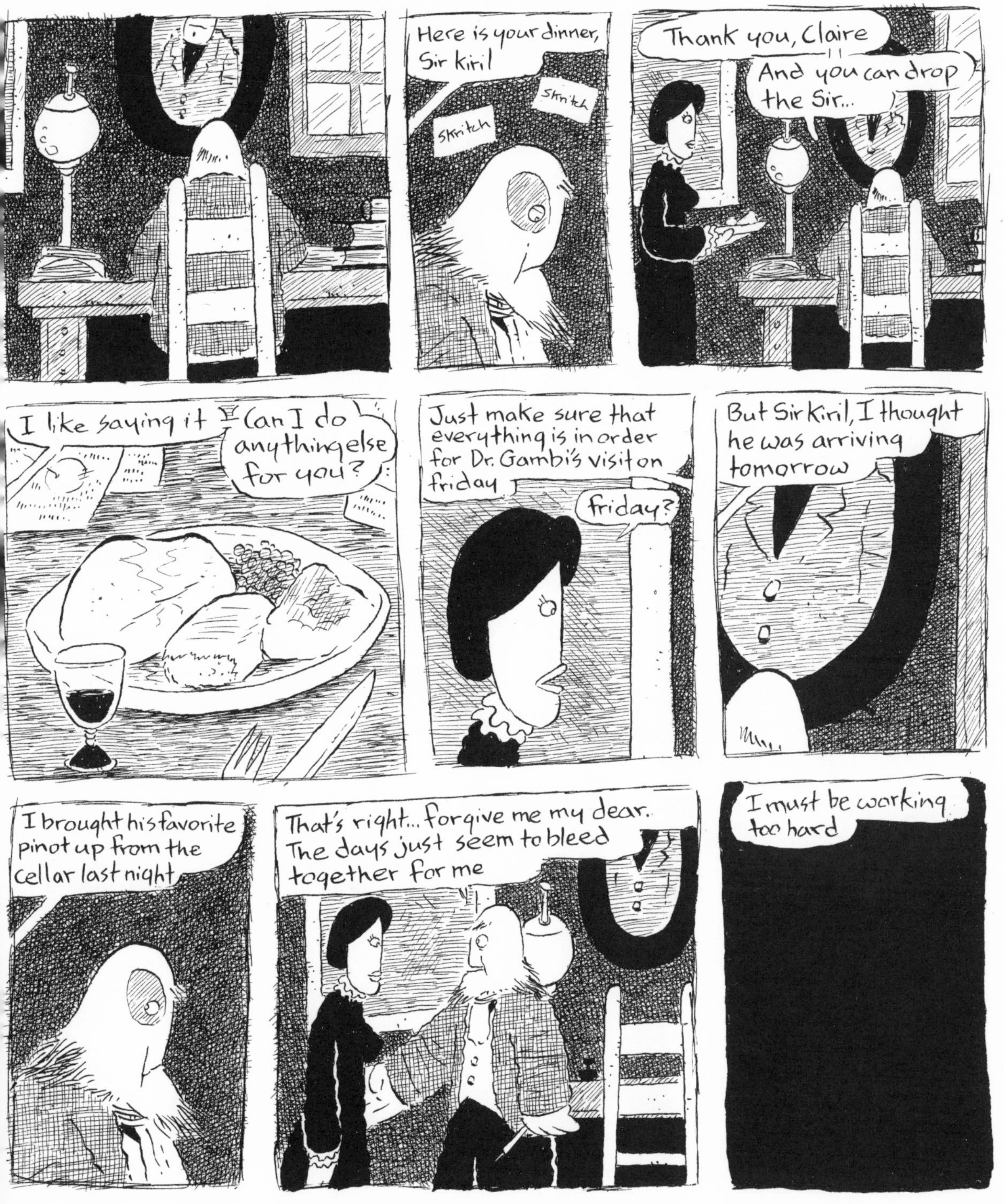

Here is your dinner, Sir Kiril
Skritch
Skritch
Thank you, Claire
And you can drop the Sir...
I like saying it
Can I do anythingelse for you?
Just make sure that everything is in order for Dr. Gambi's visit on friday
friday?
But Sir Kiril, I thought he was arriving tomorrow
I brought his favorite pinot up from the cellar last night
That's right... forgive me my dear. The days just seem to bleed together for me
I must be working too hard

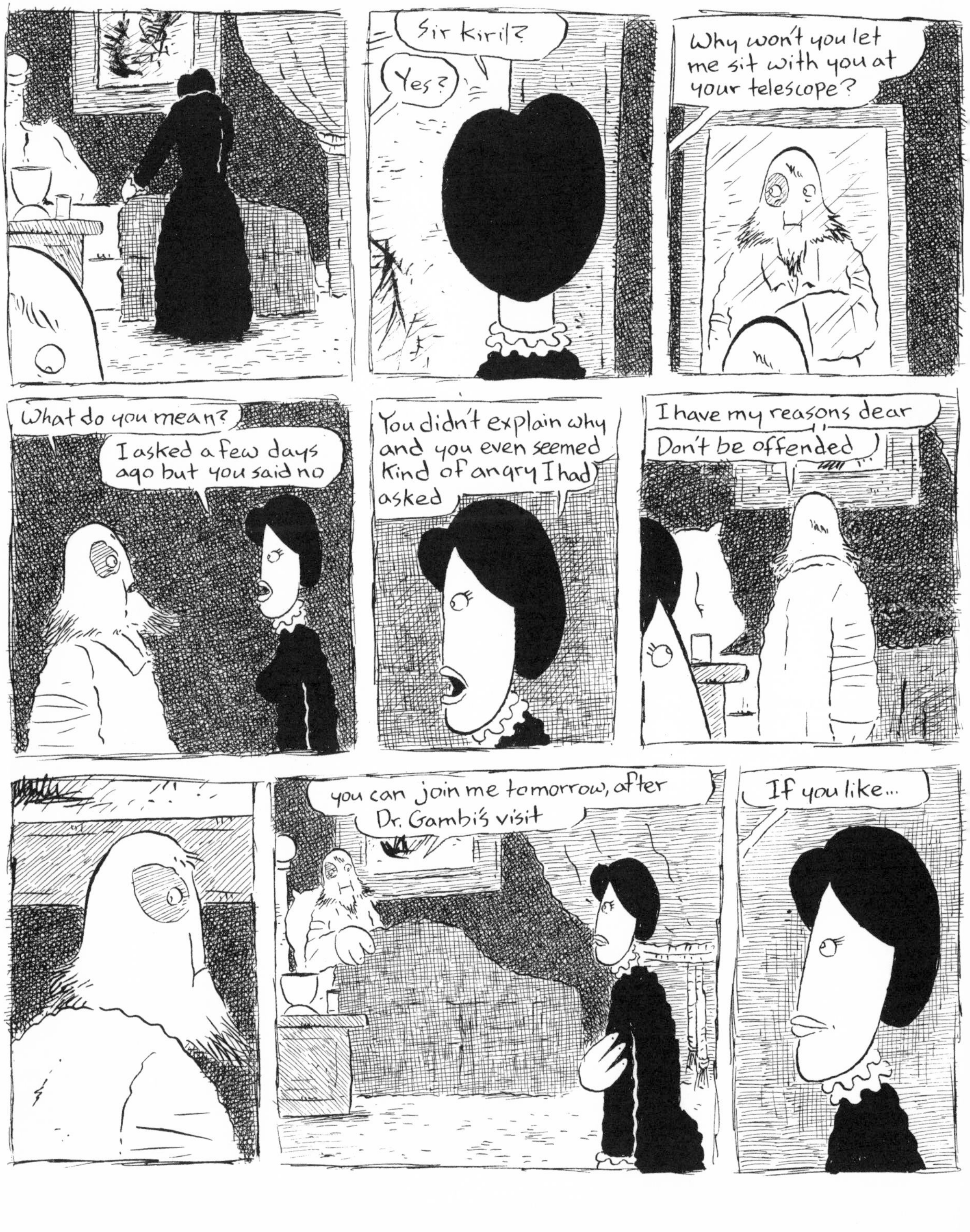

Sir Kiril?
Yes?
Why won't you let me sit with you at your telescope?
What do you mean?
I asked a few days ago but you said no
You didn't explain why and you even seemed Kind of angry I had asked
I have my reasons dear
Don't be offended
you can join me tomorrow, after Dr. Gambi's visit
If you like...

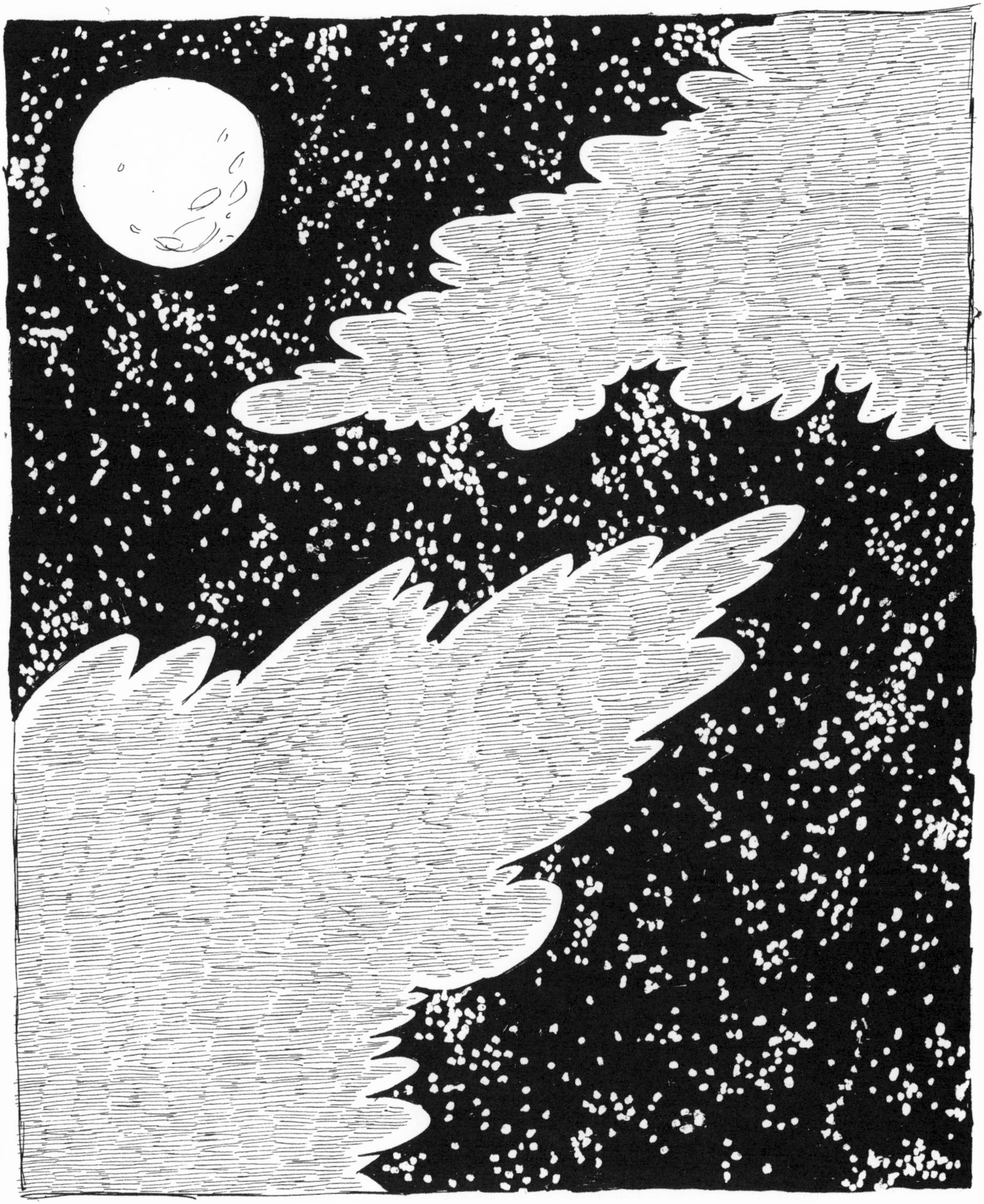

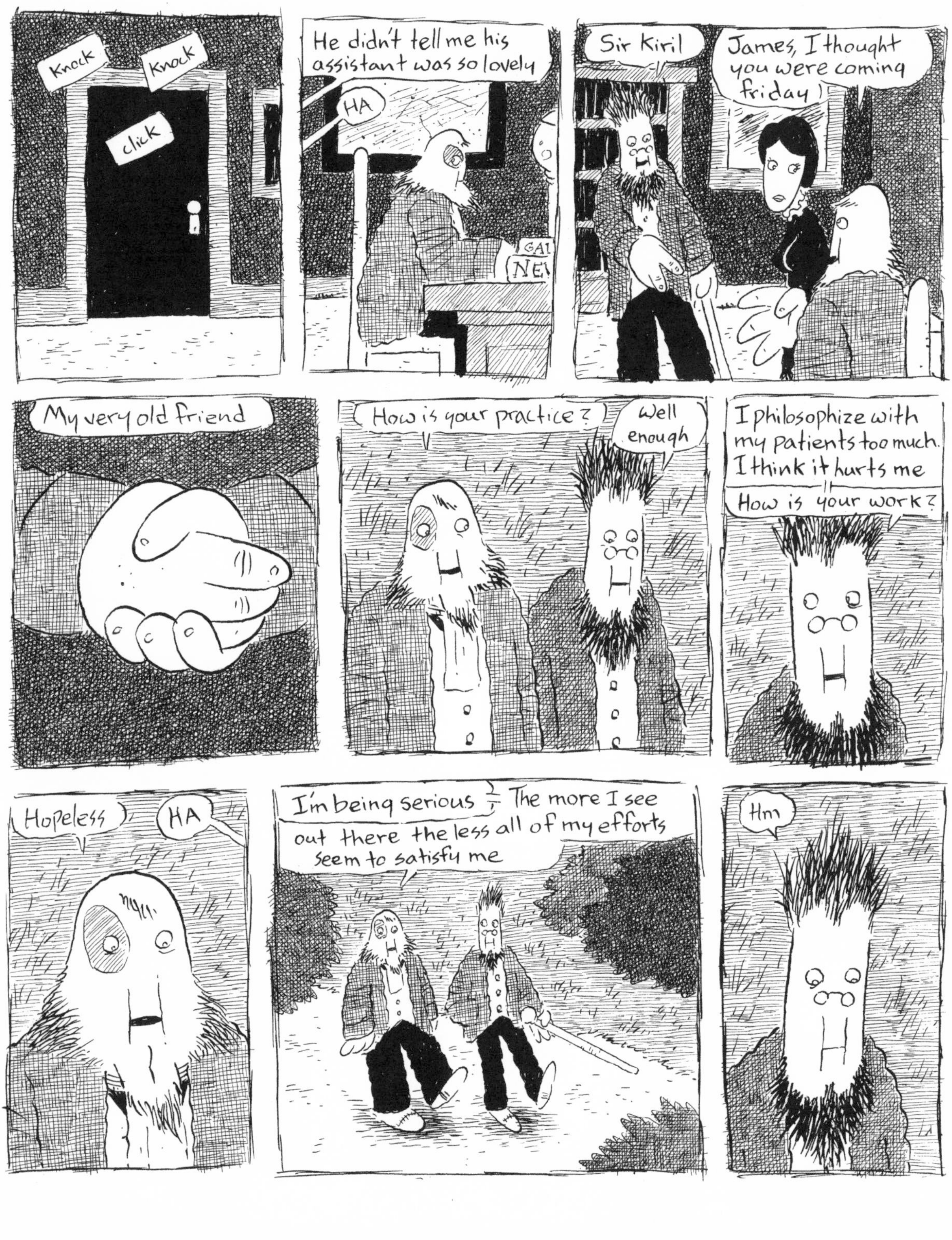

Knock
Knock
click
He didn't tell me his assistant was so lovely
HA
Sir Kiril
James, I thought you were coming friday!
My very old friend
How is your practice?
Well enough
I philosophize with my patients too much. I think it hurts me
How is your work?
Hopeless
HA
I'm being serious
The more I see out there the less all of my efforts seem to satisfy me
Hm

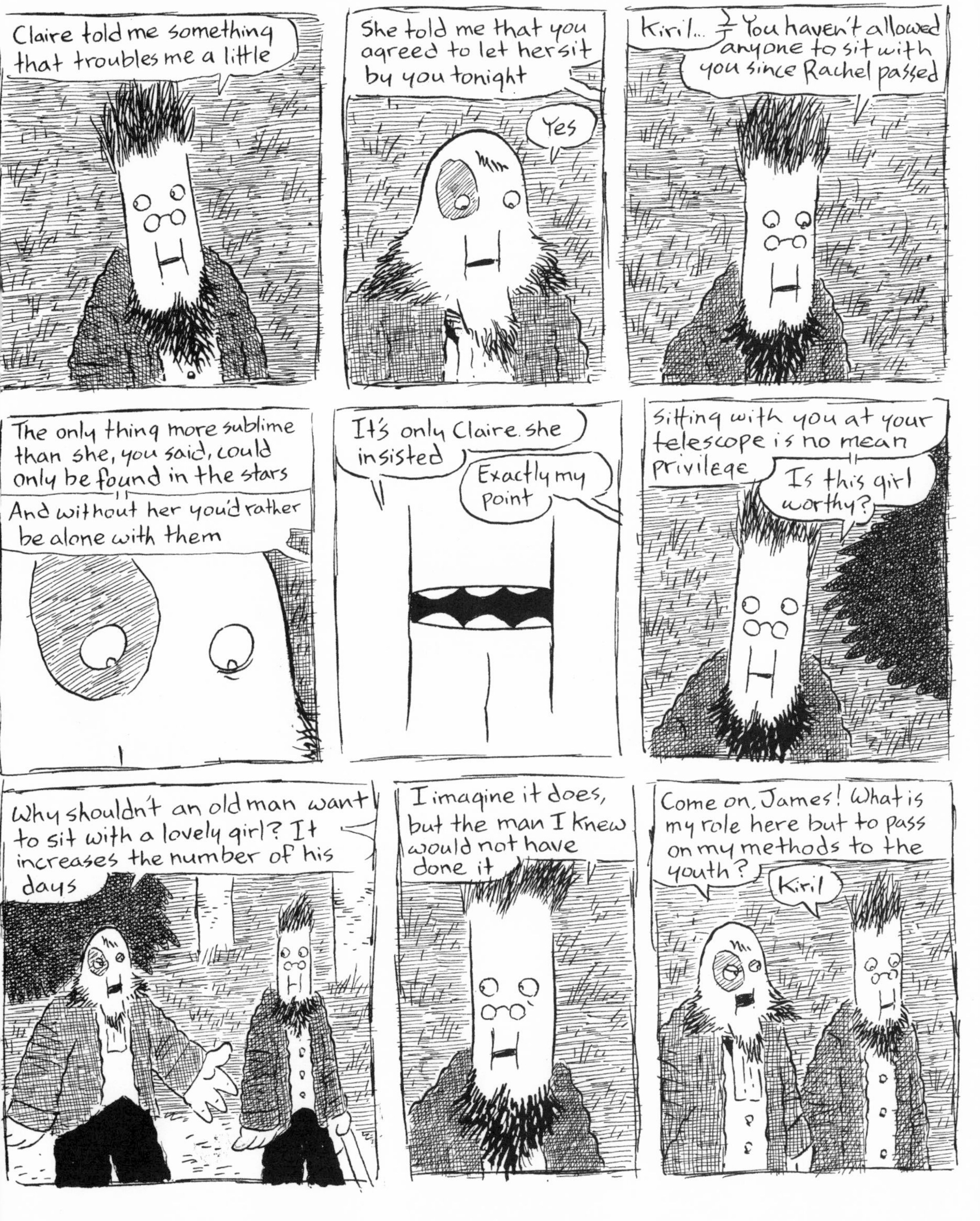
Claire told me something that troubles me a little
She told me that you agreed to let her sit by you tonight
Yes
Kiril...
You haven't allowed anyone to sit with you since Rachel passed
The only thing more sublime than she, you said, could only be found in the stars
And without her you'd rather be alone with them
It's only Claire. she insisted
Exactly my point
Sitting with you at your telescope is no mean privilege
Is this girl worthy?
Why shouldn't an old man want to sit with a lovely girl? It increases the number of his days
I imagine it does, but the man I knew would not have done it
Come on, James! What is my role here but to pass on my methods to the youth?
Kiril

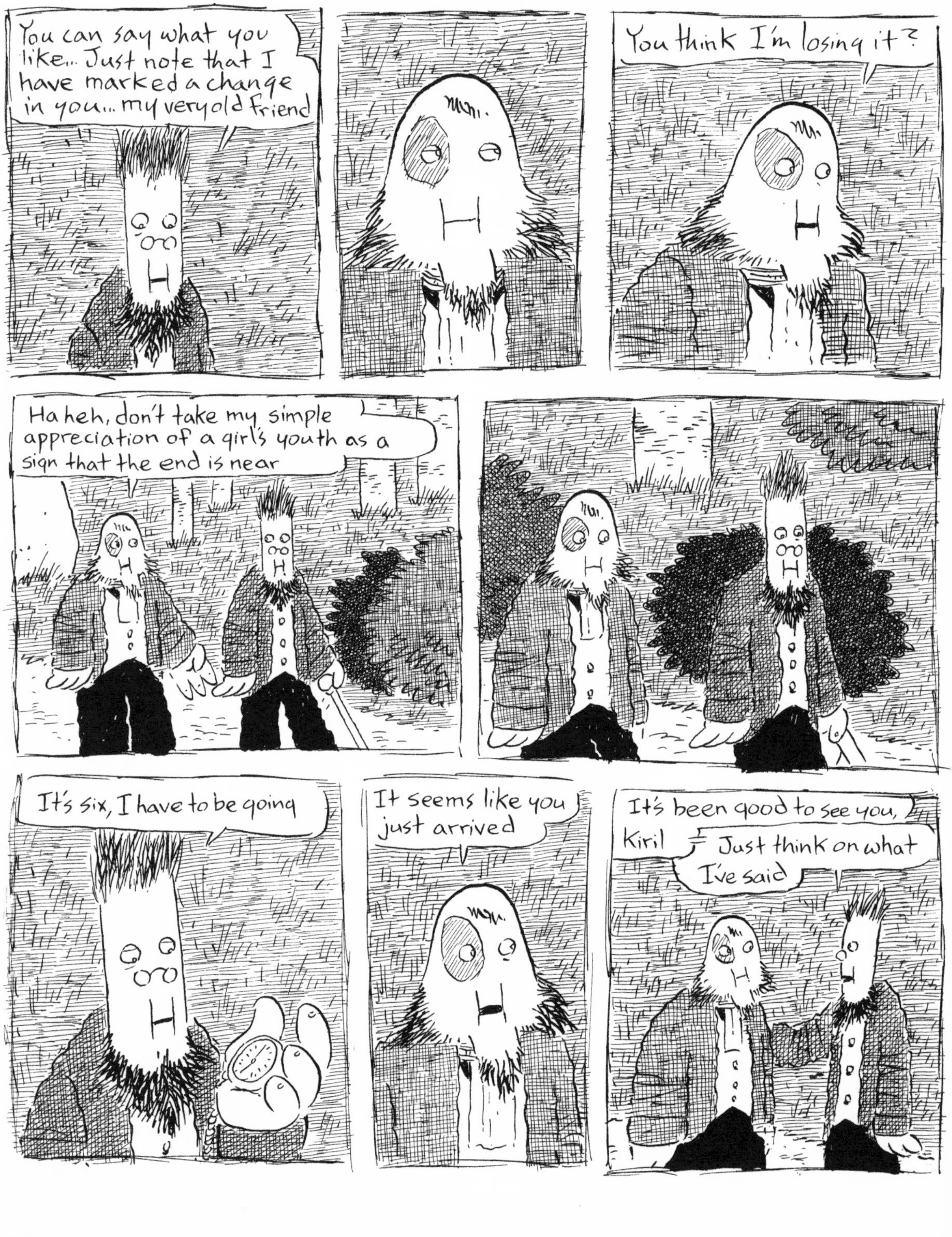
You can say what you like... Just note that I have marked a change in you... my very old friend
You think I'm losing it?
Ha heh, don't take my simple appreciation of a girl's youth as a sign that the end is near
It's six, I have to be going
It seems like you just arrived
It's been good to see you, Kiril
Just think on what I've said

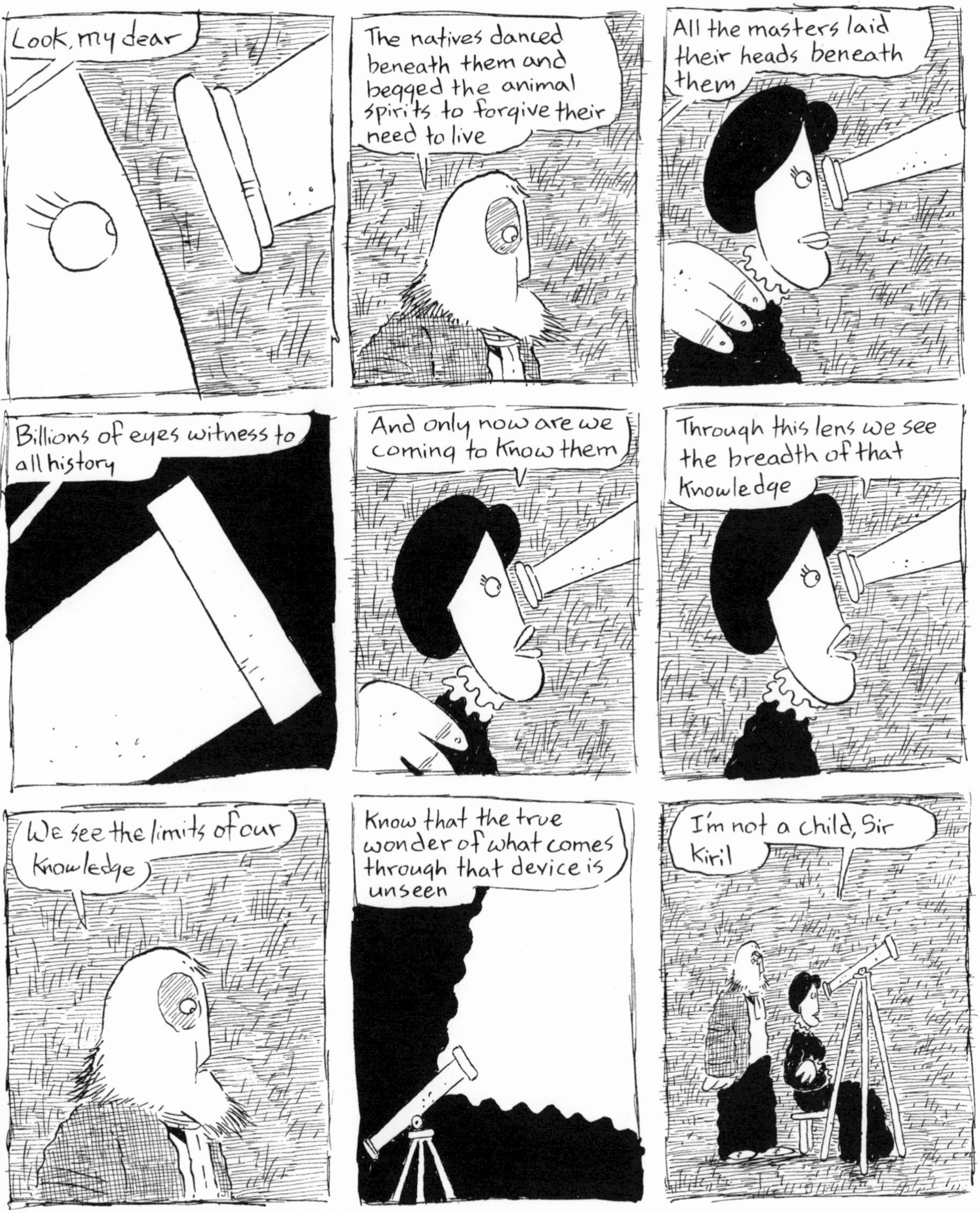

Look, my dear
The natives danced beneath them and begged the animal spirits to forgive their need to live
All the masters laid their heads beneath them
Billions of eyes witness to all history
And only now are we coming to know them
Through this lens we see the breadth of that knowledge
We see the limits of our knowledge
Know that the true wonder of what comes through that device is unseen
I'm not a child, Sir Kiril

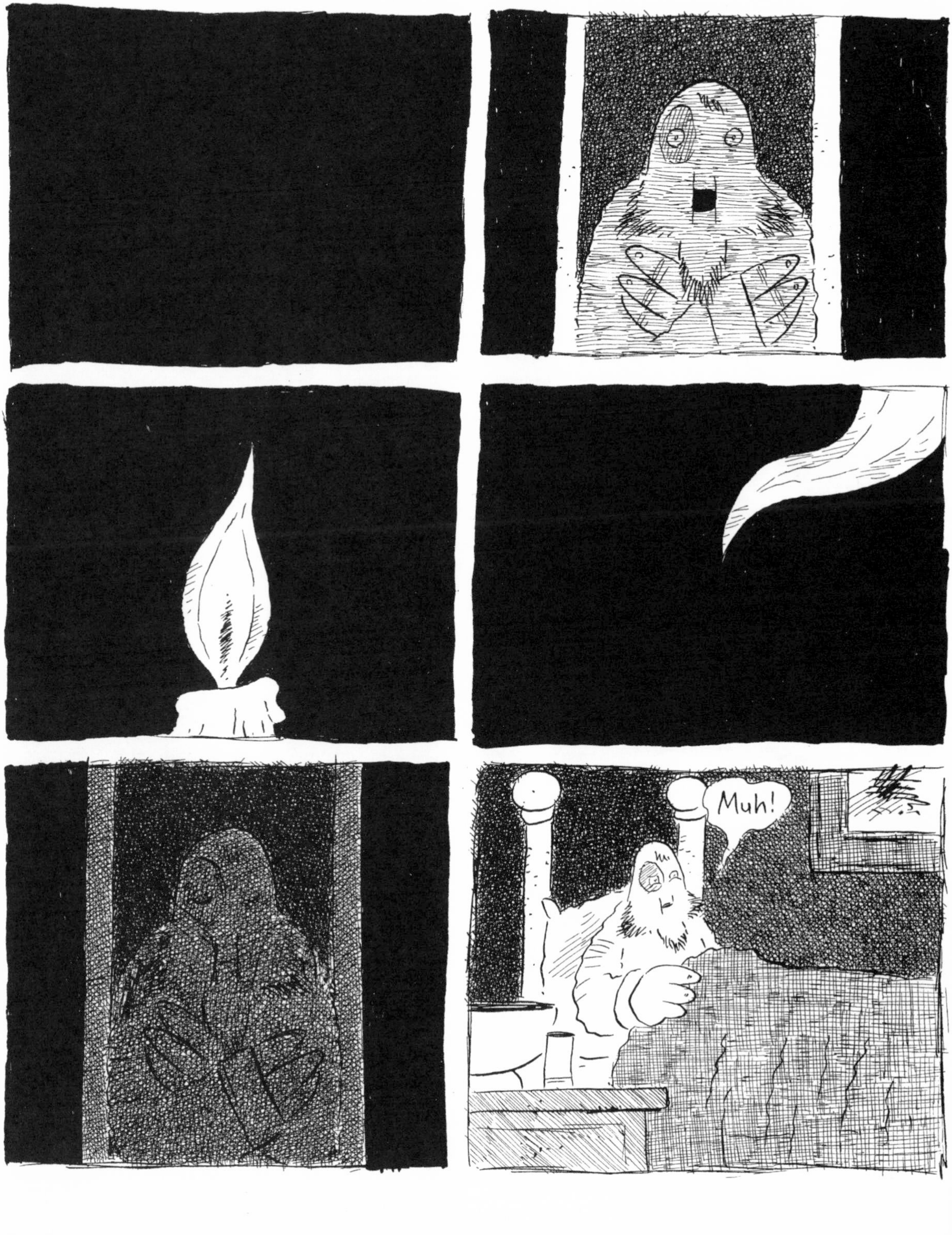
Muh!

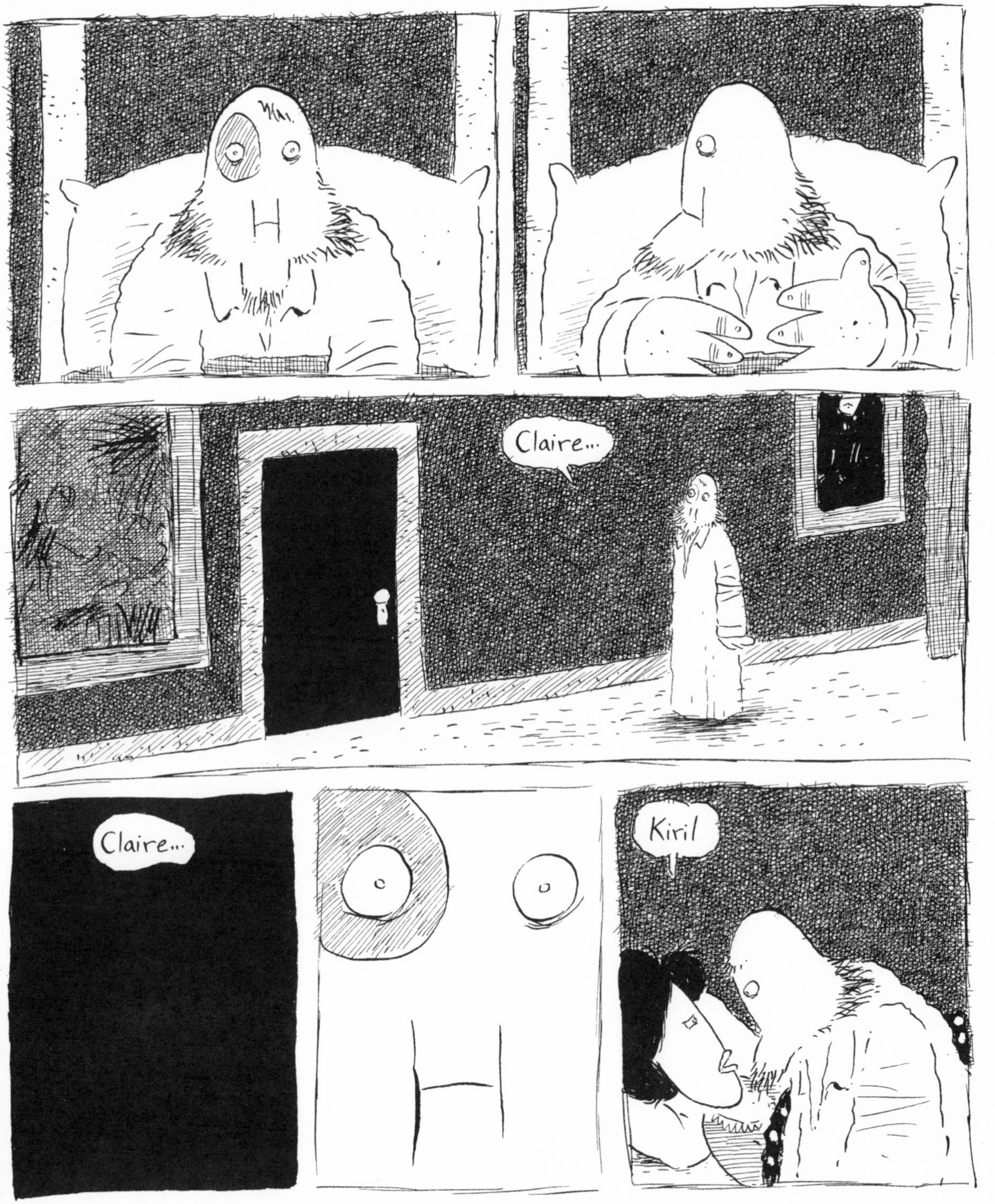
Claire...
Claire...
Kiril

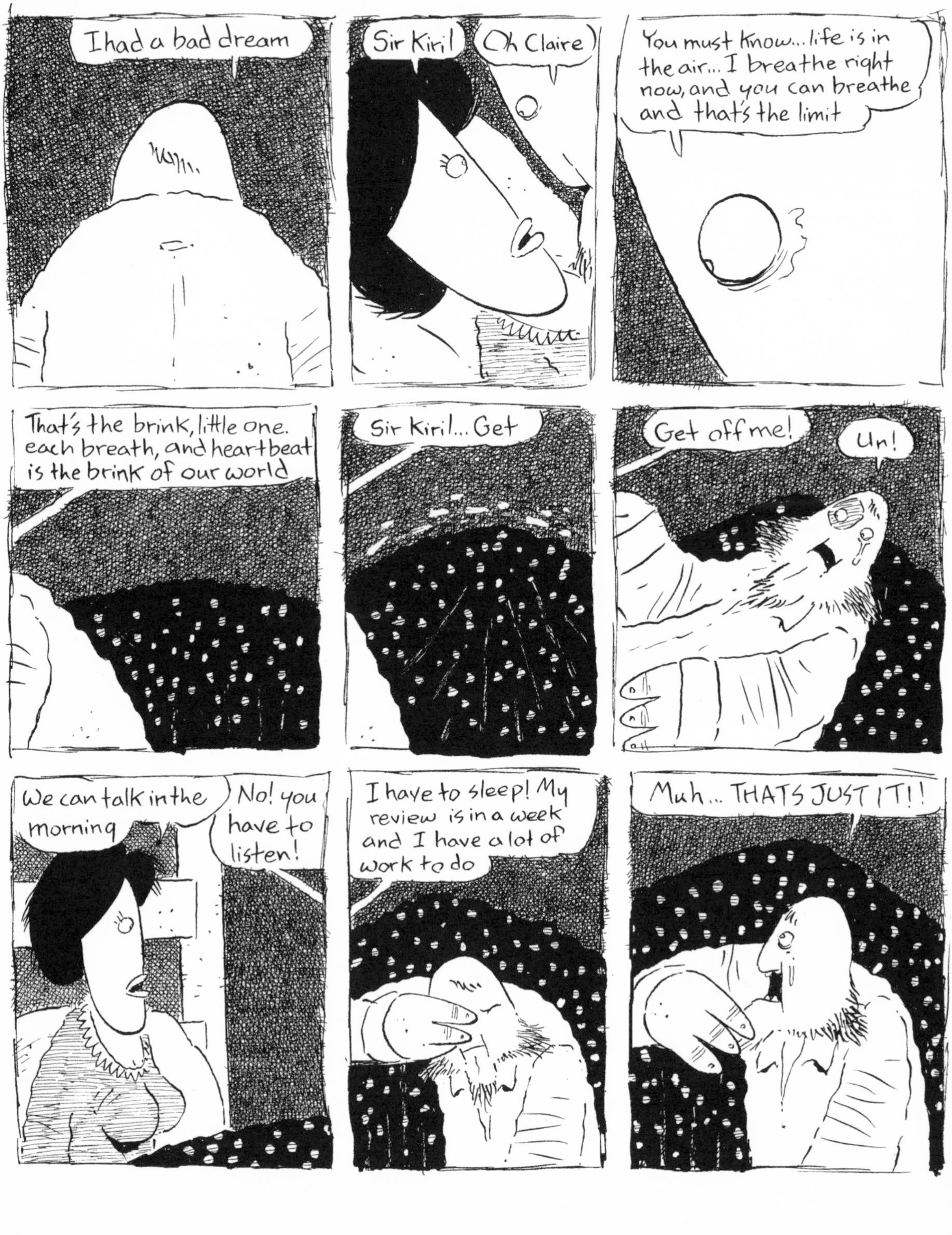
I had a bad dream
Sir Kiril
Oh Claire
You must know... life is in the air... I breathe right now, and you can breathe and that's the limit
That's the brink, little one. each breath, and heartbeat is the brink of our world
Sir Kiril... Get
Get off me!
Un!
We can talk in the morning
No! you have to listen!
I have to sleep! My review is in a week and I have a lot of work to do
Muh... THATS JUST IT!!

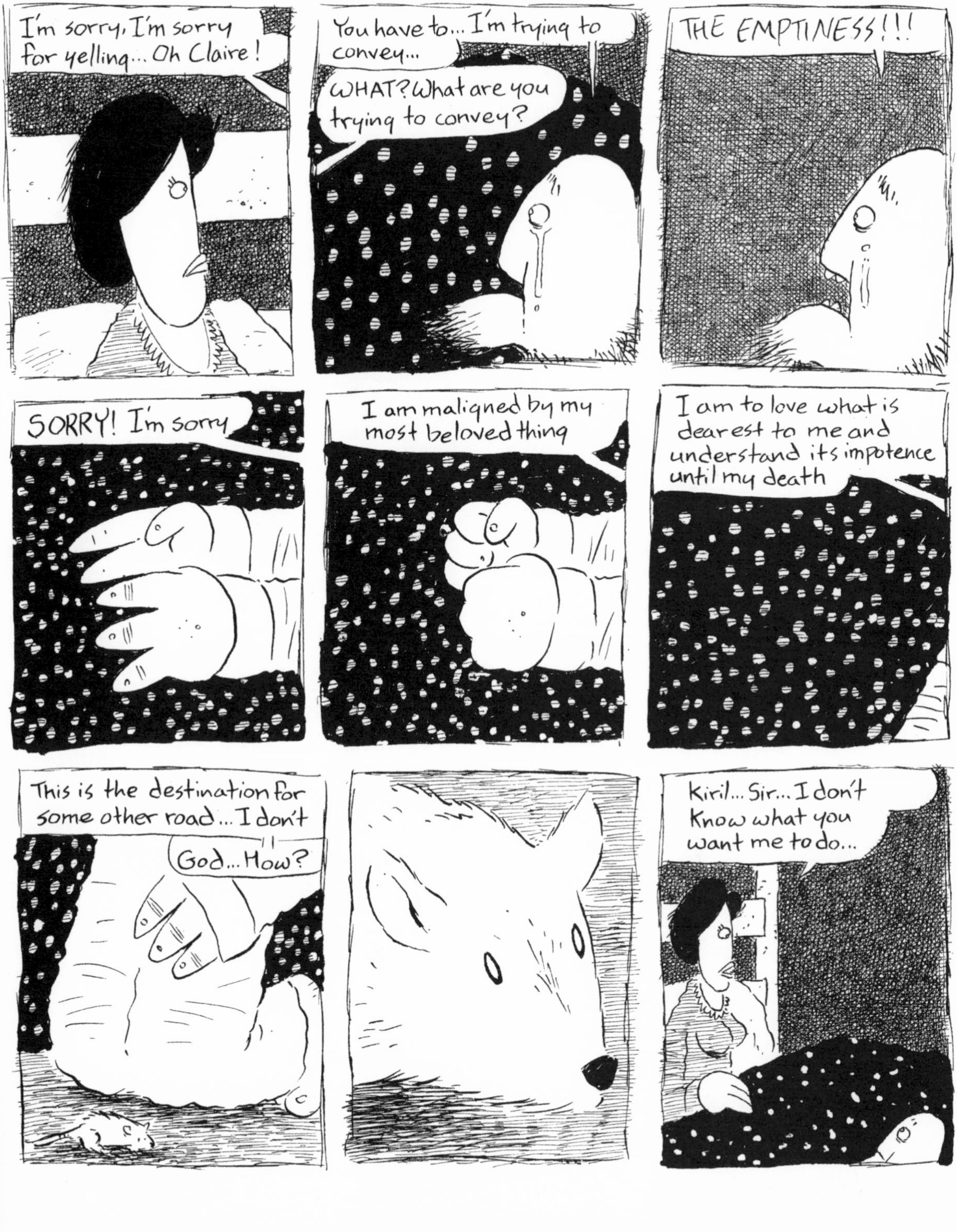

I'm sorry, I'm sorry for yelling... Oh Claire!
You have to... I'm trying to convey...
WHAT? What are you trying to convey?
THE EMPTINESS!!!
SORRY! I'm sorry
I am maligned by my most beloved thing
I am to love what is dearest to me and understand its impotence until my death
This is the destination for some other road... I don't
God... How?
Kiril... Sir... I don't Know what you want me to do...

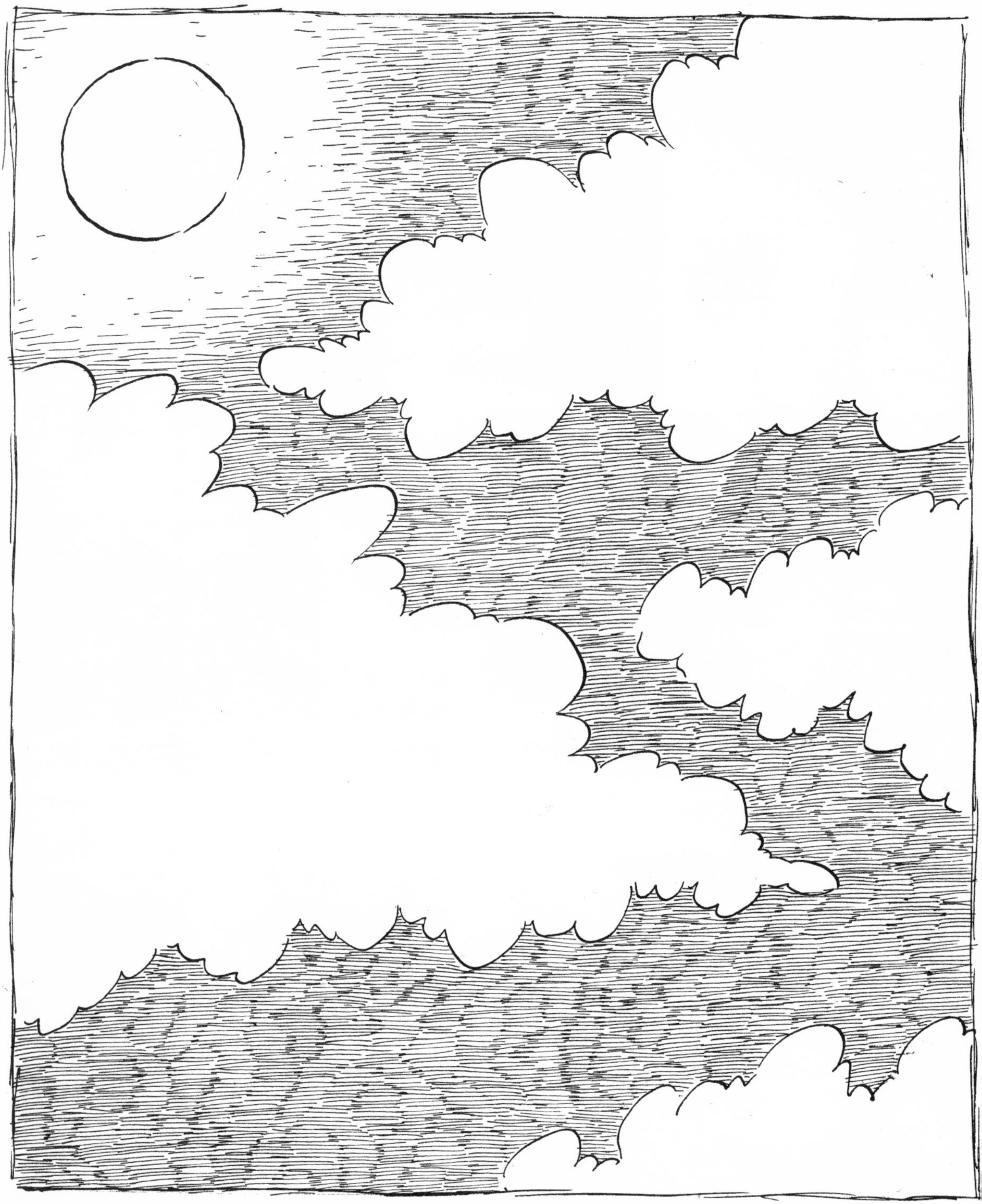

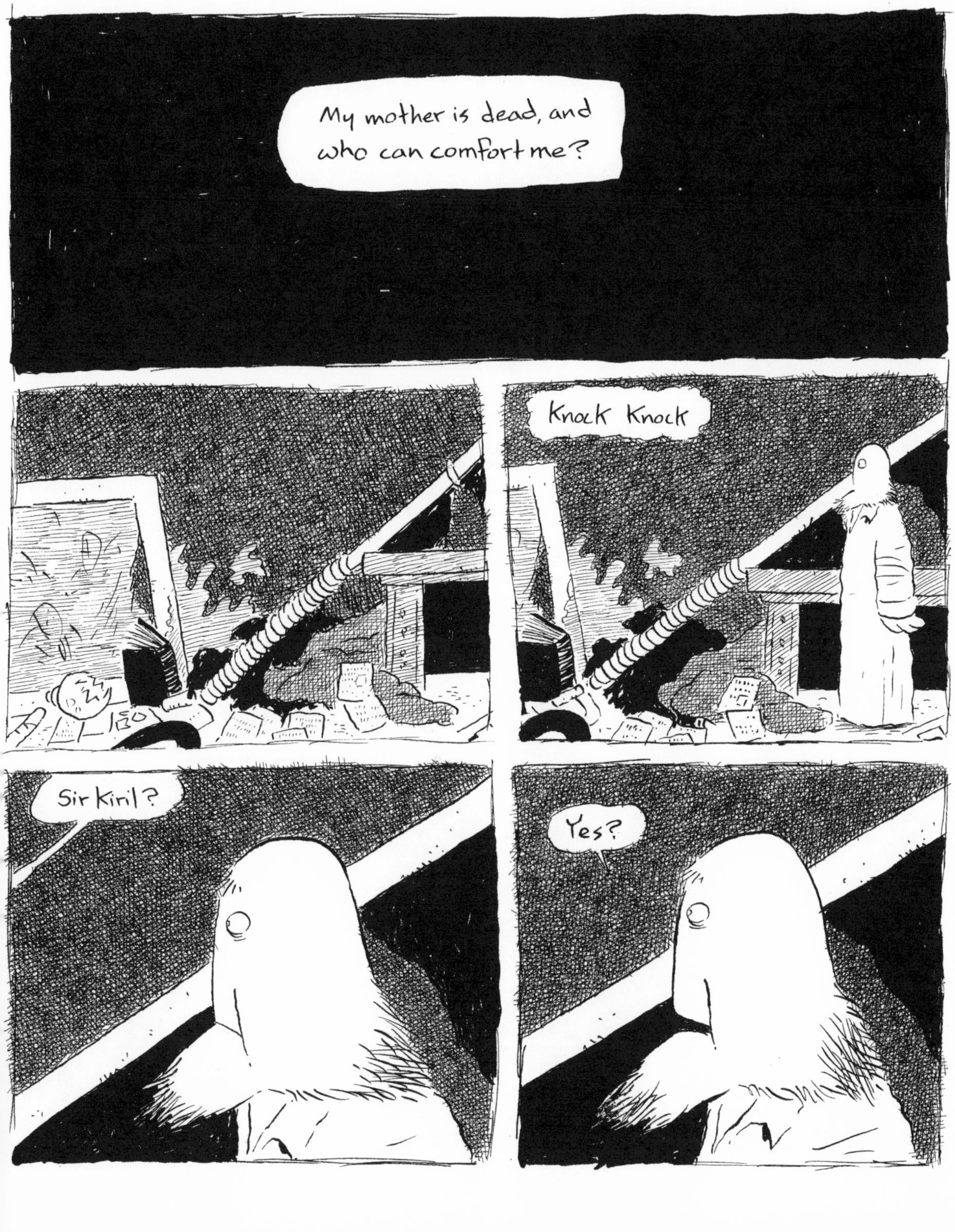
My mother is dead, and who can comfort me?
Knock Knock
Sir Kiril?
Yes?

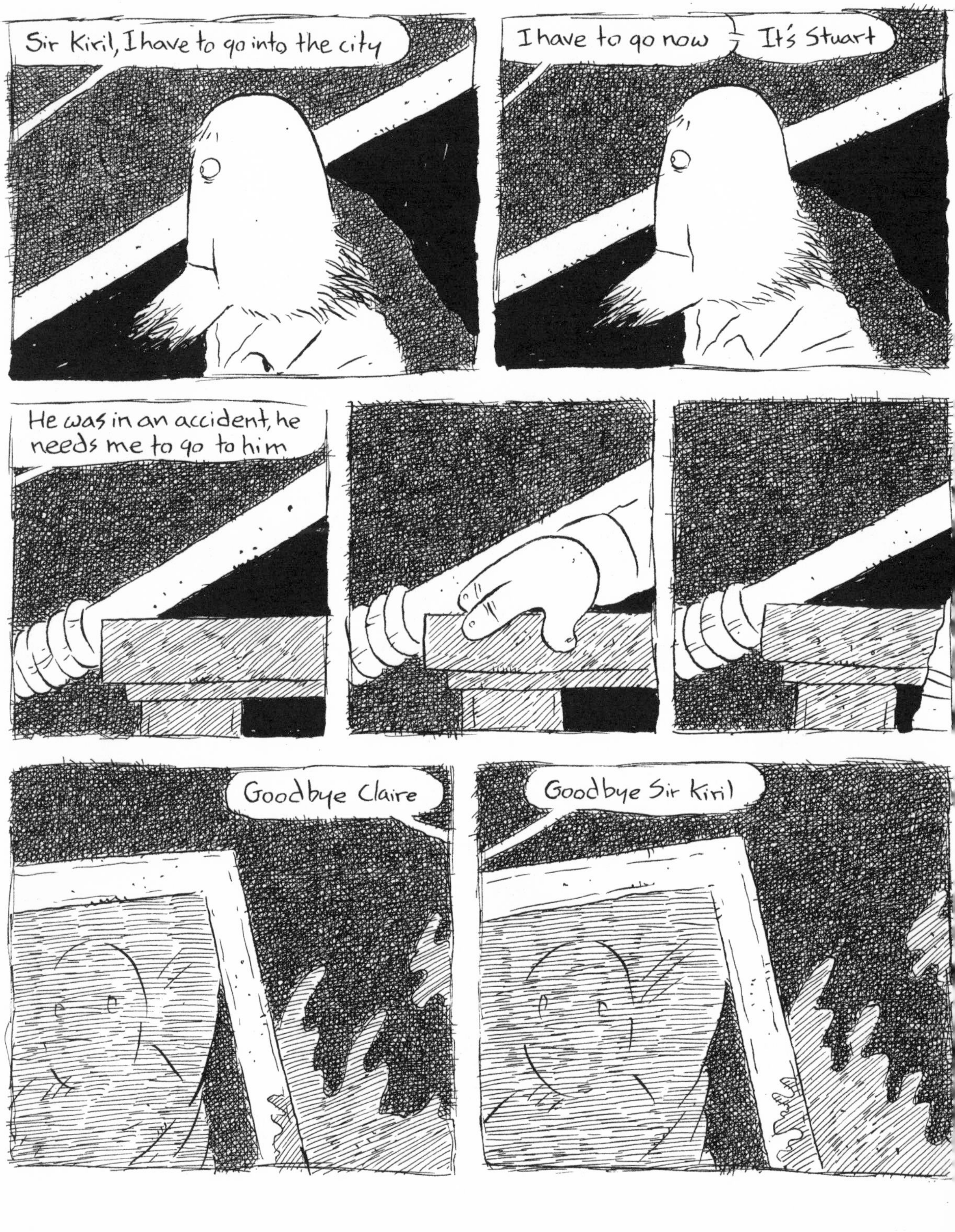
Sir Kiril, I have to go into the city
I have to go now
It's Stuart
He was in an accident, he needs me to go to him
Goodbye Claire
Goodbye Sir Kiril

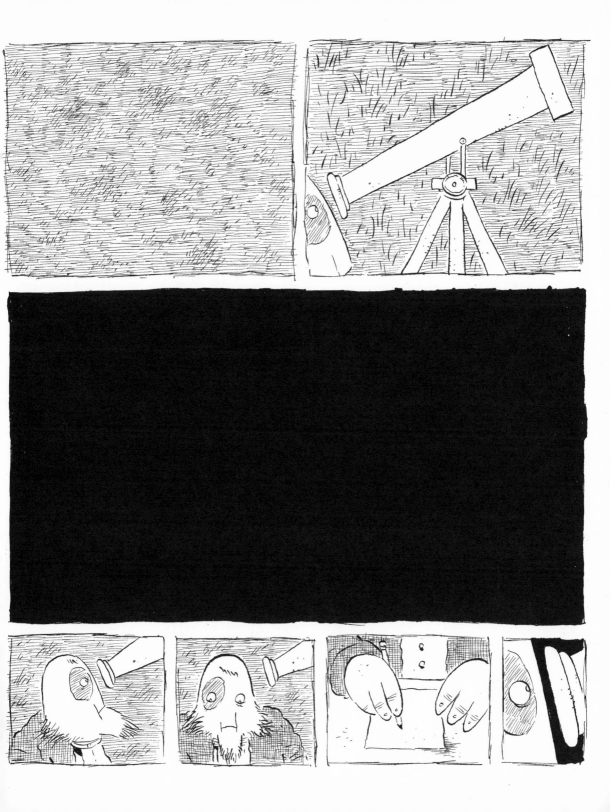

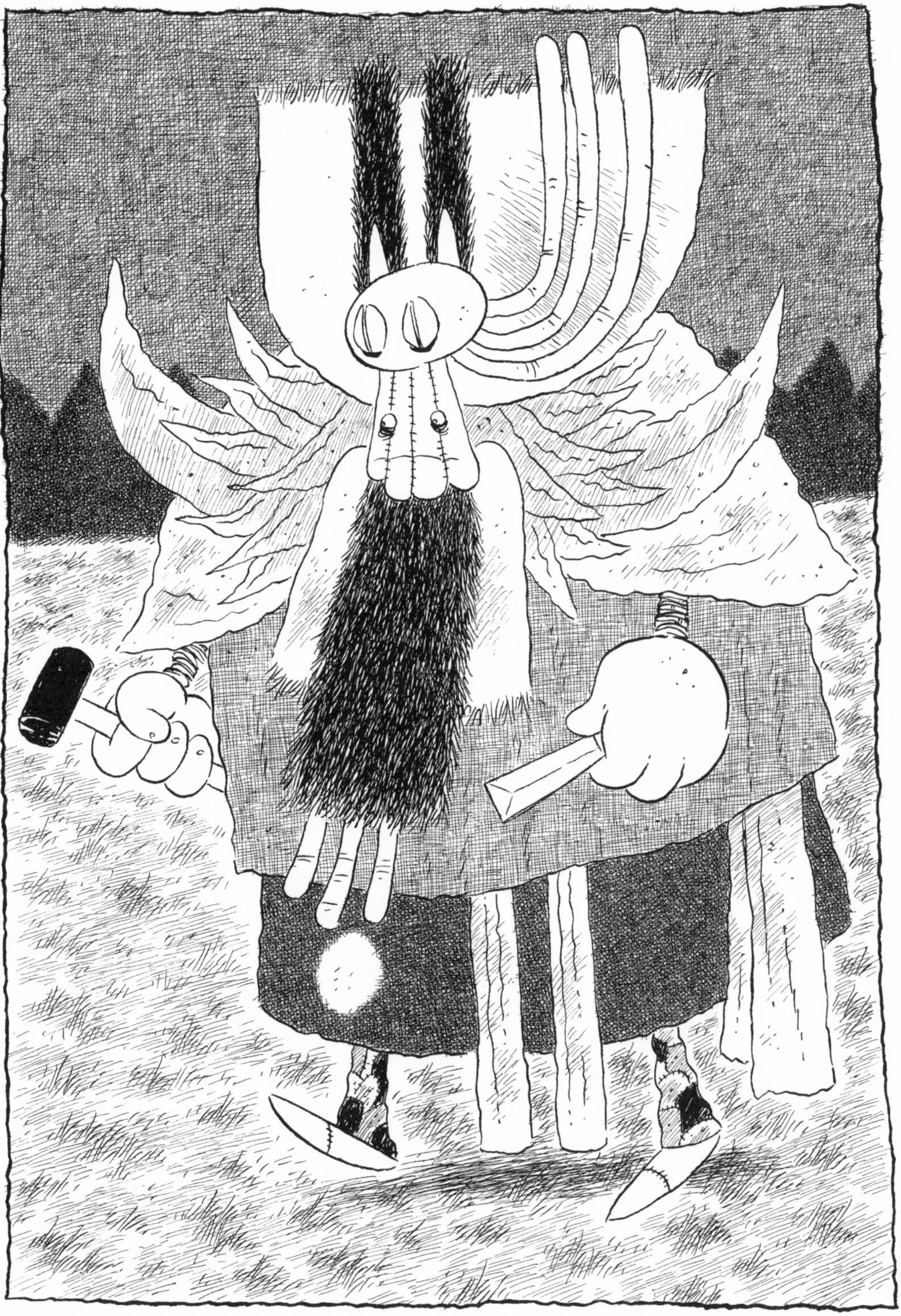

The Snake

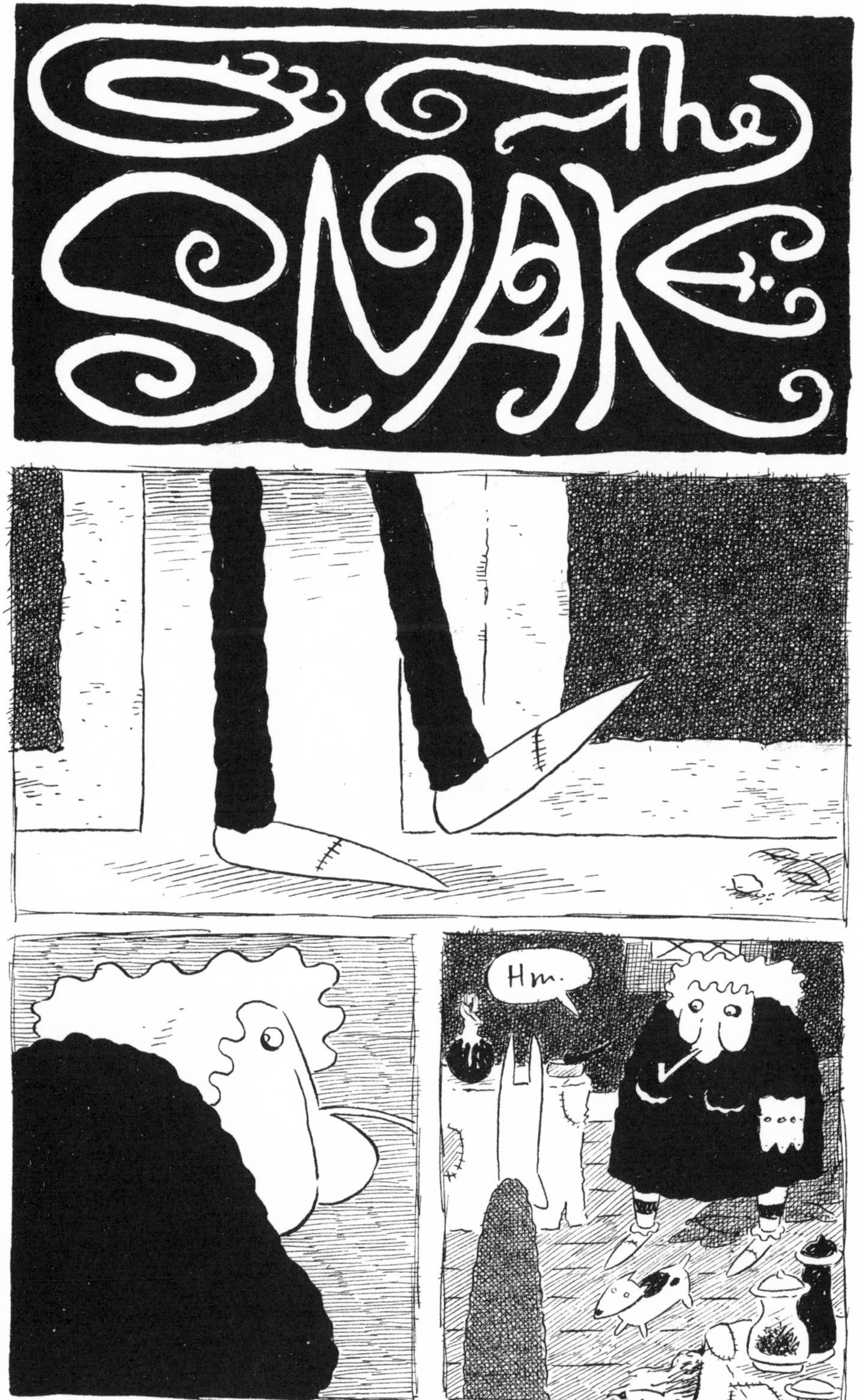
the
SNAKE
Hm.

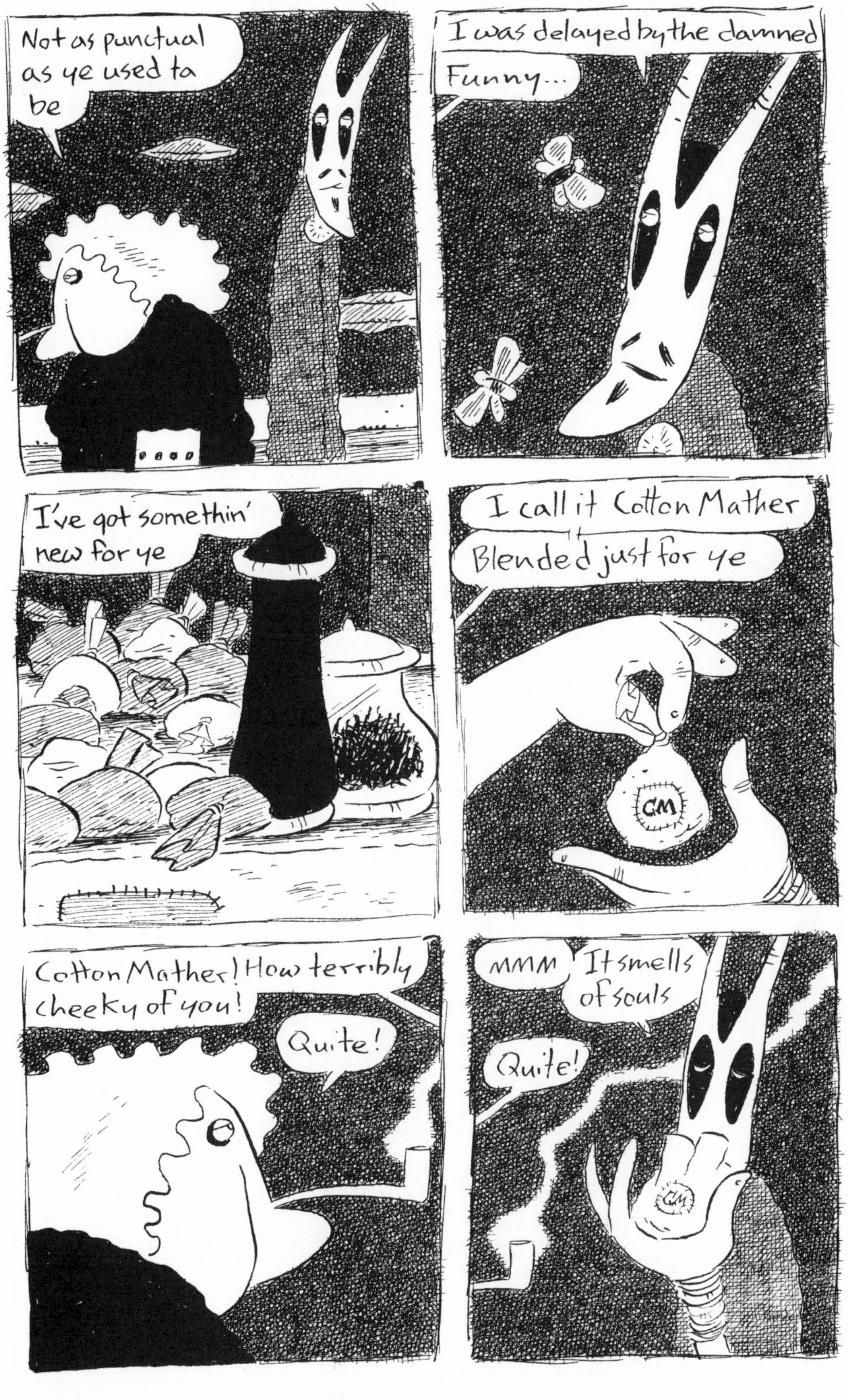
Not as punctual as ye used ta be
I was delayed by the damned
Funny...
I've got somethin' new for ye
I call it Cotton Mather
Blended just for ye
CM
Cotton Mather! How terribly cheeky of you!
Quite!
MMM
It smells of souls
Quite!
CM

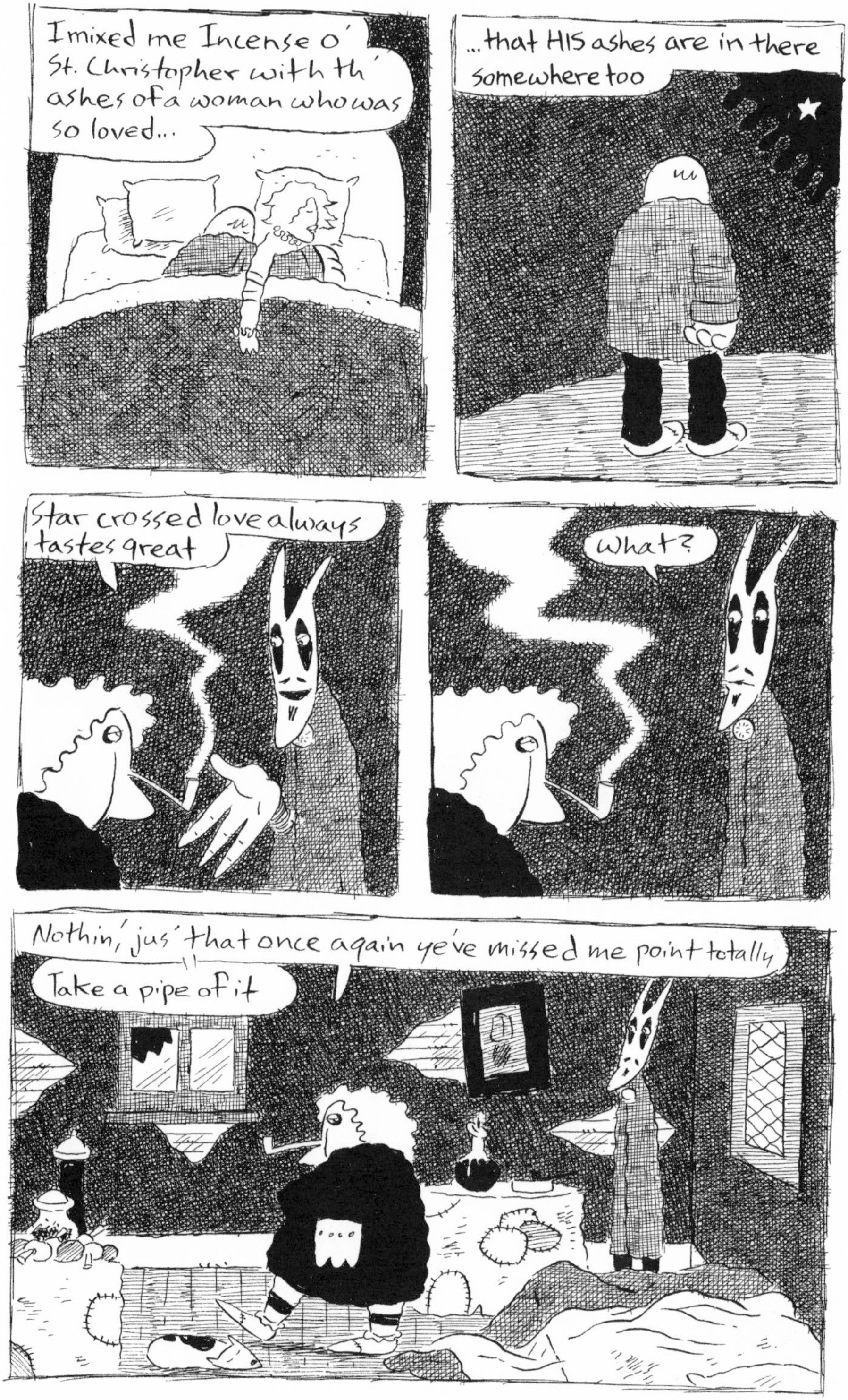
I mixed me Incense o' St. Christopher with th' ashes of a woman who was so loved...
...that HIS ashes are in there somewhere too
Star crossed love always tastes great
What?
Nothin', jus' that once again ye've missed me point totally
Take a pipe of it

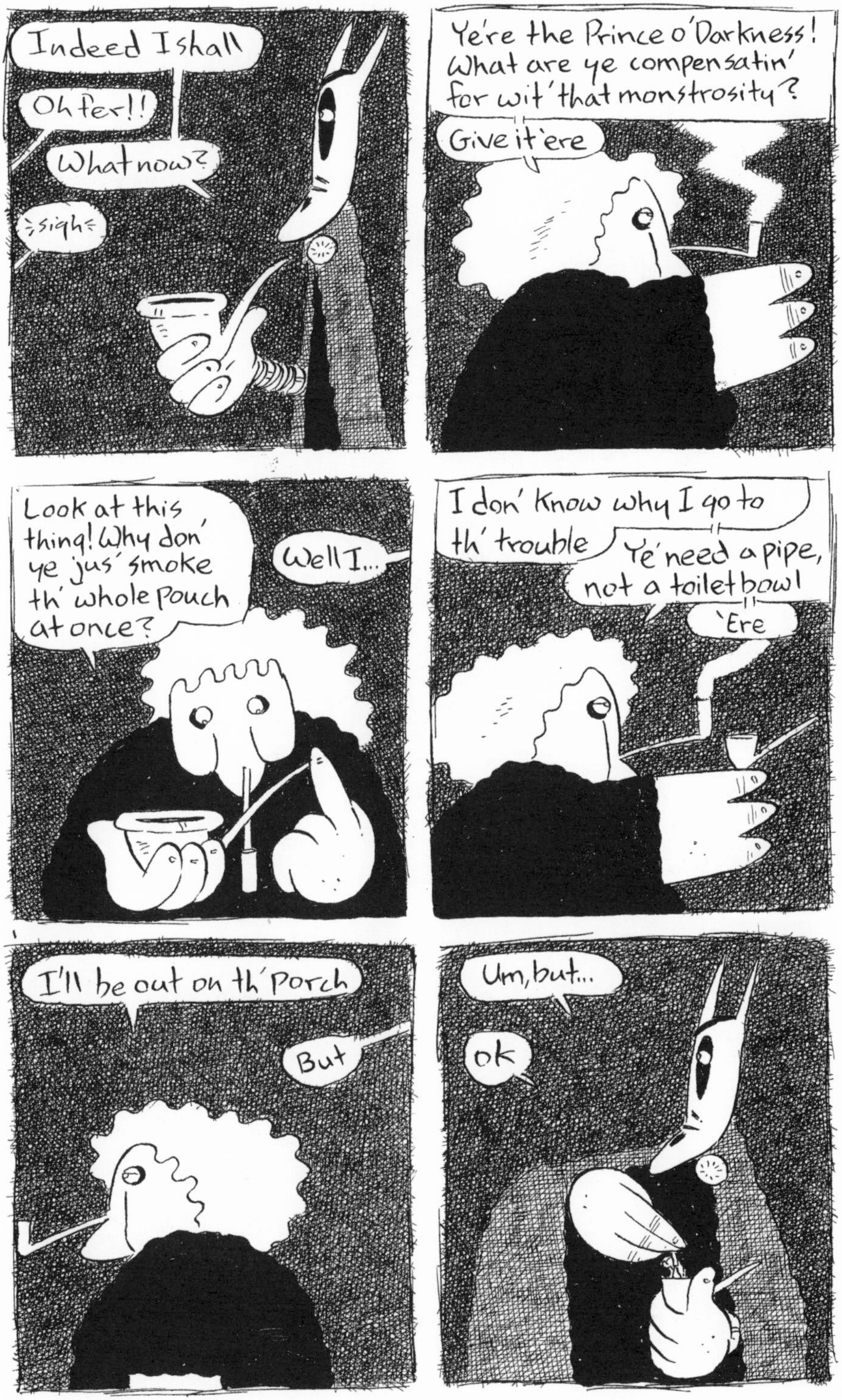
Indeed I shall
Oh fer!!
What now?
sigh
Ye're the Prince o'Darkness! What are ye compensatin' for wit' that monstrosity?
Give it 'ere
Look at this thing! Why don' ye jus' smoke th' whole pouch at once?
Well I...
I don' know why I go to th' trouble
Ye' need a pipe, not a toilet bowl
'Ere
I'll be out on th' porch
But
Um, but...
ok

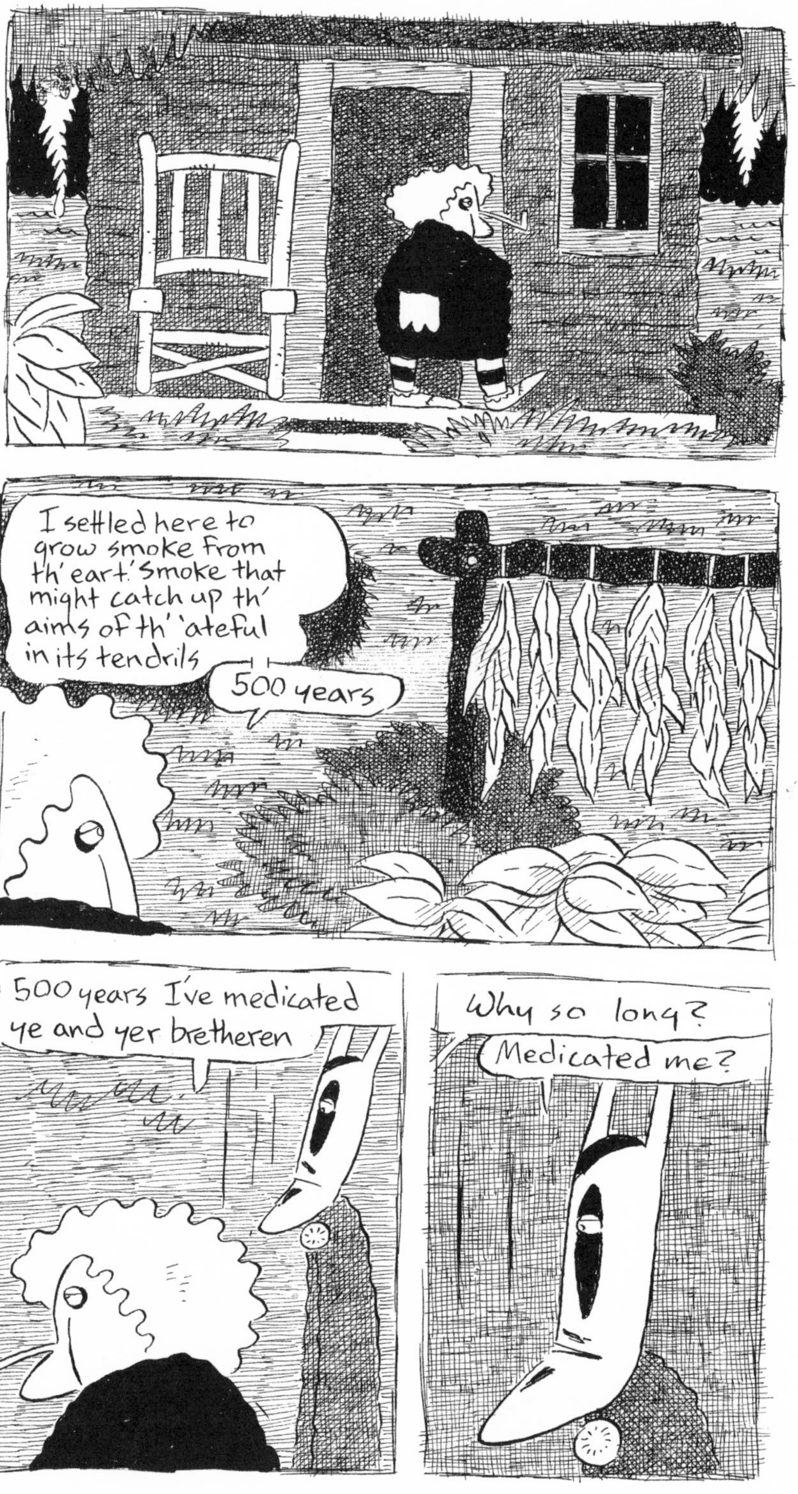
I settled here to grow smoke from th' eart.' Smoke that might catch up th' aims of th' 'ateful in its tendrils
500 years
500 years I've medicated ye and yer bretheren
Why so long?
Medicated me?

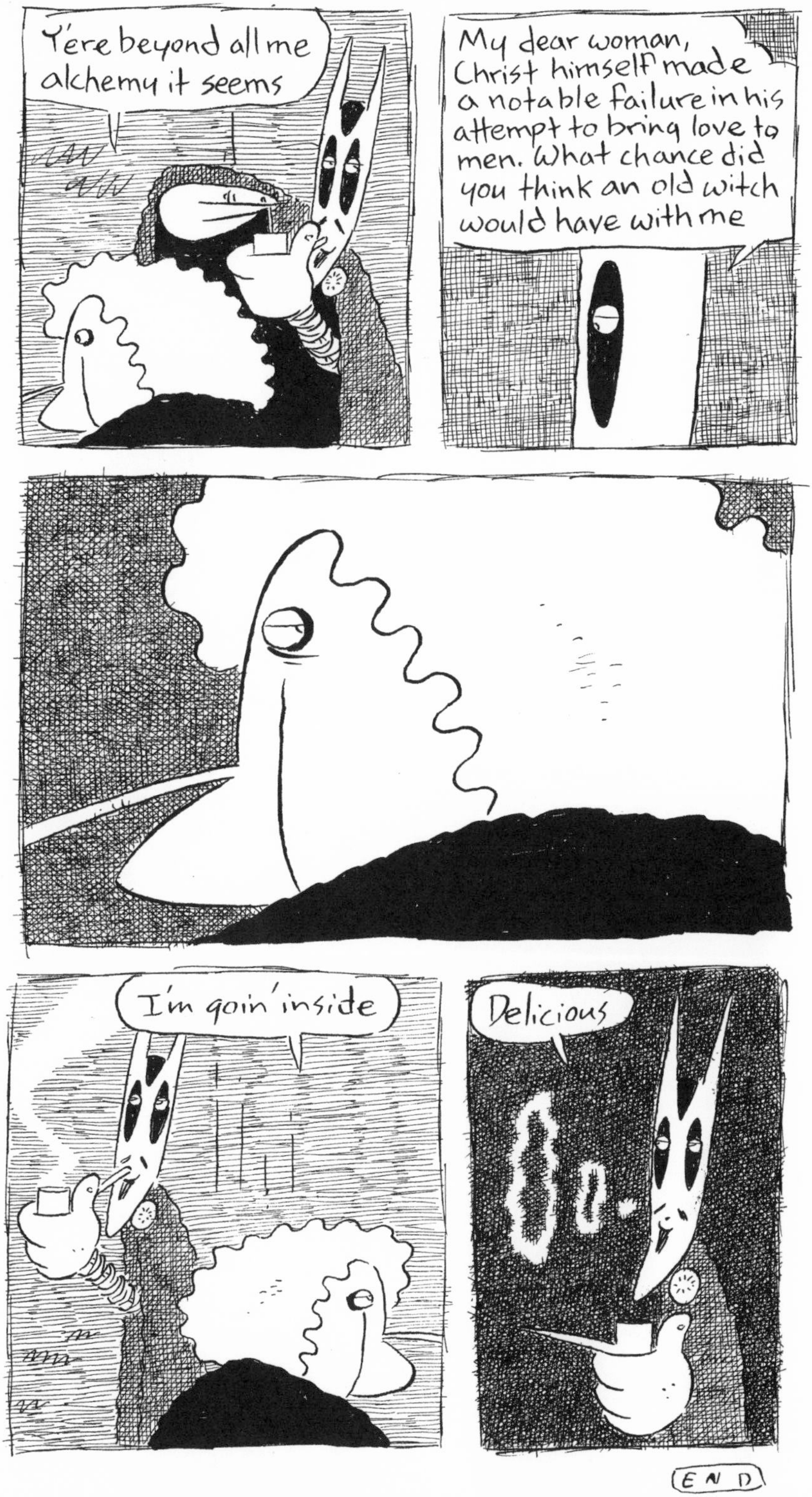
Y'ere beyond all me alchemy it seems
My dear woman, Christ himself made a notable failure in his attempt to bring love to men. What chance did you think an old witch would have with me
I'm goin' inside
Delicious
END

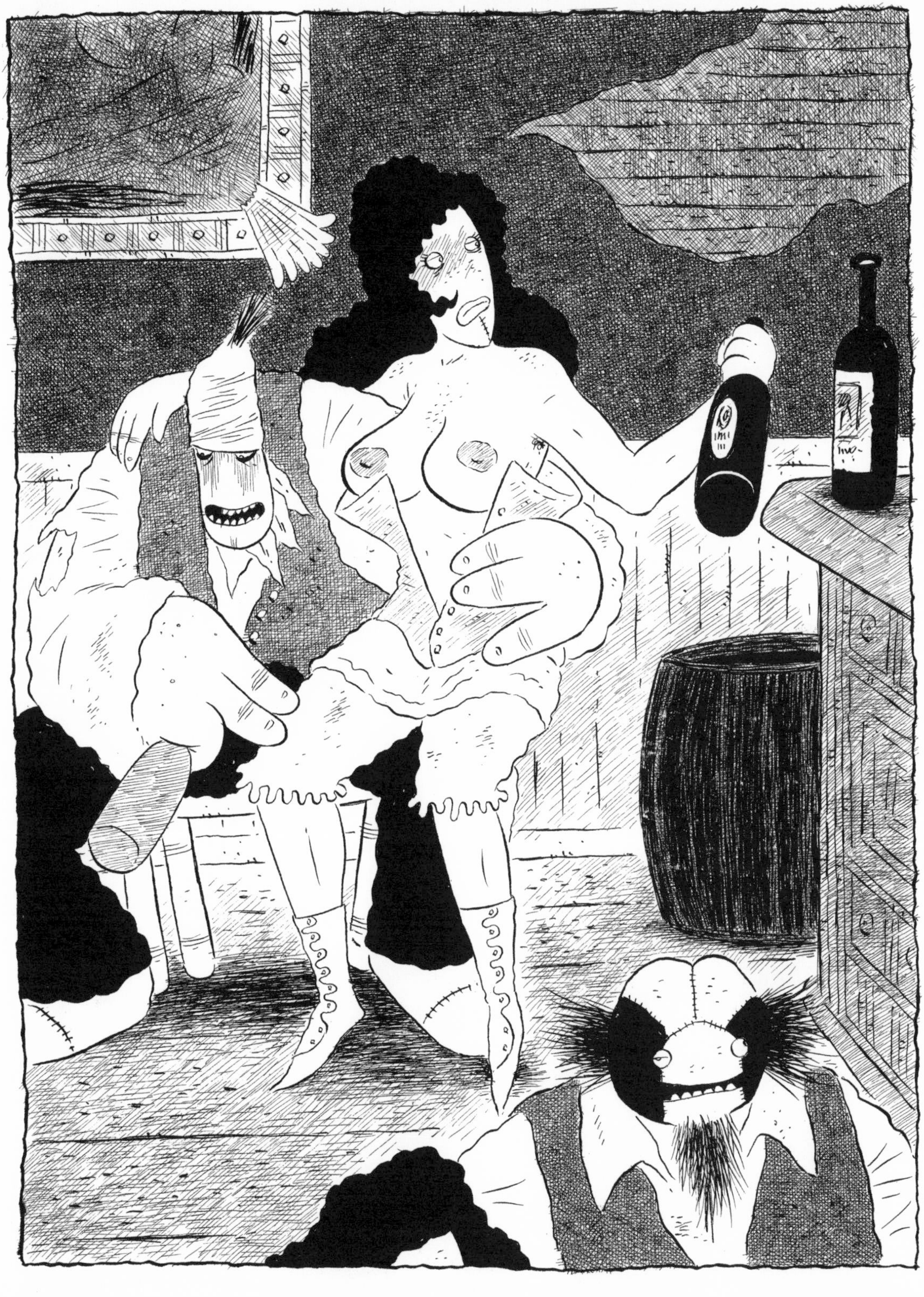

Truth

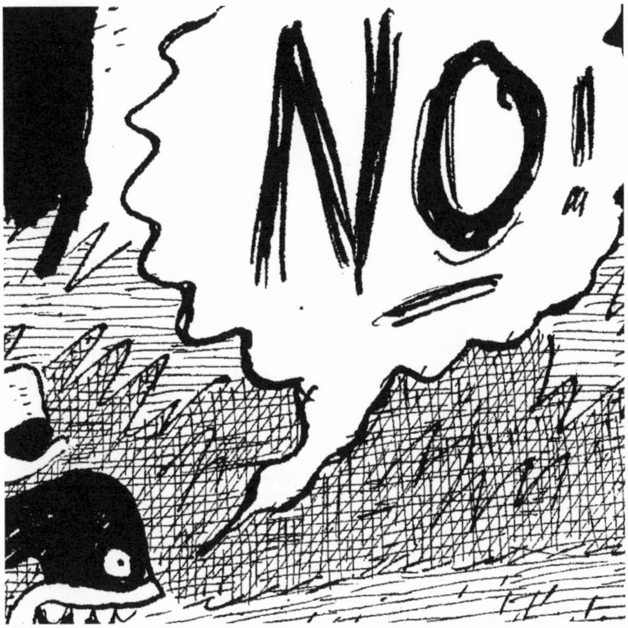
NO!

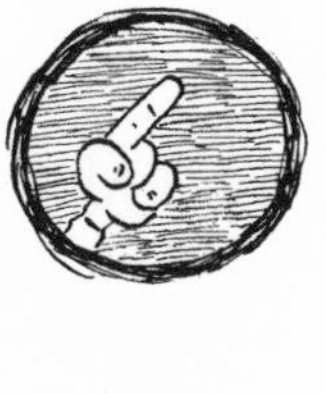

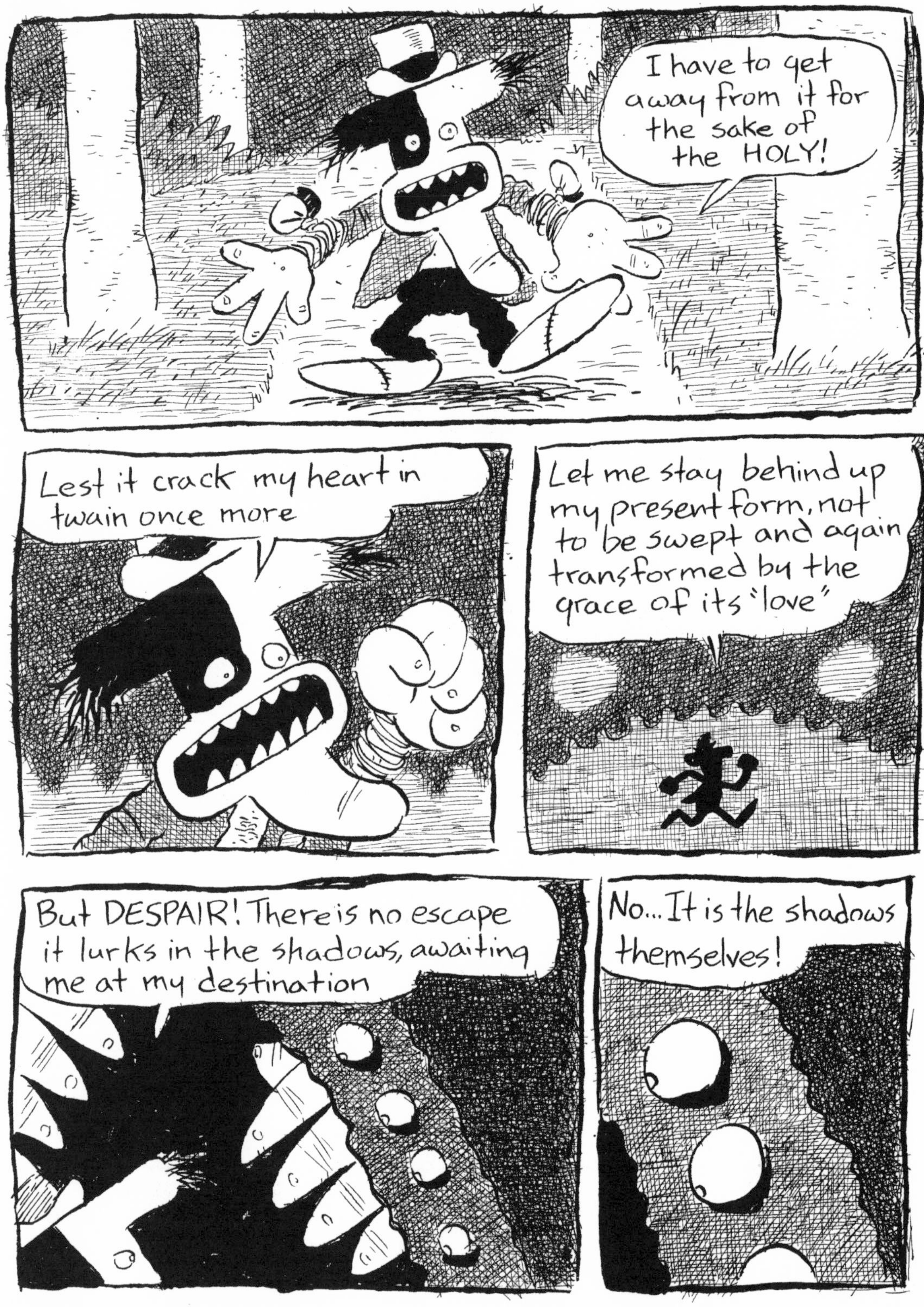
I have to get away from it for the sake of the HOLY!
Lest it crack my heart in twain once more
Let me stay behind up my present form, not to be swept and again transformed by the grace of its "love"
But DESPAIR! There is no escape it lurks in the shadows, awaiting me at my destination
No... It is the shadows themselves!

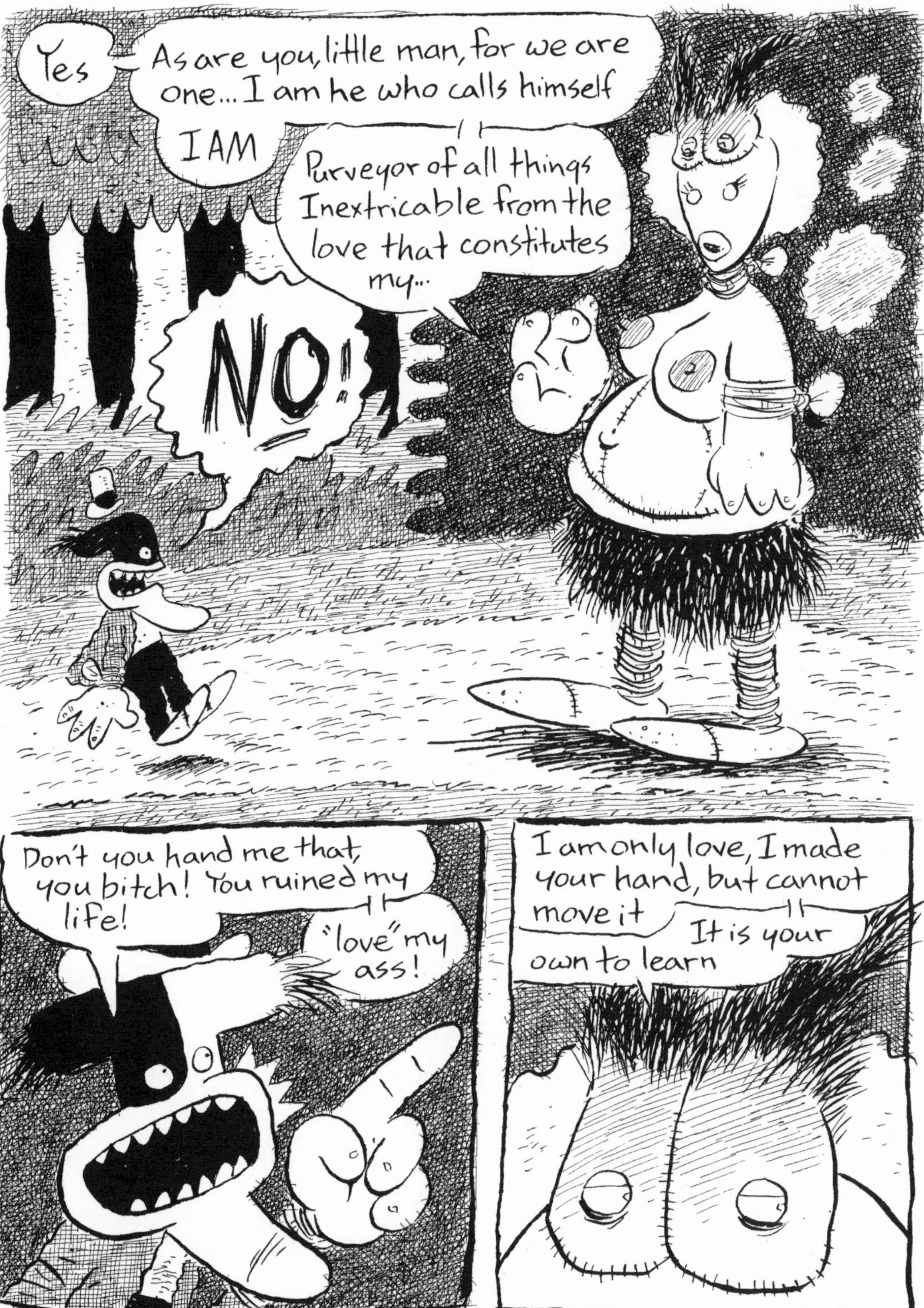
Yes
As are you, little man, for we are one... I am he who calls himself
IAM
Purveyor of all things Inextricable from the love that constitutes my...
NO!
Don't you hand me that, you bitch! You ruined my life!
"love" my ass!
I am only love, I made your hand, but cannot move it
It is your own to learn

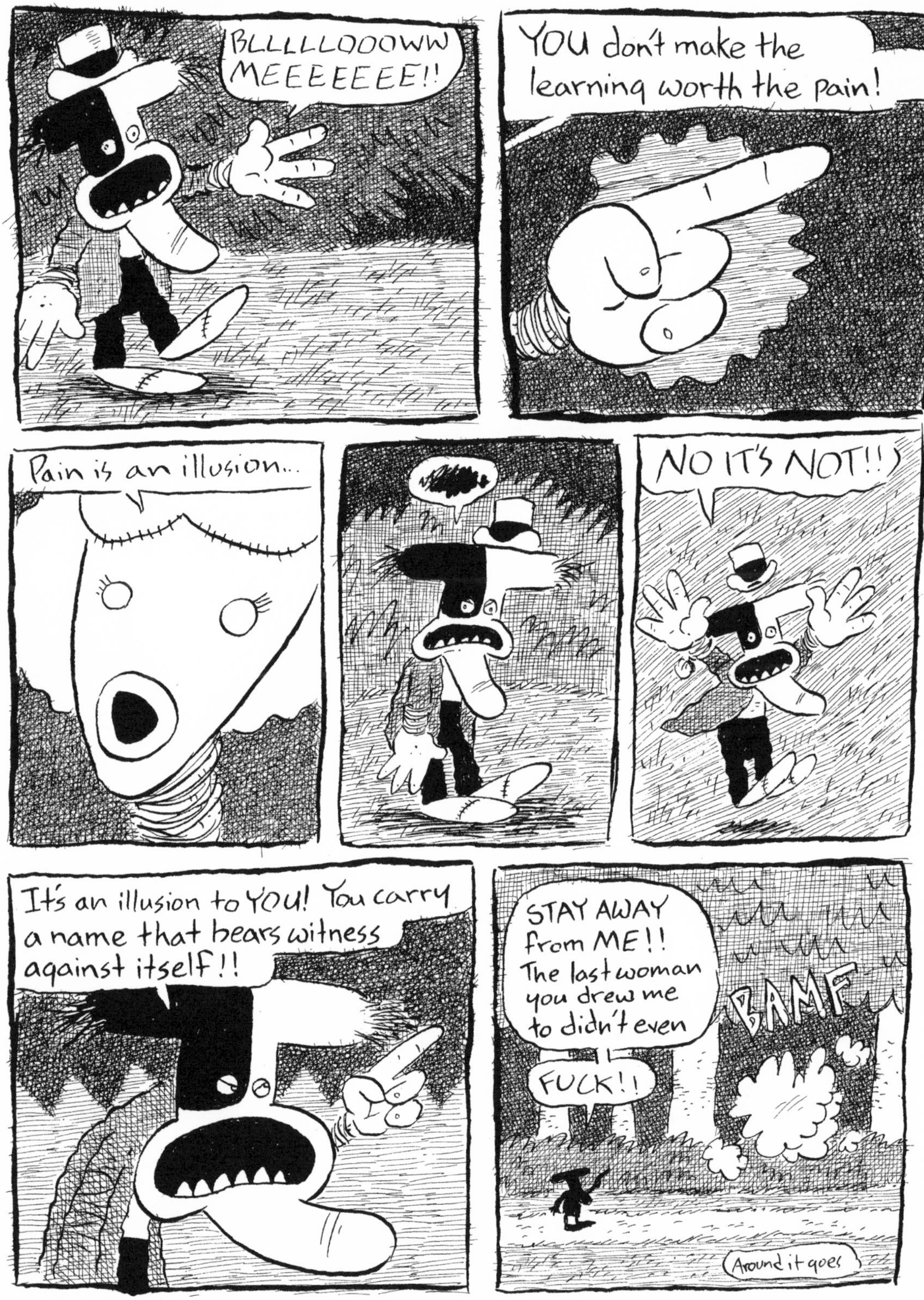
BLLLLLOOOWW MEEEEEEE!!
YOU don't make the learning worth the pain!
Pain is an illusion...
NO IT'S NOT!!
It's an illusion to YOU! You carry a name that bears witness against itself!!
STAY AWAY from ME!! The last woman you drew me to didn't even
FUCK!!
BAMF
Around it goes

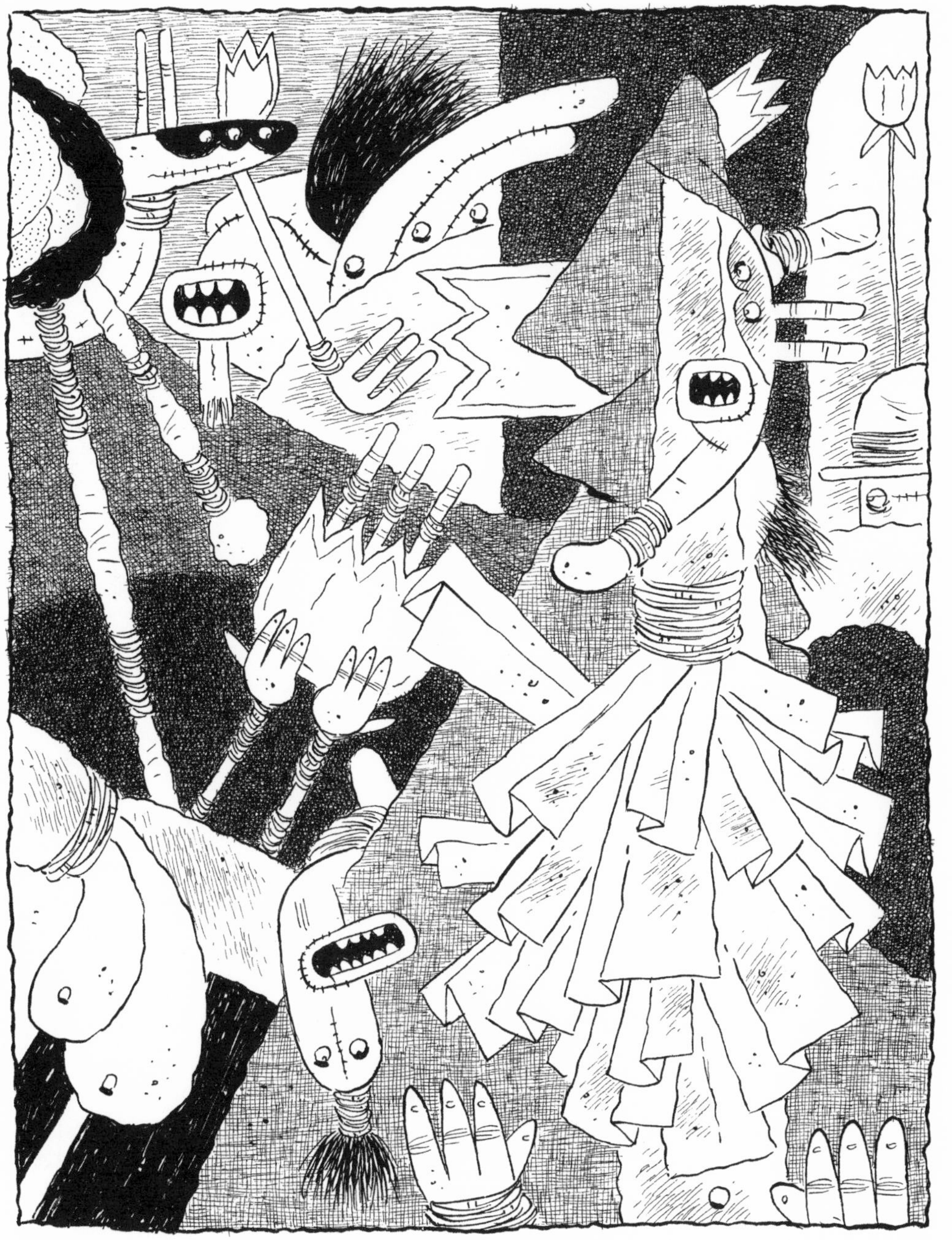

The Urn

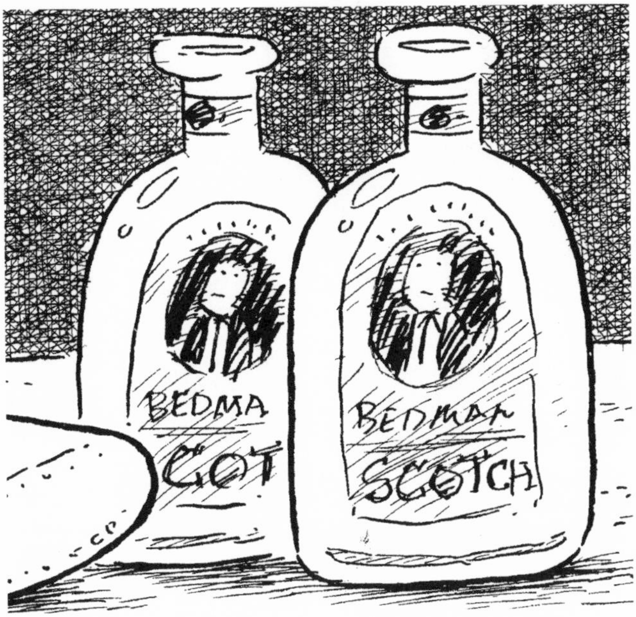
BEDMA
GOT
BEDMAN
SCOTCH

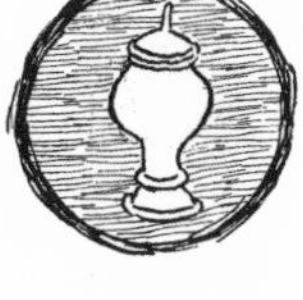

There is a spot on the urn

It is rust colored

But it is not rust

If you touch it it will come off on your fingers

A thin red, yellow liquid

Containing bits of sand

There is no corrosion

It will not be wiped away

If it is not tended to it will bubble and run down its silver host

Like a living thing that is grieving

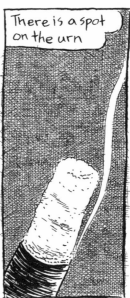

There is a spot on the urn

That contains his ashes

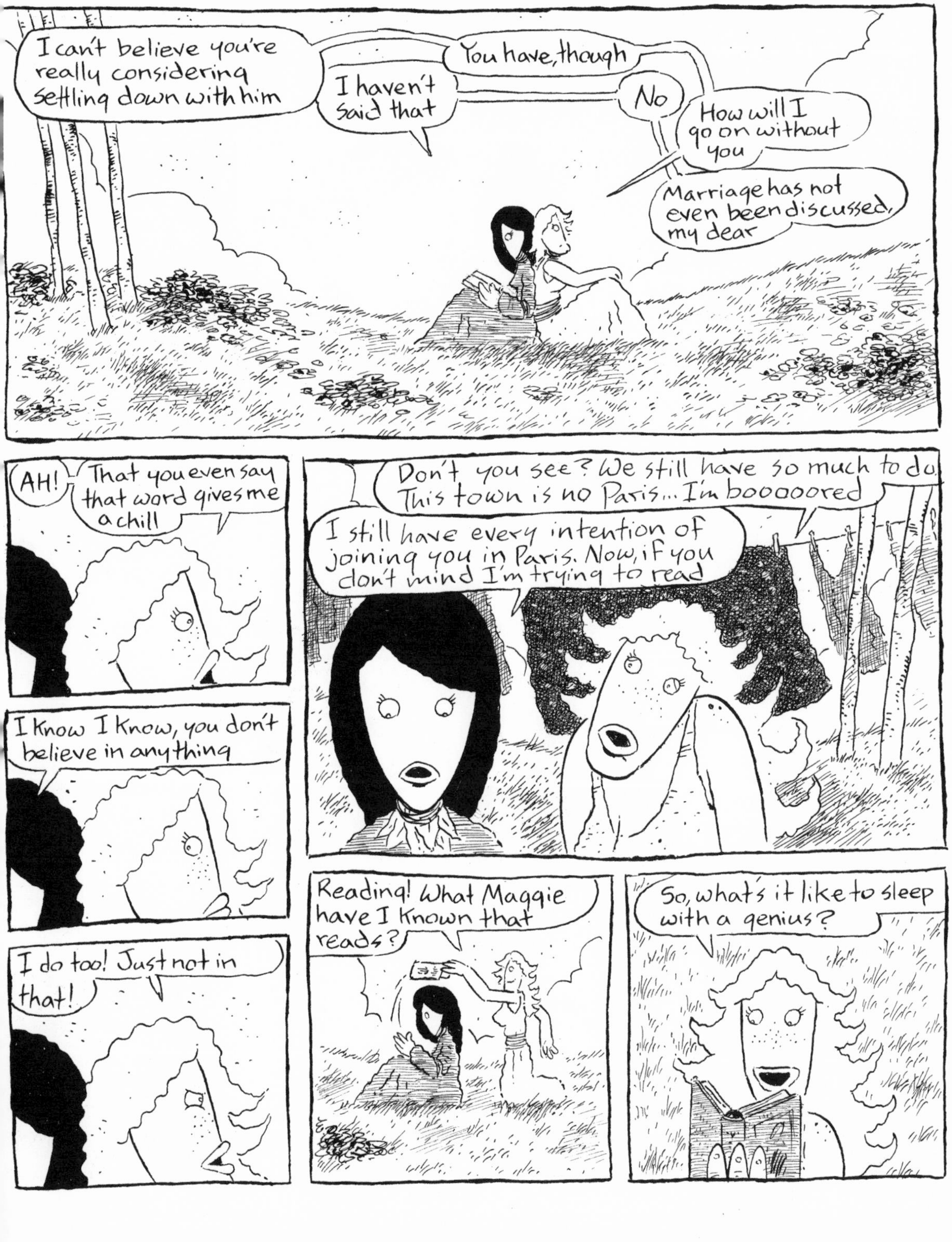

I can't believe you're really considering settling down with him
I haven't said that
You have, though
No
How will I go on without you
Marriage has not even been discussed, my dear
AH!
That you even say that word gives me a chill
Don't you see? We still have so much to do. This town is no Paris... I'm boooooored
I still have every intention of joining you in Paris. Now, if you don't mind I'm trying to read
I Know I Know, you don't believe in anything
I do too! Just not in that!
Reading! What Maggie have I Known that reads?
So, what's it like to sleep with a genius?

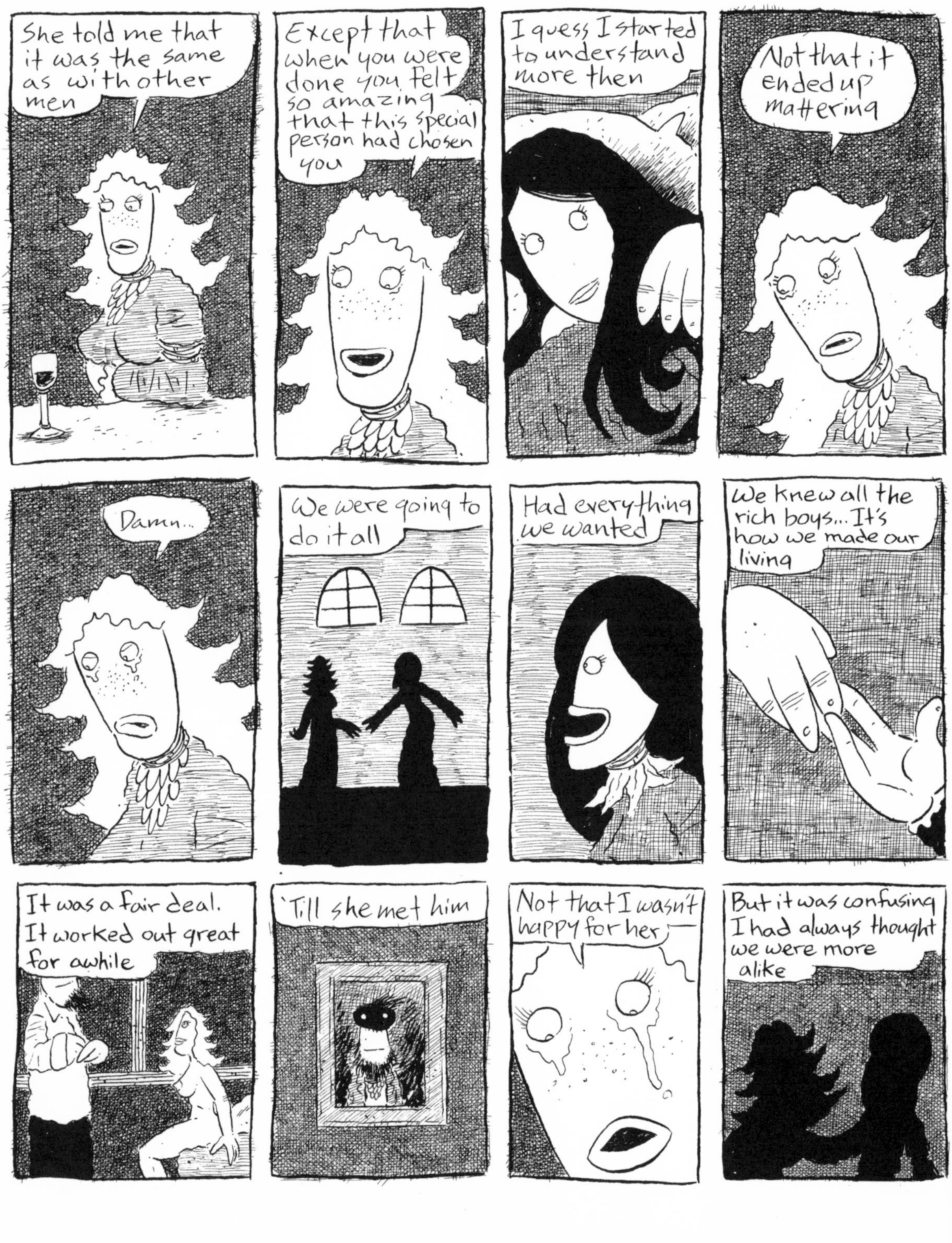
She told me that it was the same as with other men
Except that when you were done you felt so amazing that this special person had chosen you
I guess I started to understand more then
Not that it ended up mattering
Damn...
We were going to do it all
Had everything we wanted
We knew all the rich boys... It's how we made our living
It was a fair deal. It worked out great for awhile
'Till she met him
Not that I wasn't happy for her
But it was confusing I had always thought we were more alike

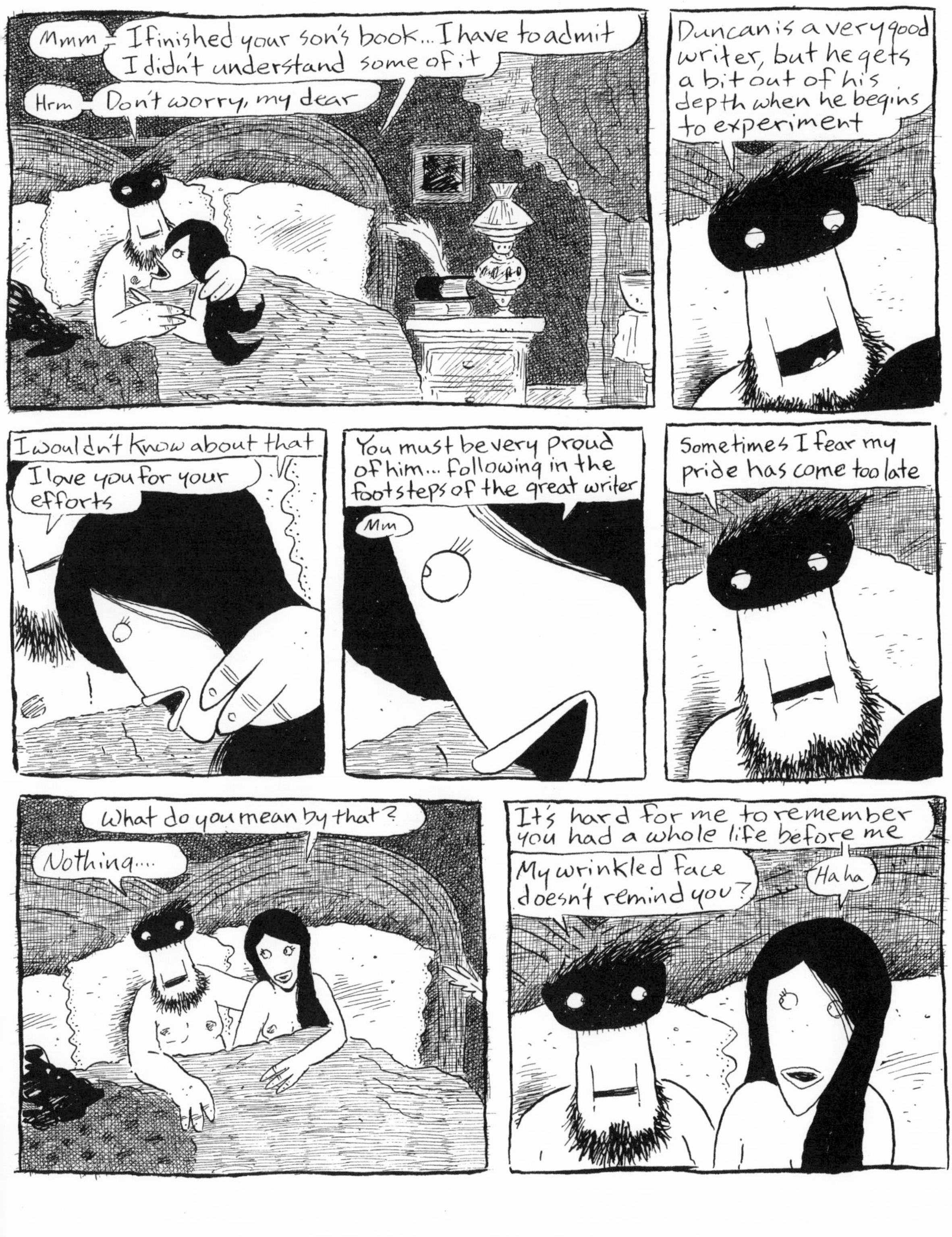
Mmm
I finished your son's book... I have to admit I didn't understand some of it
Hrm
Don't worry, my dear
Duncan is a very good writer, but he gets a bit out of his depth when he begins to experiment
I wouldn't know about that
I love you for your efforts
You must be very proud of him... following in the footsteps of the great writer
Mm
Sometimes I fear my pride has come too late
What do you mean by that?
Nothing....
It's hard for me to remember you had a whole life before me
My wrinkled face doesn't remind you?
Haha

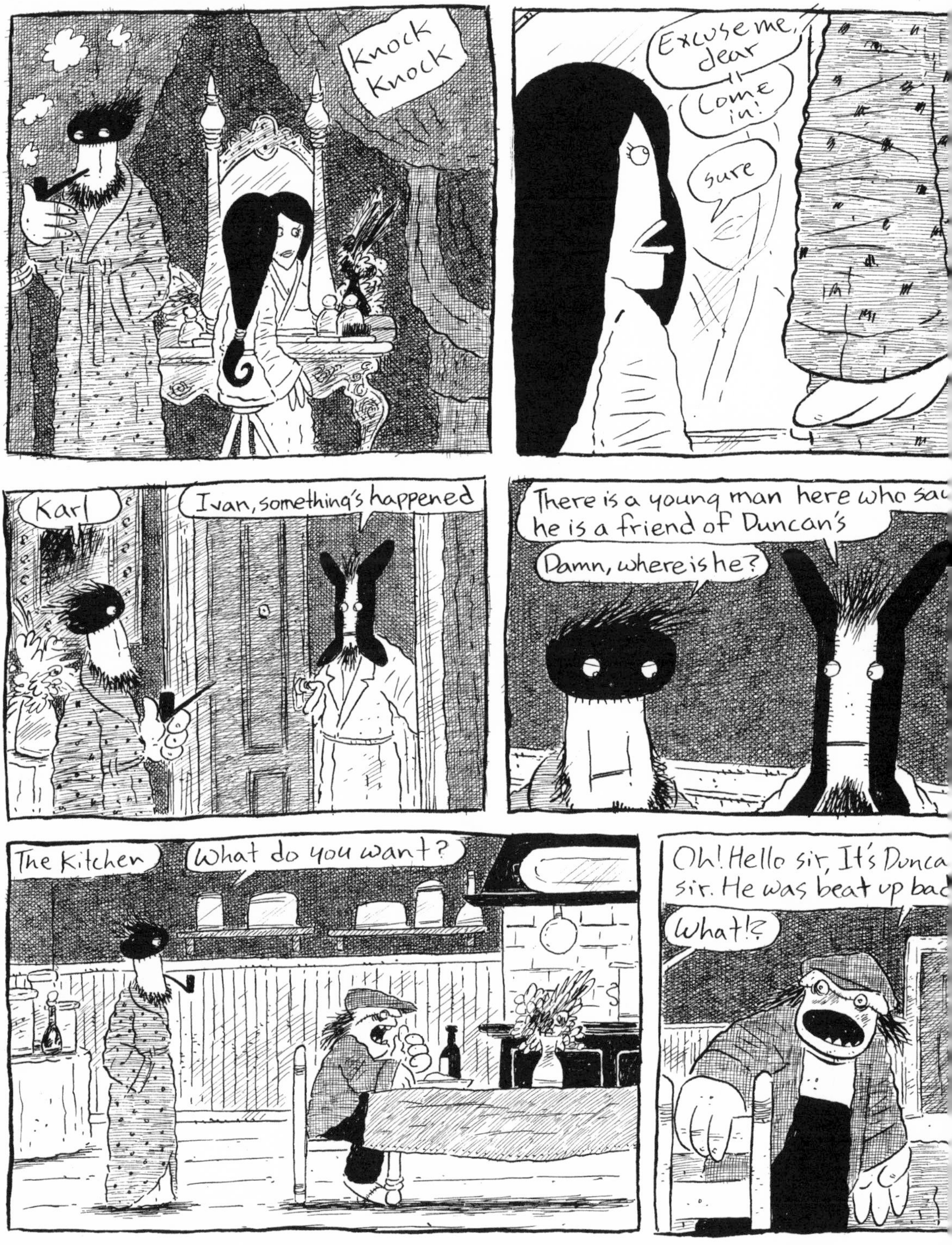

Knock Knock
Excuse me, dear
Come in!
sure
Karl
Ivan, something's happened
There is a young man here who sa
he is a friend of Duncan's
Damn, where is he?
The Kitchen
What do you want?
Oh! Hello sir, It's Dunca
sir. He was beat up bad
What!?

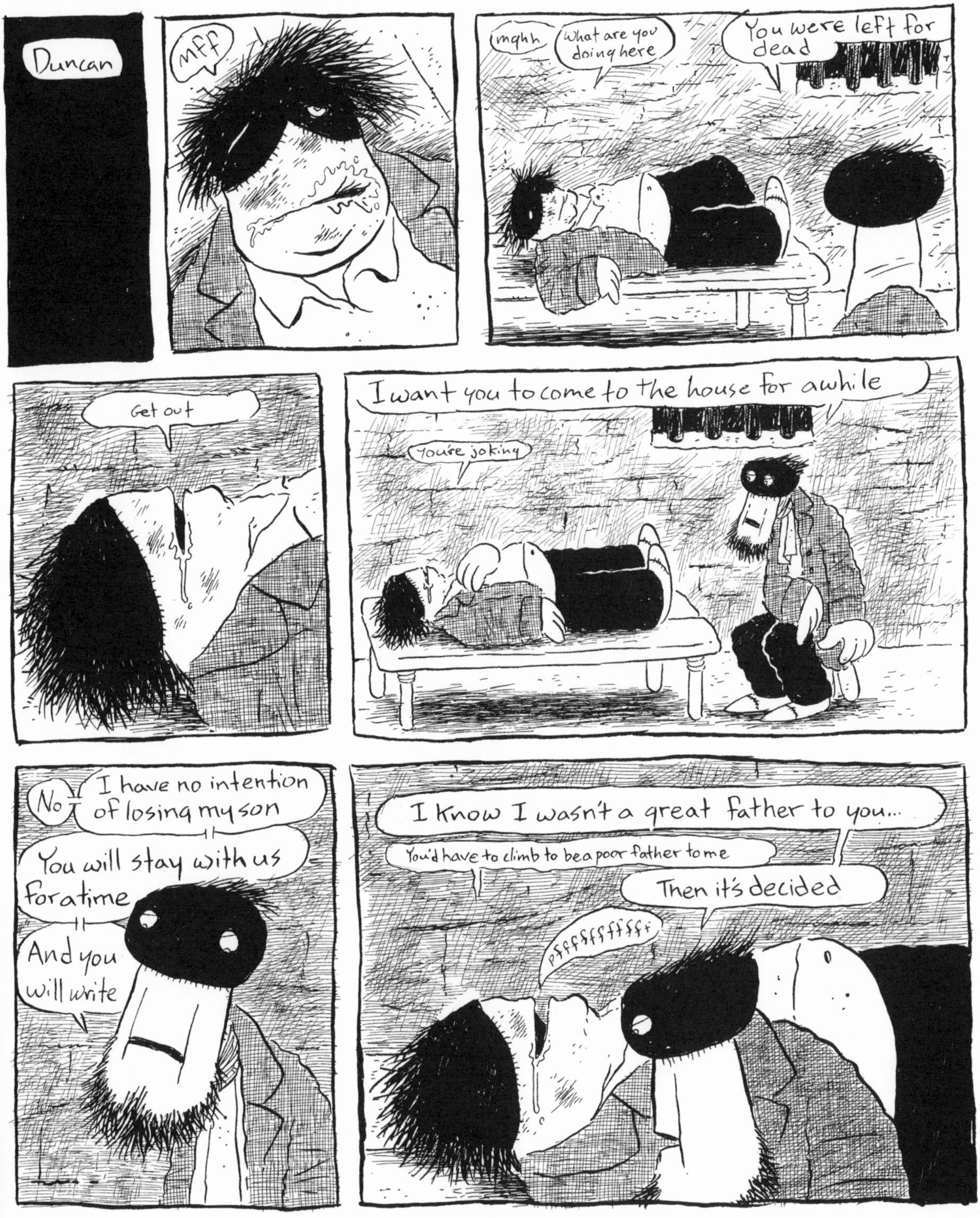
Duncan
mff
mqhh
What are you doing here
You were left for dead
Get out
I want you to come to the house for awhile
You're joking
No
I have no intention of losing my son
You will stay with us for a time
And you will write
I know I wasn't a great father to you...
You'd have to climb to be a poor father to me
Then it's decided
pfffffffffff

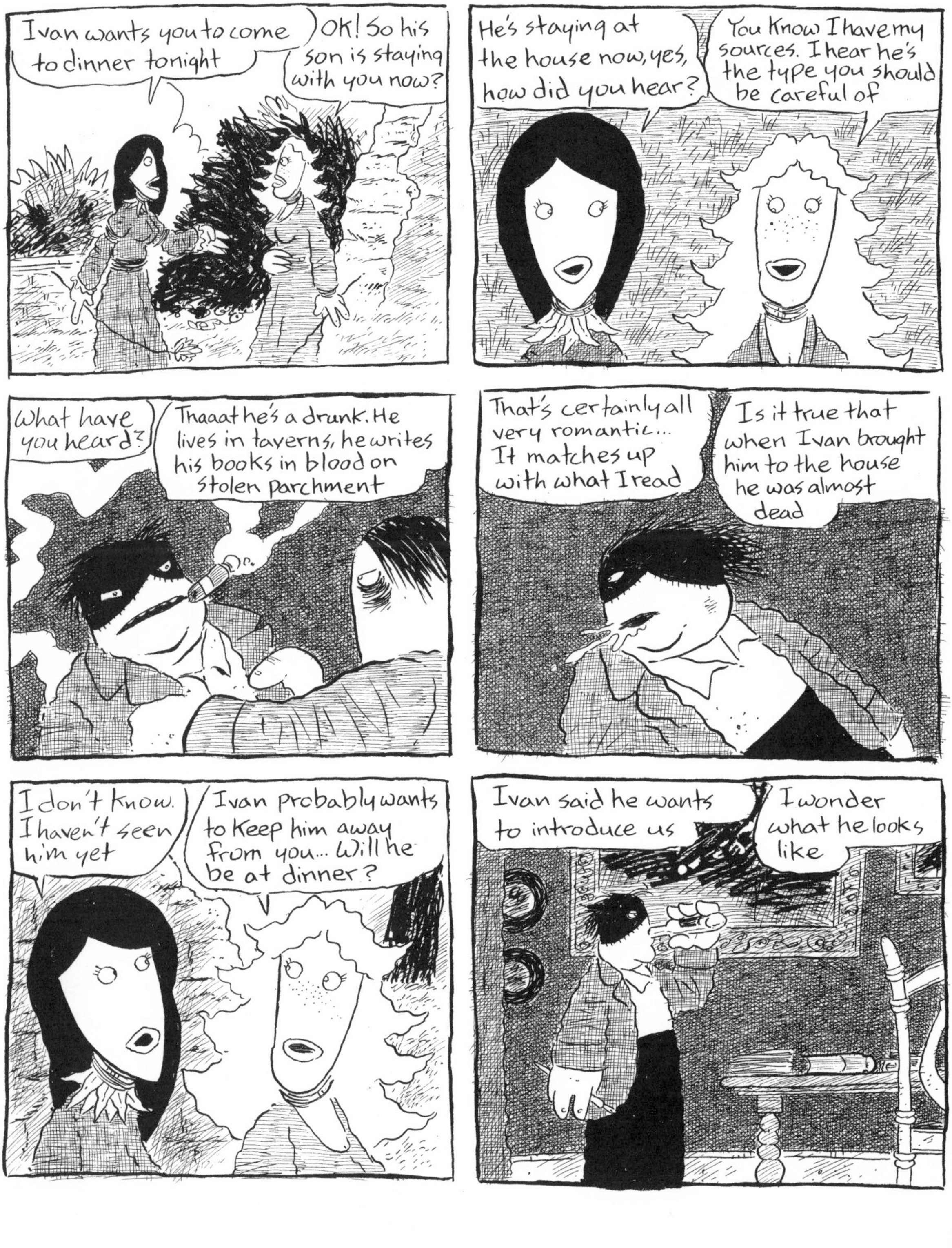
Ivan wants you to come to dinner tonight
OK! So his son is staying with you now?
He's staying at the house now, yes, how did you hear?
You know I have my sources. I hear he's the type you should be careful of
What have you heard?
Thaaat he's a drunk. He lives in taverns, he writes his books in blood on stolen parchment
That's certainly all very romantic... It matches up with what I read
Is it true that when Ivan brought him to the house he was almost dead
I don't know. I haven't seen him yet
Ivan probably wants to keep him away from you... Will he be at dinner?
Ivan said he wants to introduce us
I wonder what he looks like

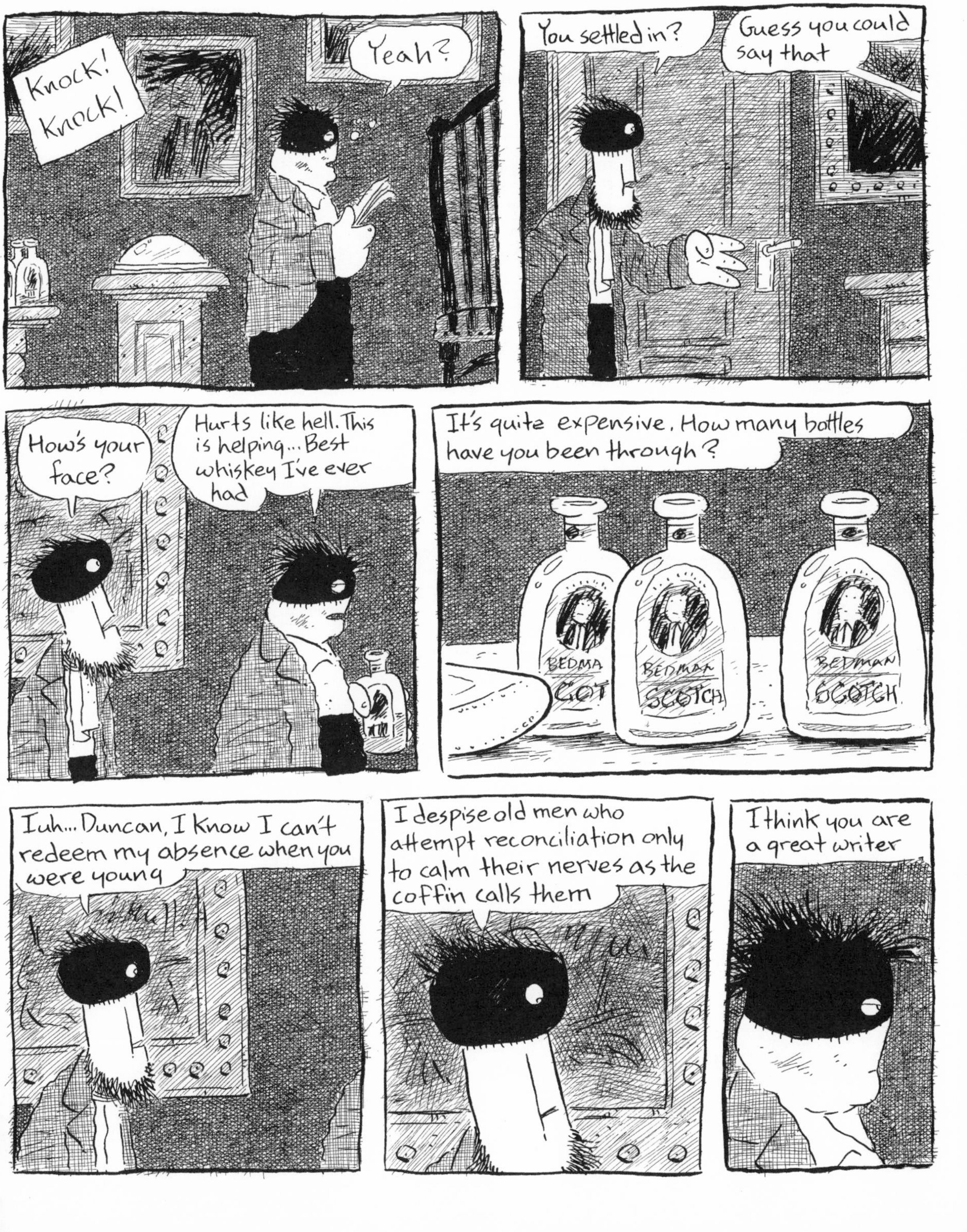
Knock! Knock!
Yeah?
You settled in?
Guess you could say that
How's your face?
Hurts like hell. This is helping... Best whiskey I've ever had
It's quite expensive. How many bottles have you been through?
BEDMA SCOT
BEDMAN SCOTCH
BEDMAN SCOTCH
Iuh... Duncan, I know I can't redeem my absence when you were young
I despise old men who attempt reconciliation only to calm their nerves as the coffin calls them
I think you are a great writer

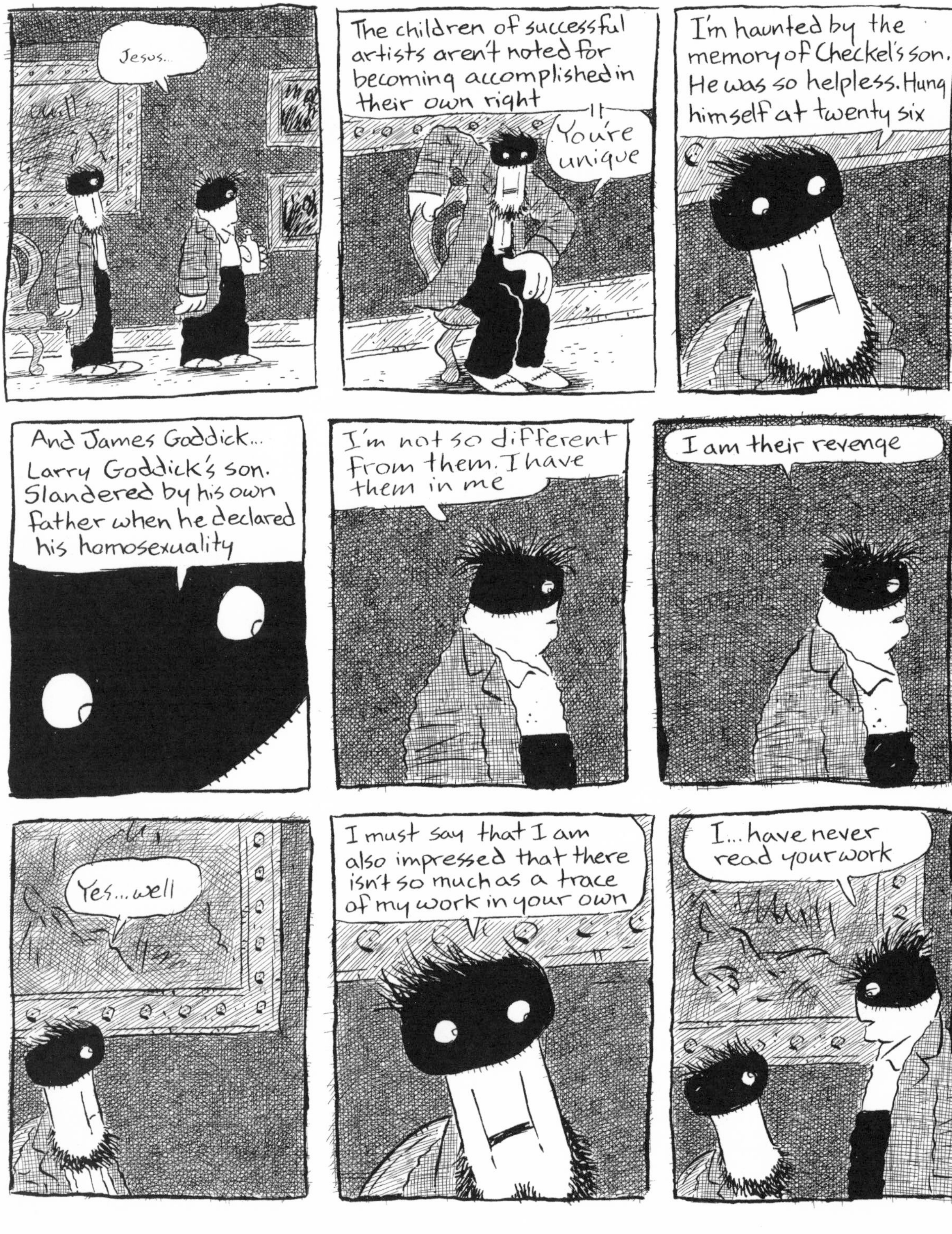

Jesus...
The children of successful artists aren't noted for becoming accomplished in their own right
You're unique
I'm haunted by the memory of Checkel's son. He was so helpless. Hung himself at twenty six
And James Goddick... Larry Goddick's son. Slandered by his own father when he declared his homosexuality
I'm not so different from them. I have them in me
I am their revenge
Yes... well
I must say that I am also impressed that there isn't so much as a trace of my work in your own
I... have never read your work

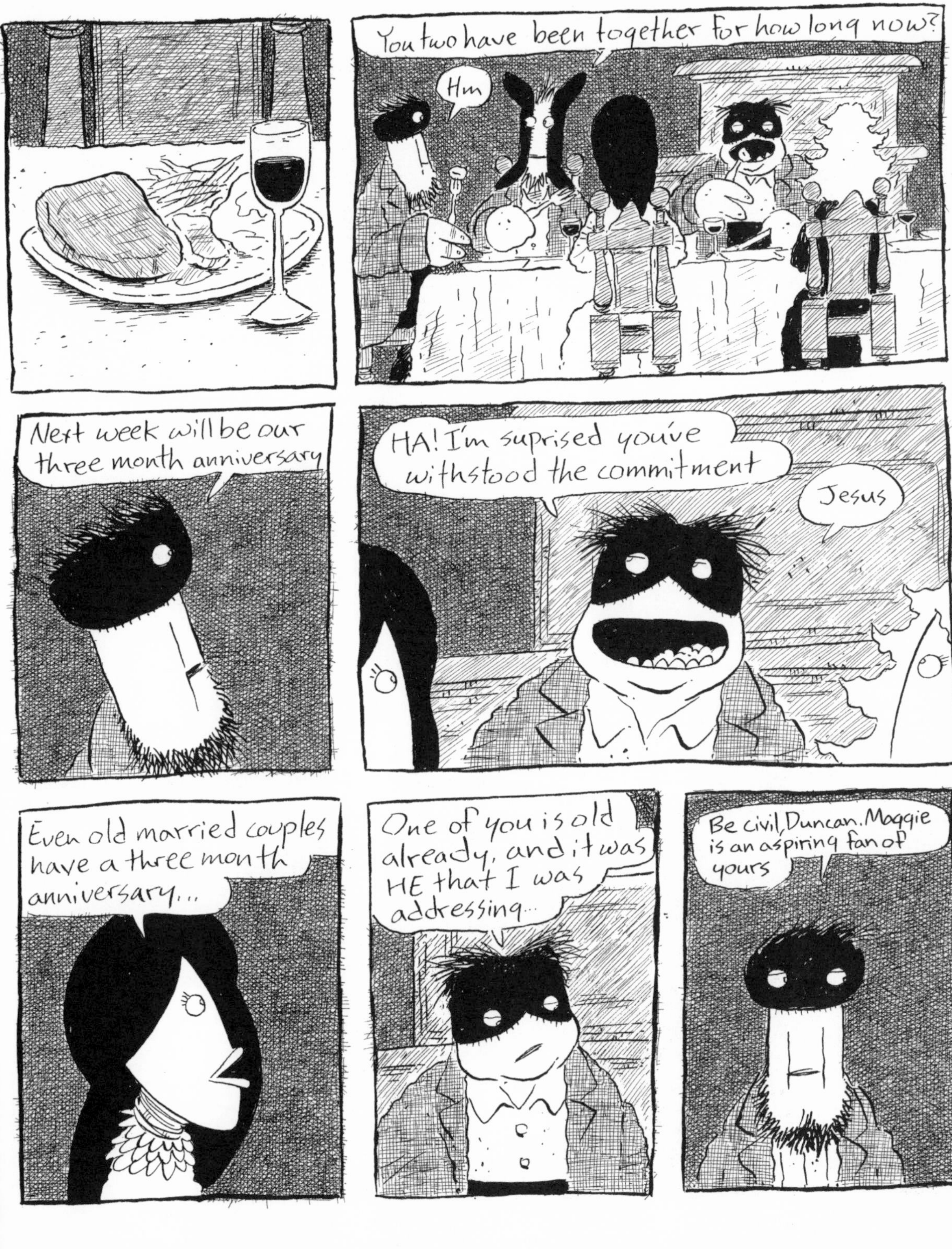
You two have been together for how long now?
Hm
Next week will be our three month anniversary
HA! I'm suprised you've withstood the commitment
Jesus
Even old married couples have a three month anniversary...
One of you is old already, and it was HE that I was addressing...
Be civil, Duncan. Maggie is an aspiring fan of yours

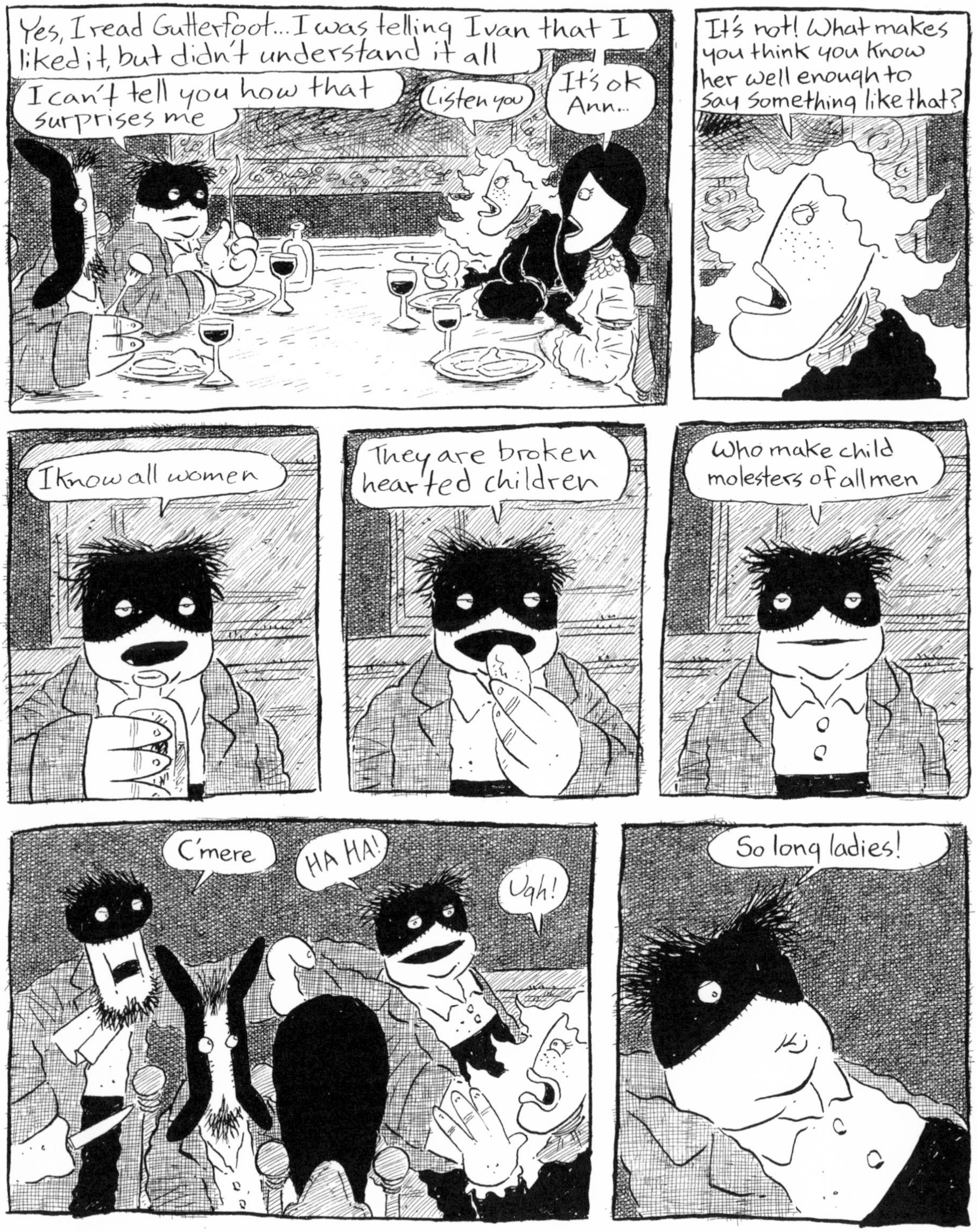
Yes, I read Gutterfoot... I was telling Ivan that I liked it, but didn't understand it all
I can't tell you how that surprises me
Listen you
It's ok Ann...
It's not! What makes you think you know her well enough to say something like that?
I know all women
They are broken hearted children
Who make child molesters of all men
C'mere
HA HA!
Ugh!
So long ladies!

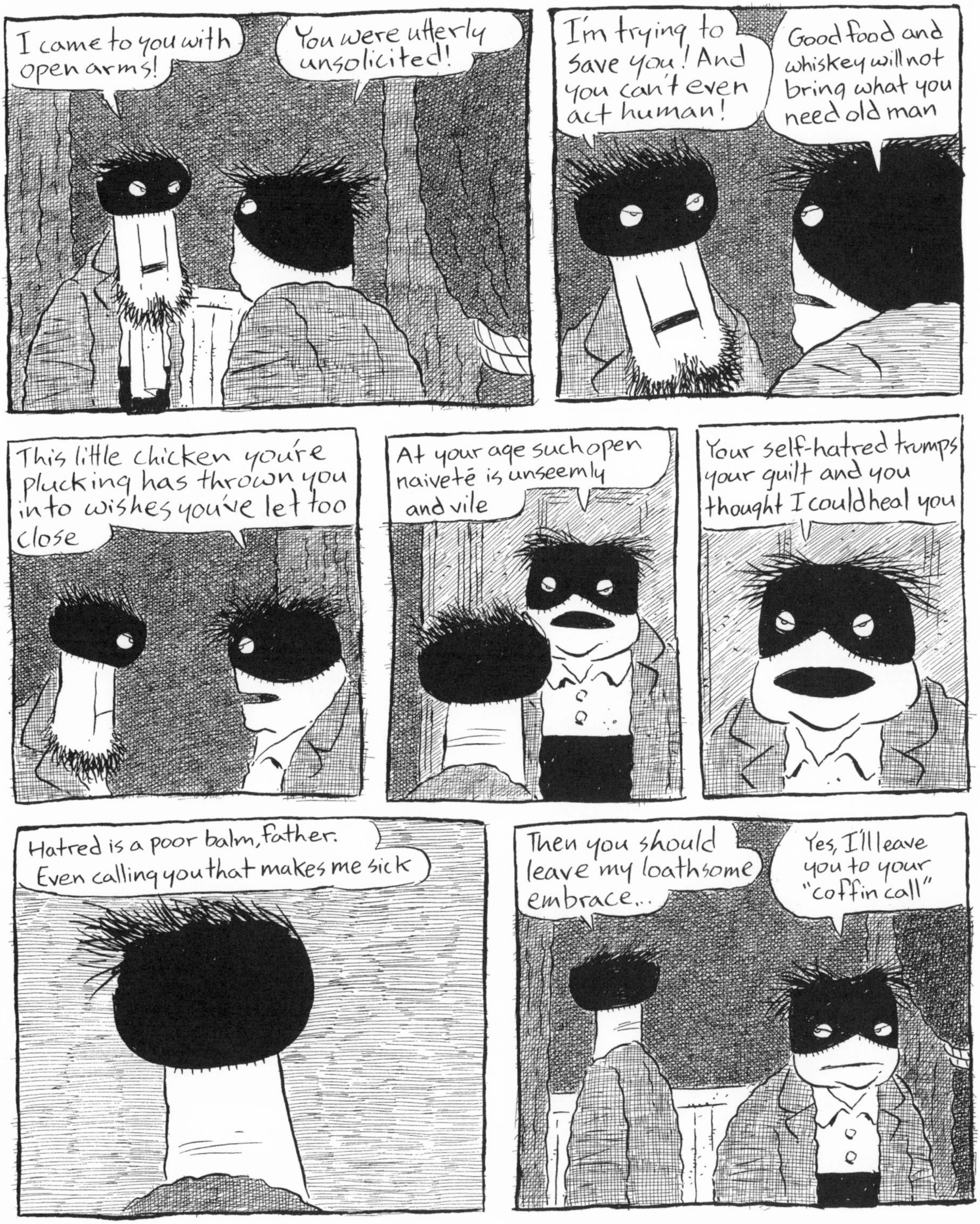
I came to you with open arms!
You were utterly unsolicited!
I'm trying to save you! And you can't even act human!
Good food and whiskey will not bring what you need old man
This little chicken you're plucking has thrown you into wishes you've let too close
At your age such open naiveté is unseemly and vile
Your self-hatred trumps your guilt and you thought I could heal you
Hatred is a poor balm, father. Even calling you that makes me sick
Then you should leave my loathsome embrace...
Yes, I'll leave you to your "coffin call"

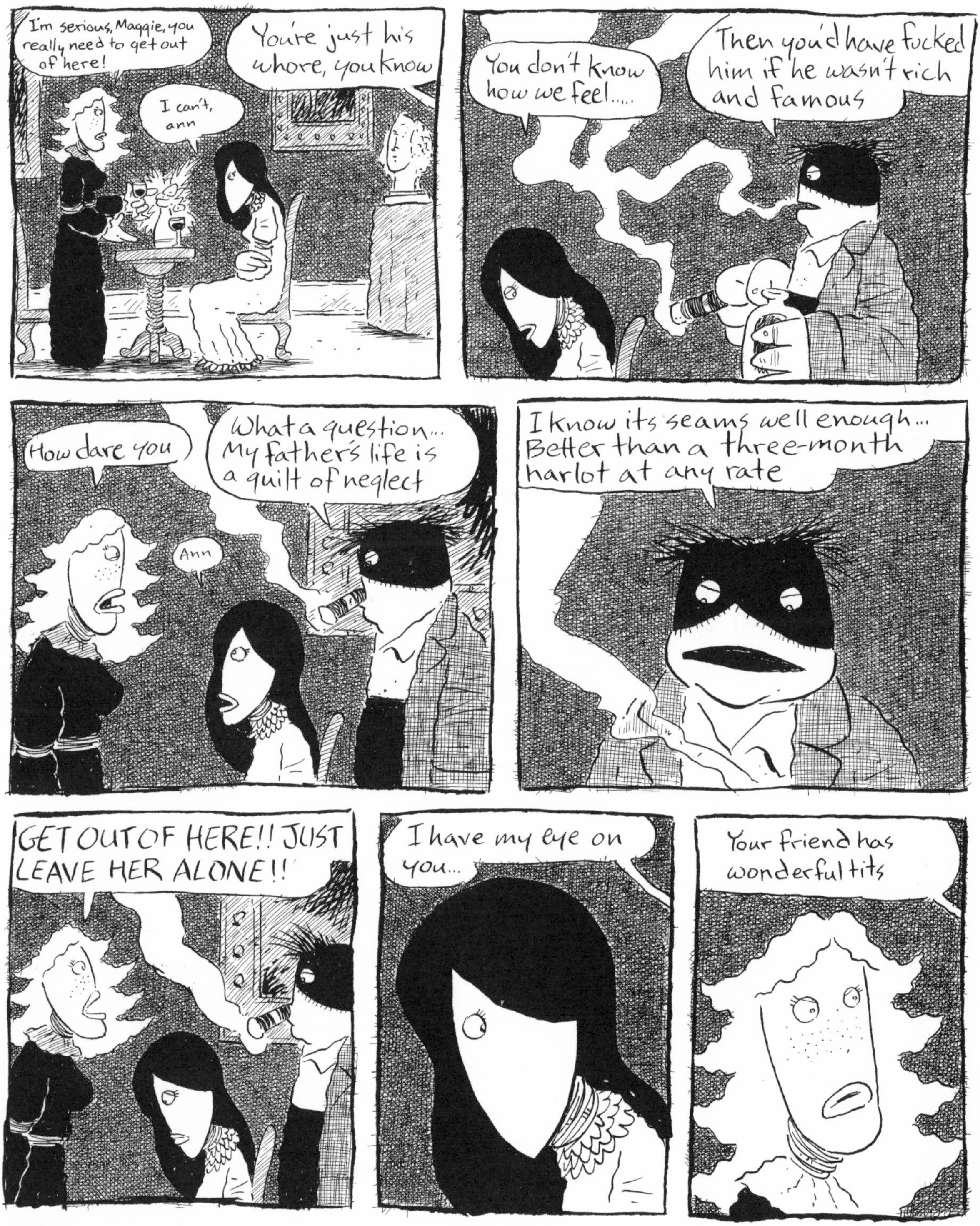
I'm serious, Maggie, you really need to get out of here!
I can't, ann
You're just his whore, you know
You don't know how we feel.....
Then you'd have fucked him if he wasn't rich and famous
How dare you
Ann
What a question... My father's life is a quilt of neglect
I know its seams well enough... Better than a three-month harlot at any rate
GET OUT OF HERE!! JUST LEAVE HER ALONE!!
I have my eye on you...
Your friend has wonderful tits

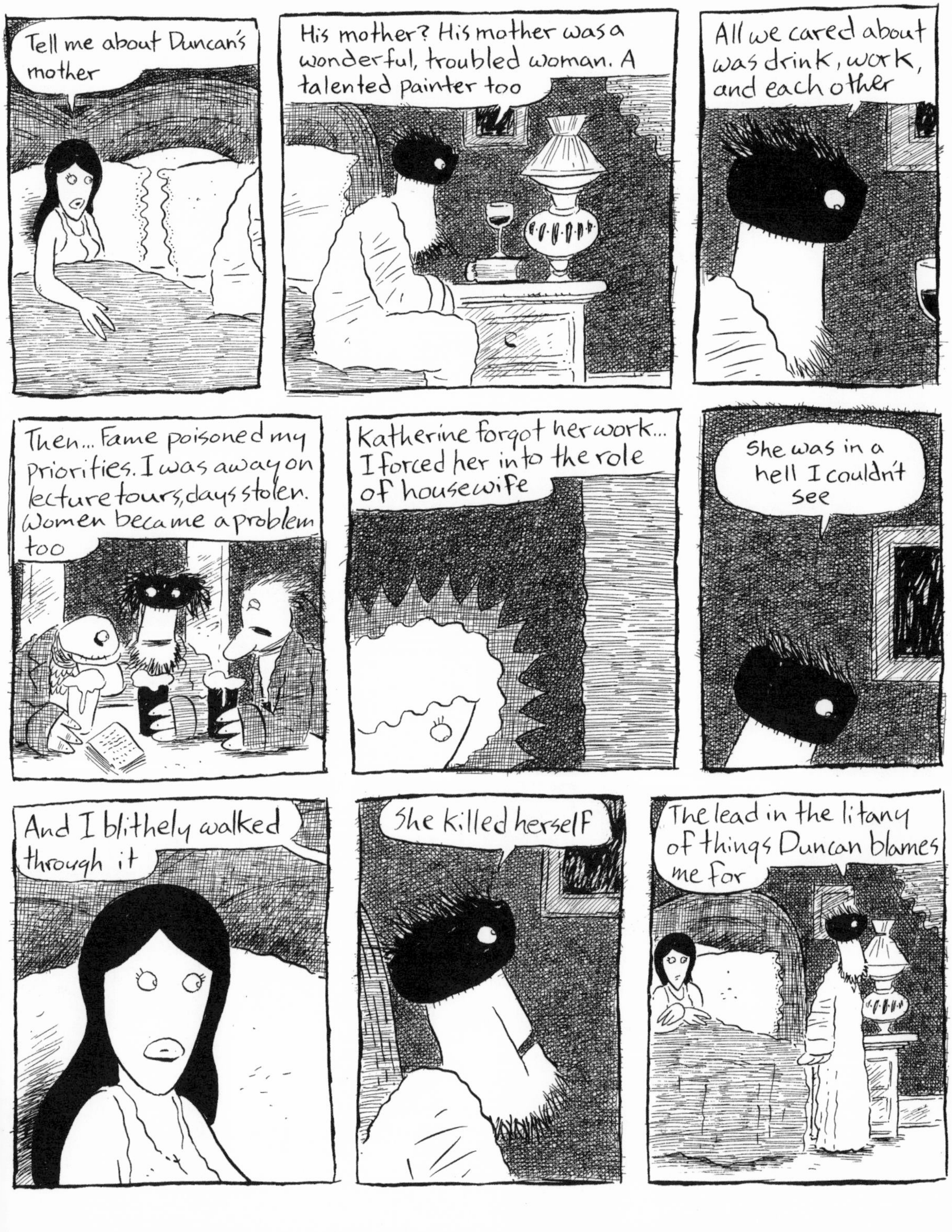

Tell me about Duncan's mother
His mother? His mother was a wonderful, troubled woman. A talented painter too
All we cared about was drink, work, and each other
Then... Fame poisoned my priorities. I was away on lecture tours, days stolen. Women became a problem too
Katherine forgot her work... I forced her into the role of housewife
She was in a hell I couldn't see
And I blithely walked through it
She killed herself
The lead in the litany of things Duncan blames me for

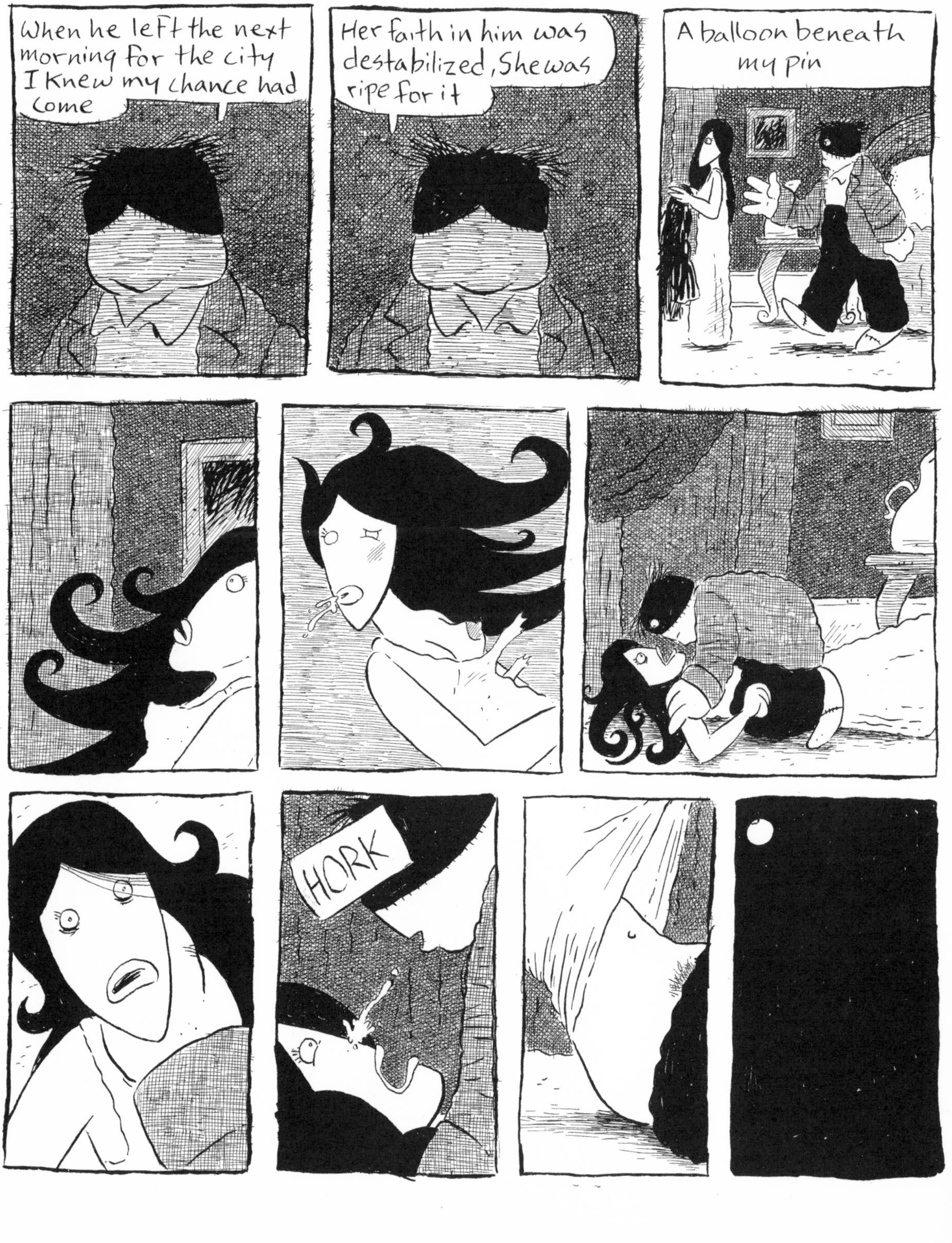
When he left the next morning for the city I Knew my chance had come
Her faith in him was destabilized, She was ripe for it
A balloon beneath my pin
HORK

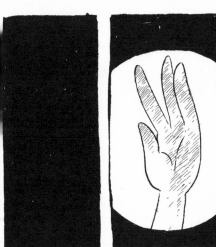

You're back early

Colin couldn't meet with me. Is Maggie up yet?

Not sure

I'll check

My dear

I've never heard a man make that sound

Of course we understood what had happened right away

Duncan was no doubt already miles away

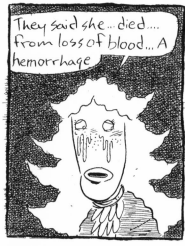

They said she...died.... from loss of blood... A hemorrhage

From the other girl, Ann I have never heard such screaming. Finally she had to be sedated

I was more her partner than Ivan could ever have been

I am ashamed and confused by the satisfaction I felt upon learning of his death

He collapsed in front of me. Right there

A heart attack. And the coroner said that she... had been...badly... torn up

Duncan absolutely vanished

I heard the monster is dead...

There is a spot on the urn that contains his ashes

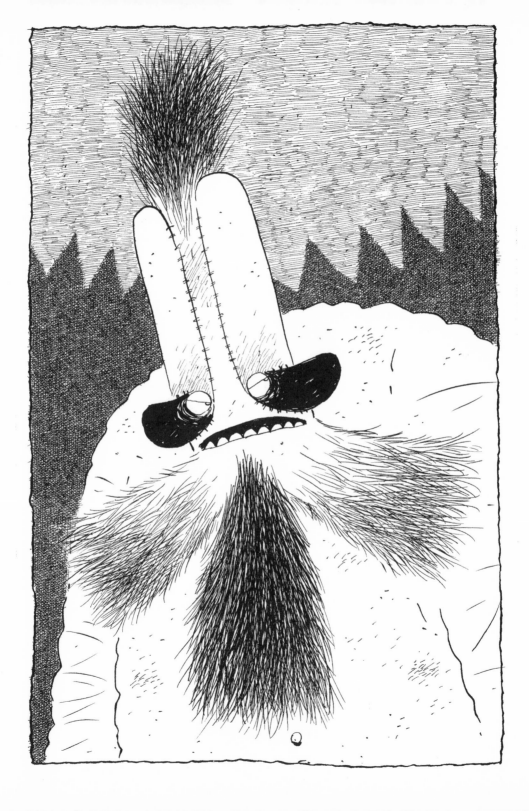

The Sea Demon

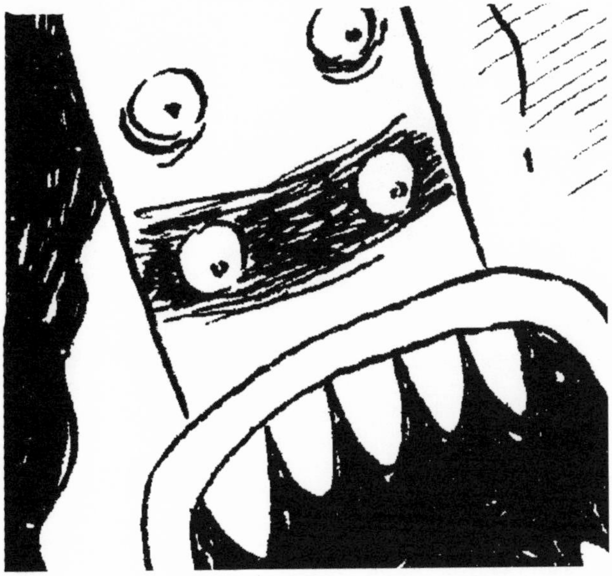

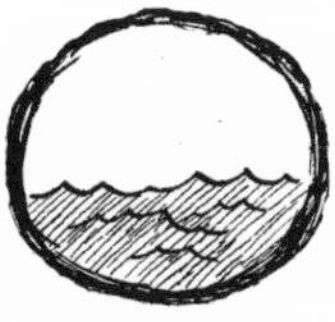

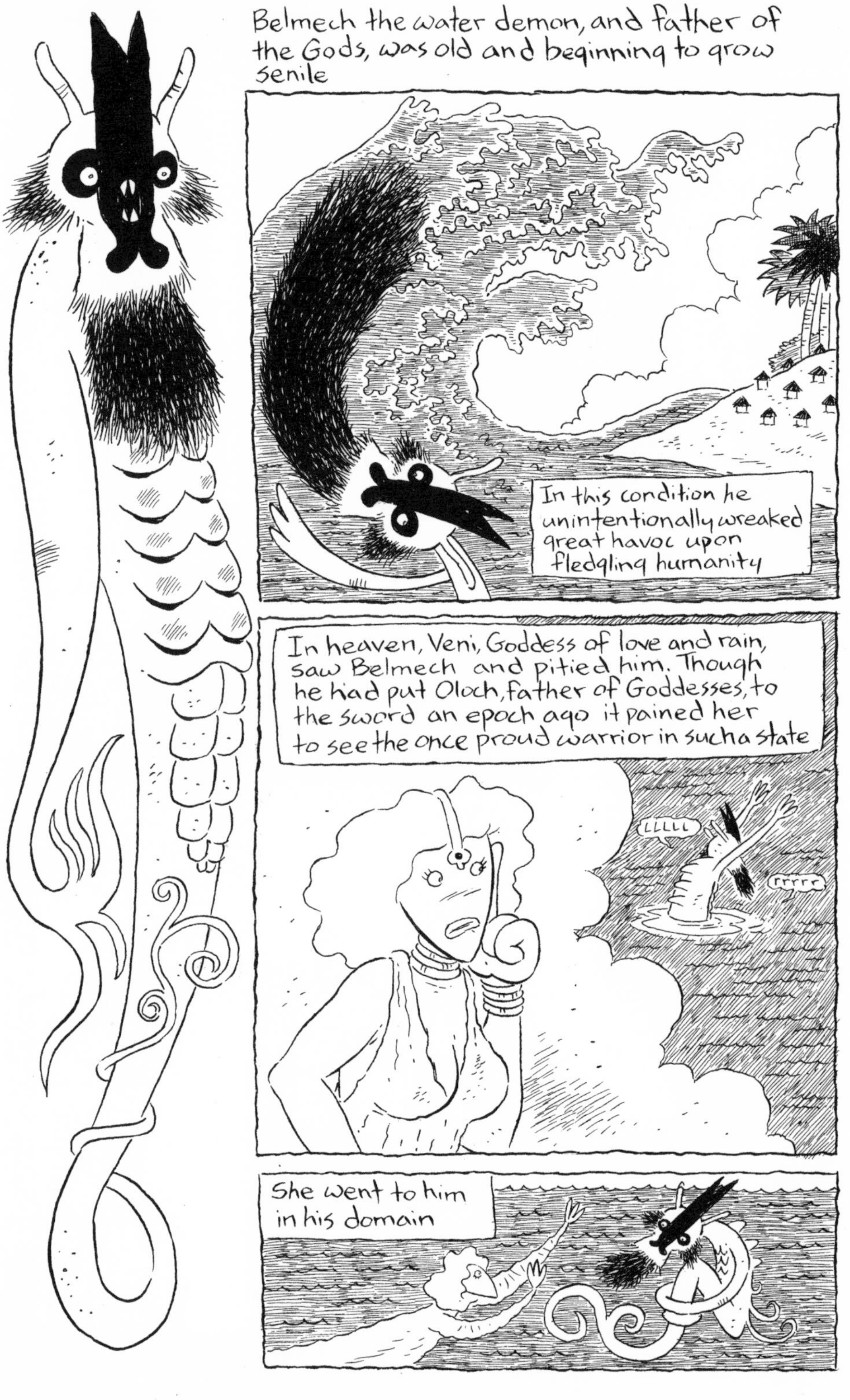

Belmech the water demon, and father of the Gods, was old and beginning to grow senile
In this condition he unintentionally wreaked great havoc upon fledgling humanity
In heaven, Veni, Goddess of love and rain, saw Belmech and pitied him. Though he had put Oloch, father of Goddesses, to the sword an epoch ago it pained her to see the once proud warrior in such a state
LLLLL
rrrrr
She went to him in his domain

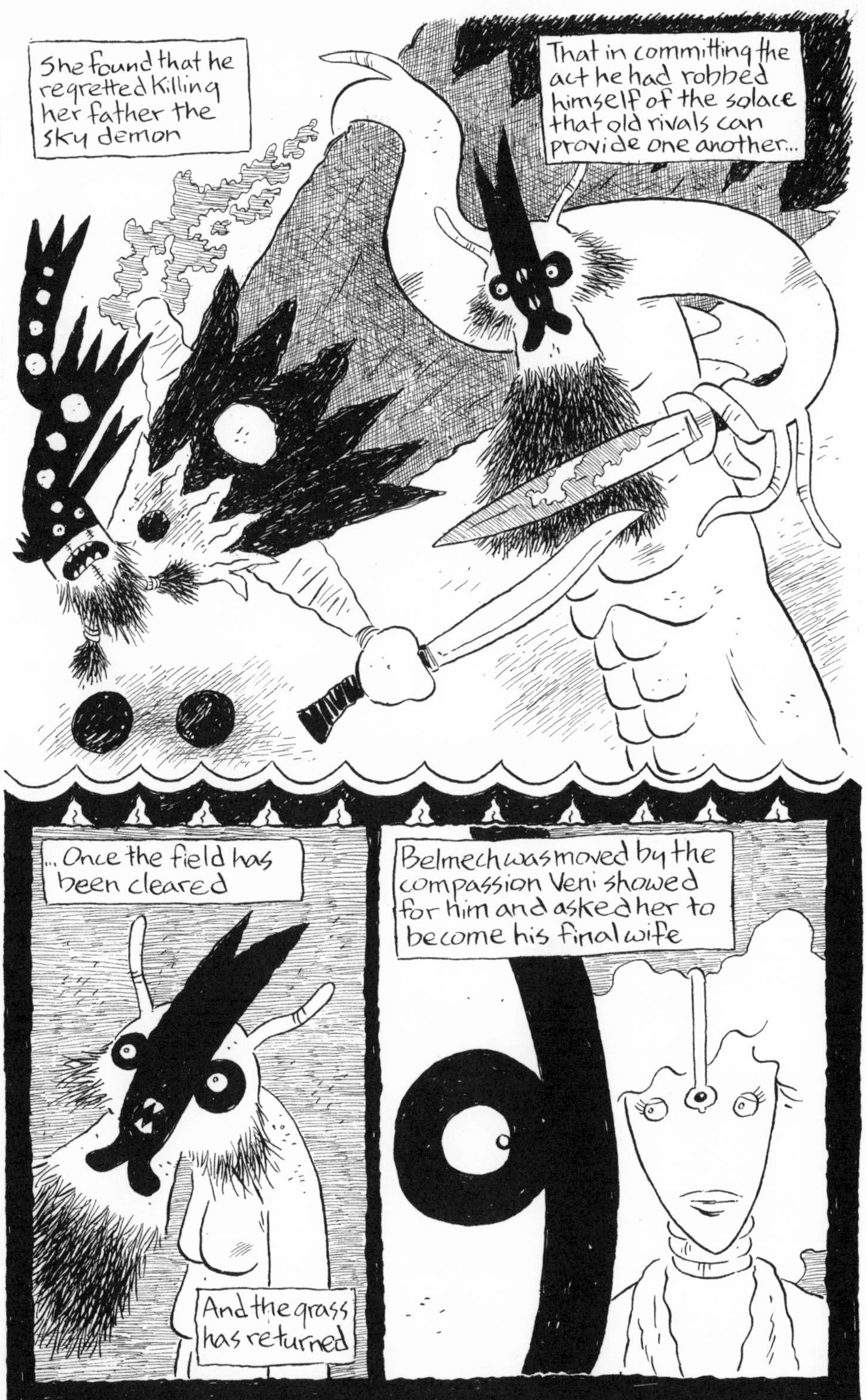
She found that he regretted killing her father the sky demon
That in committing the act he had robbed himself of the solace that old rivals can provide one another...
...Once the field has been cleared
And the grass has returned
Belmech was moved by the compassion Veni showed for him and asked her to become his final wife

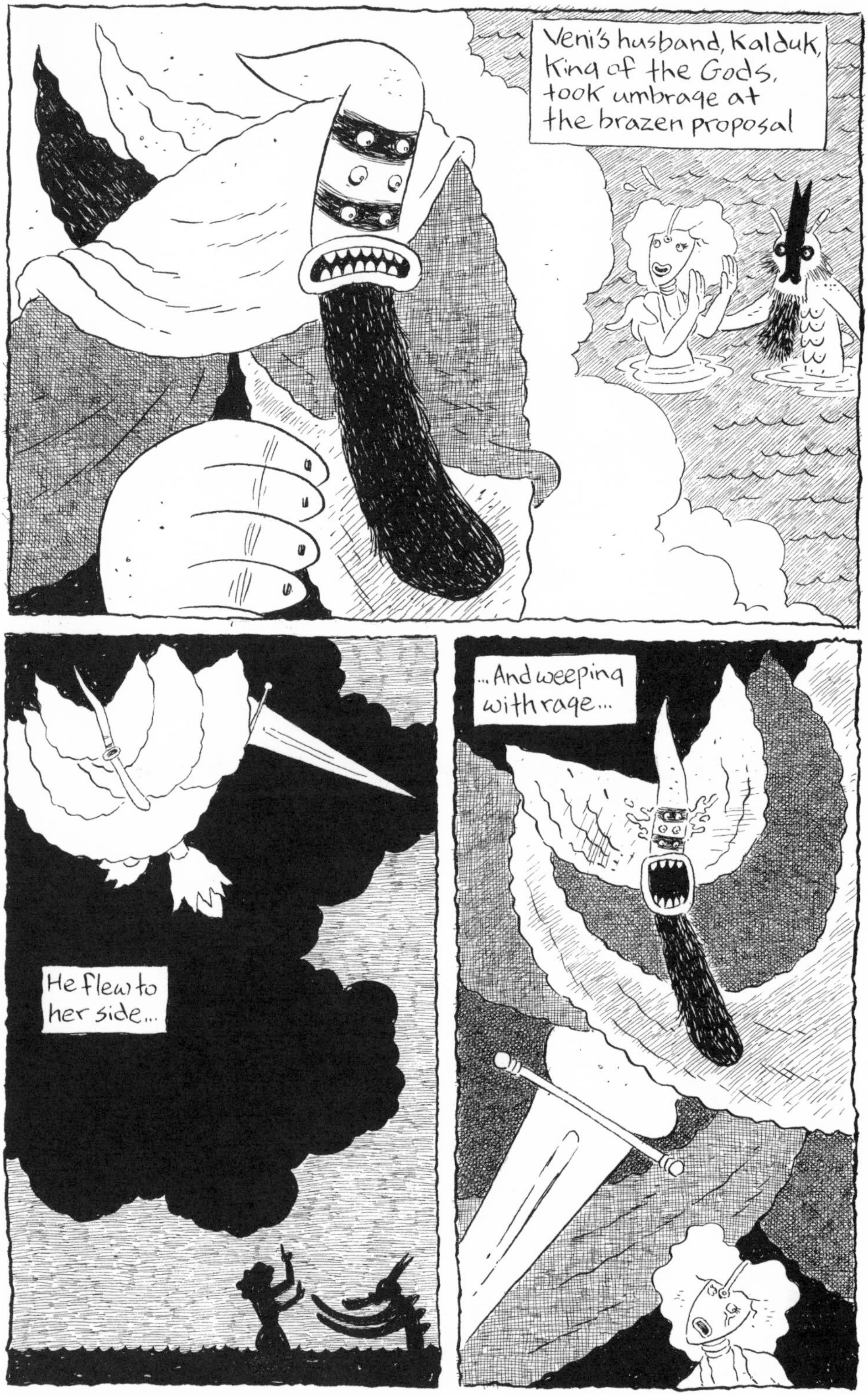
Veni's husband, Kalduk, King of the Gods, took umbrage at the brazen proposal
He flew to her side...
...And weeping with rage...

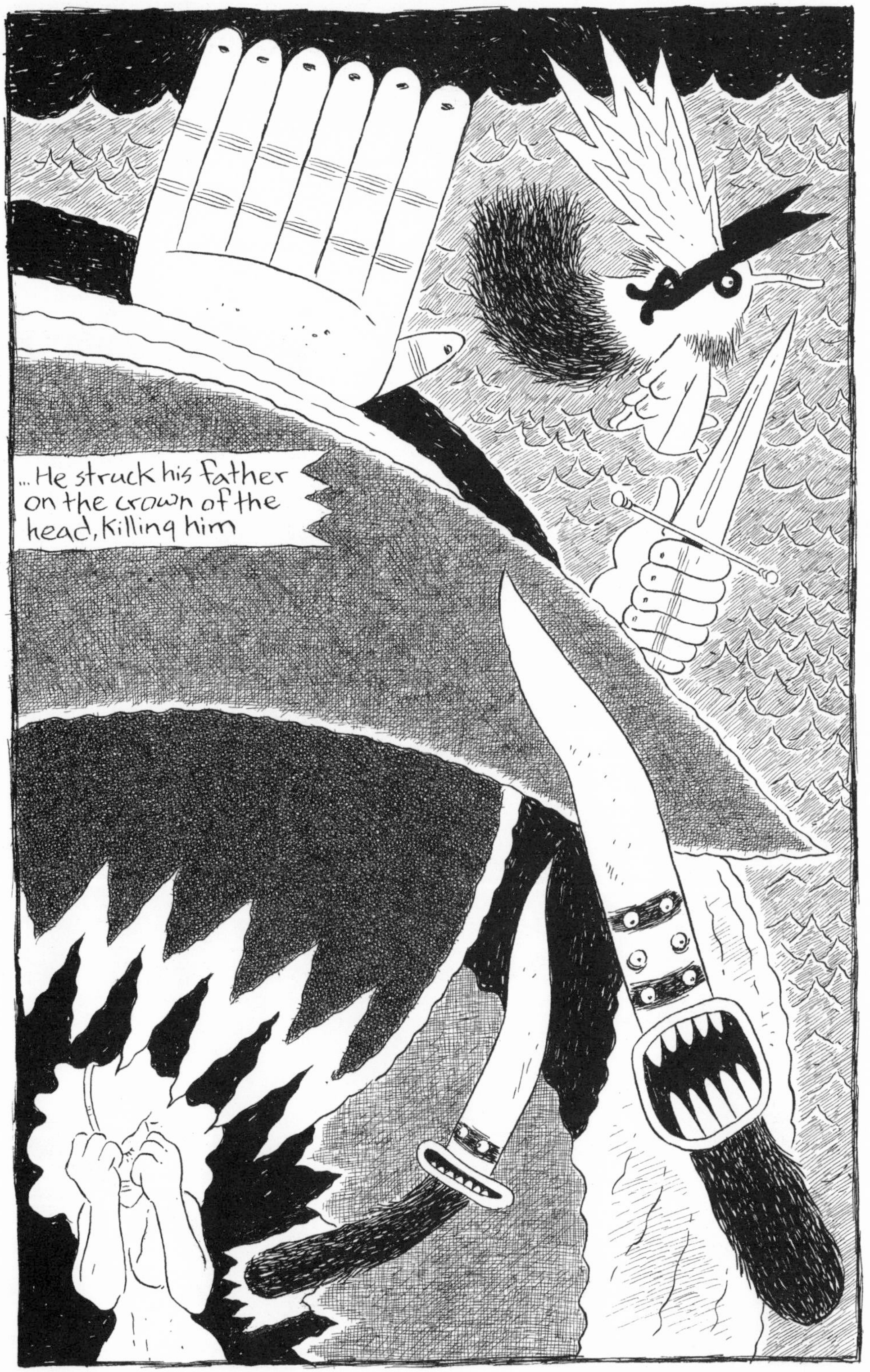
...He struck his father on the crown of the head, killing him

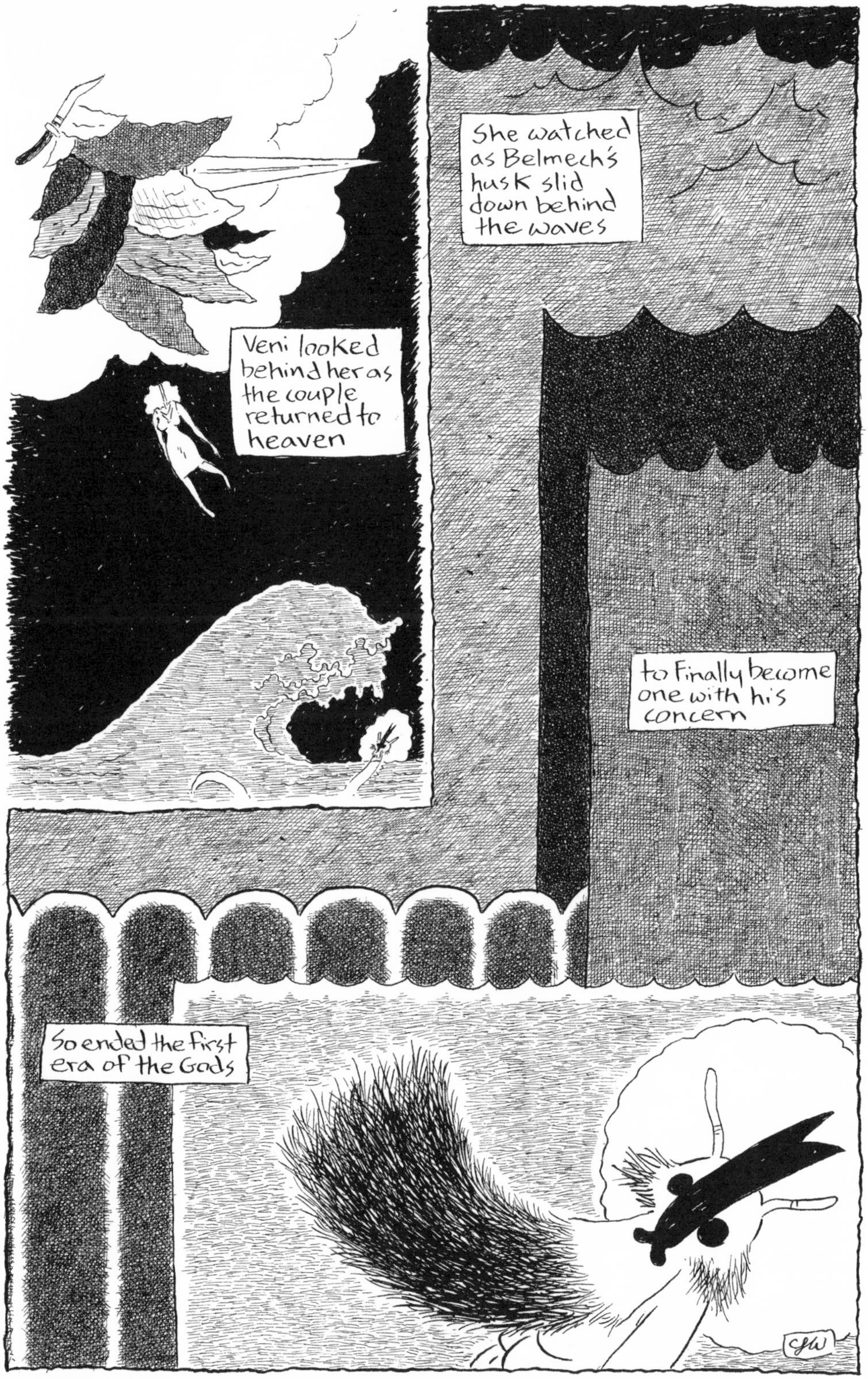
Veni looked behind her as the couple returned to heaven
She watched as Belmech's husk slid down behind the waves
to Finally become one with his concern
So ended the first era of the Gods
CJW

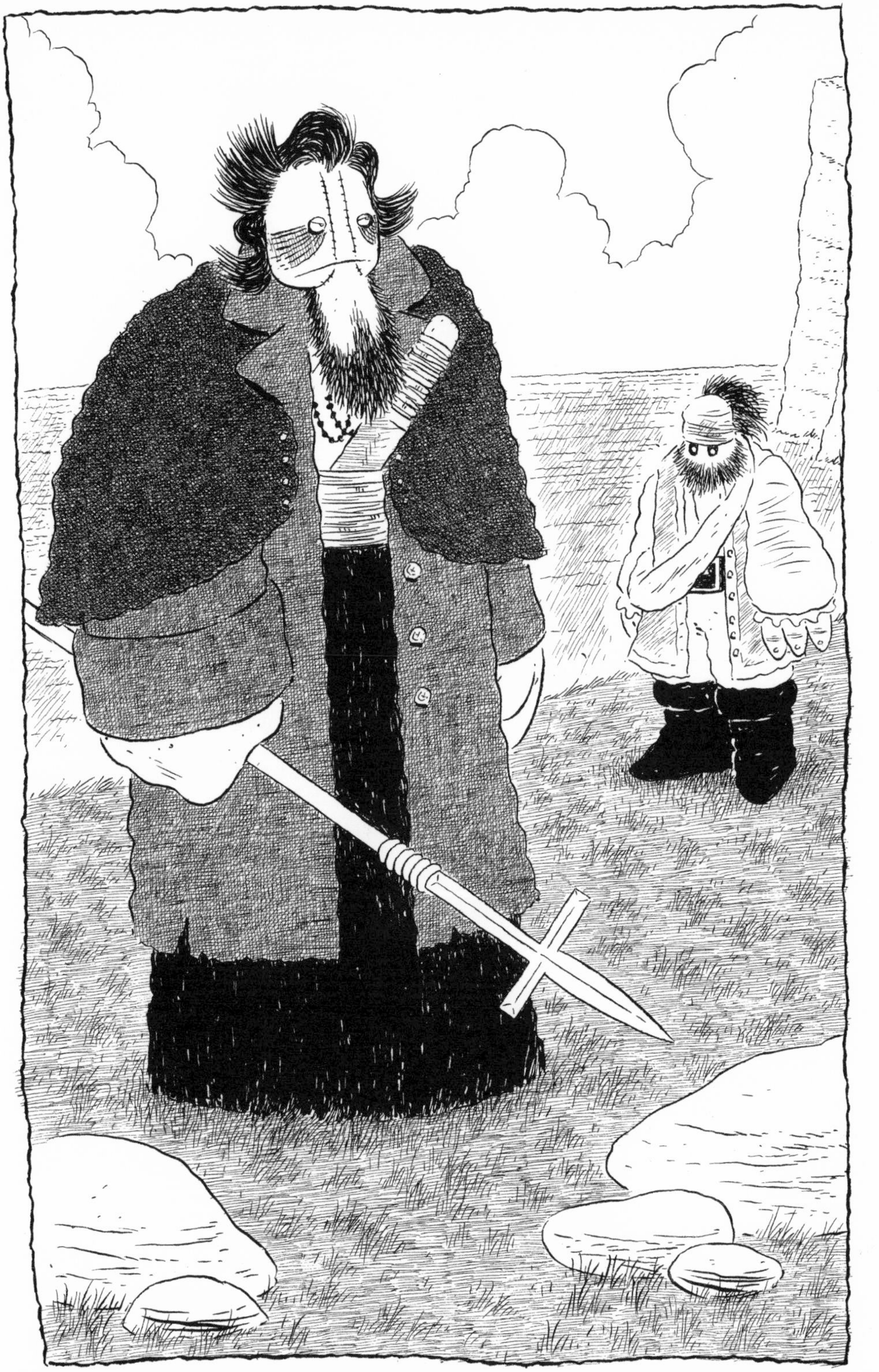

Rags and Turpentine

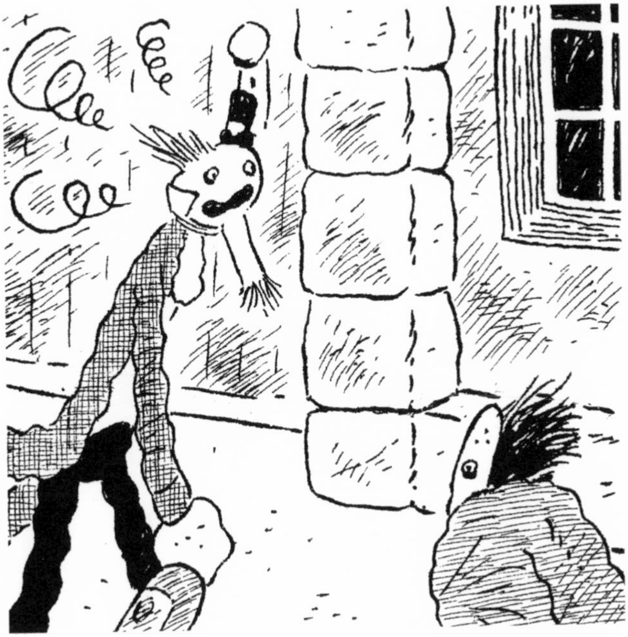

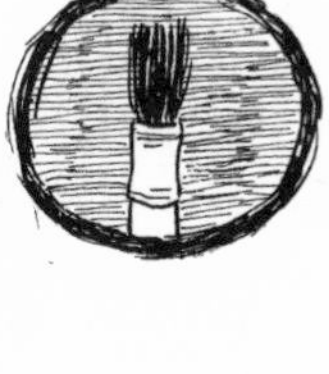

How can I push ahead when I am the product of what has come before me?
What is the line between prescience and self indulgence?

HE PAINTS..

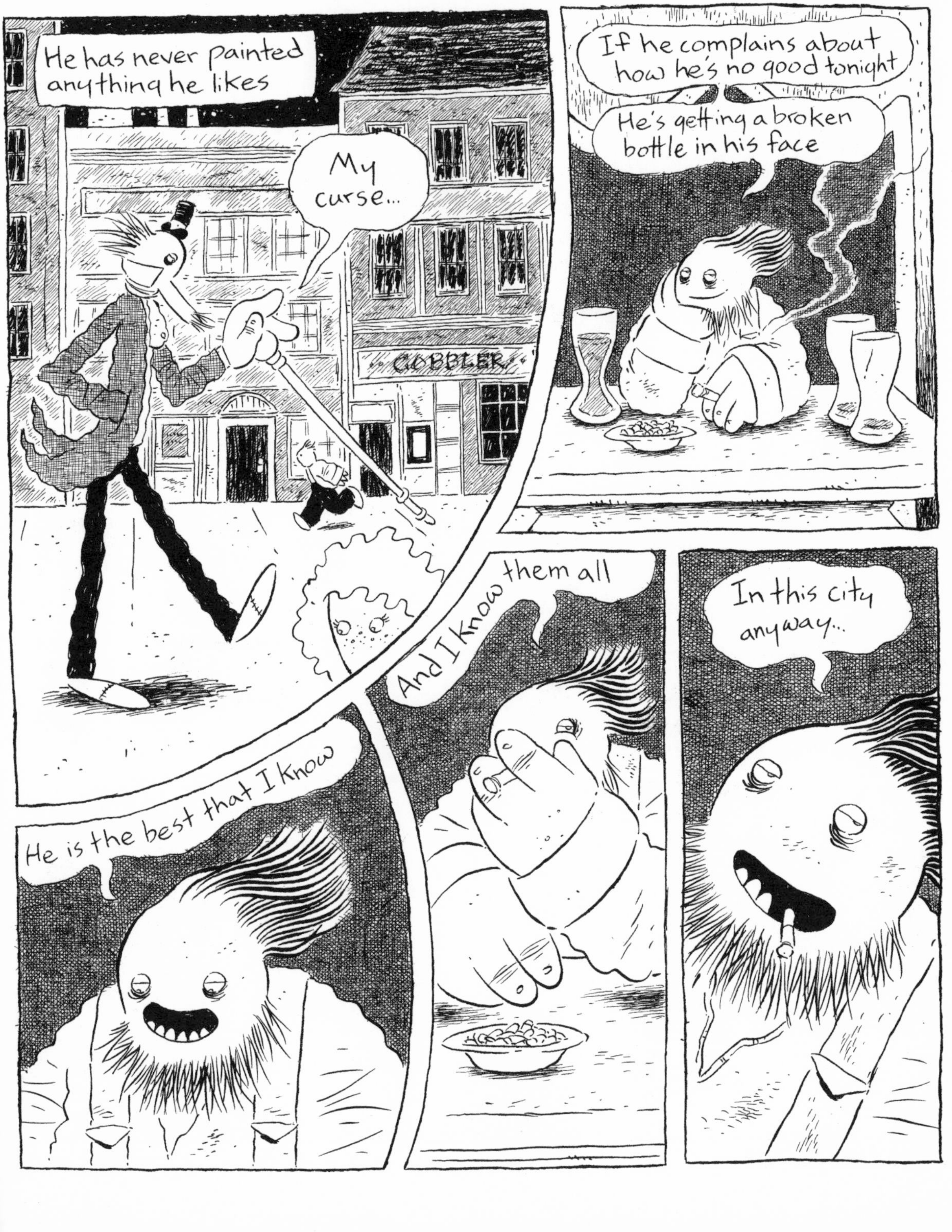
He has never painted anything he likes
My curse...
COBBLER
If he complains about how he's no good tonight
He's getting a broken bottle in his face
He is the best that I know
And I know them all
In this city anyway...

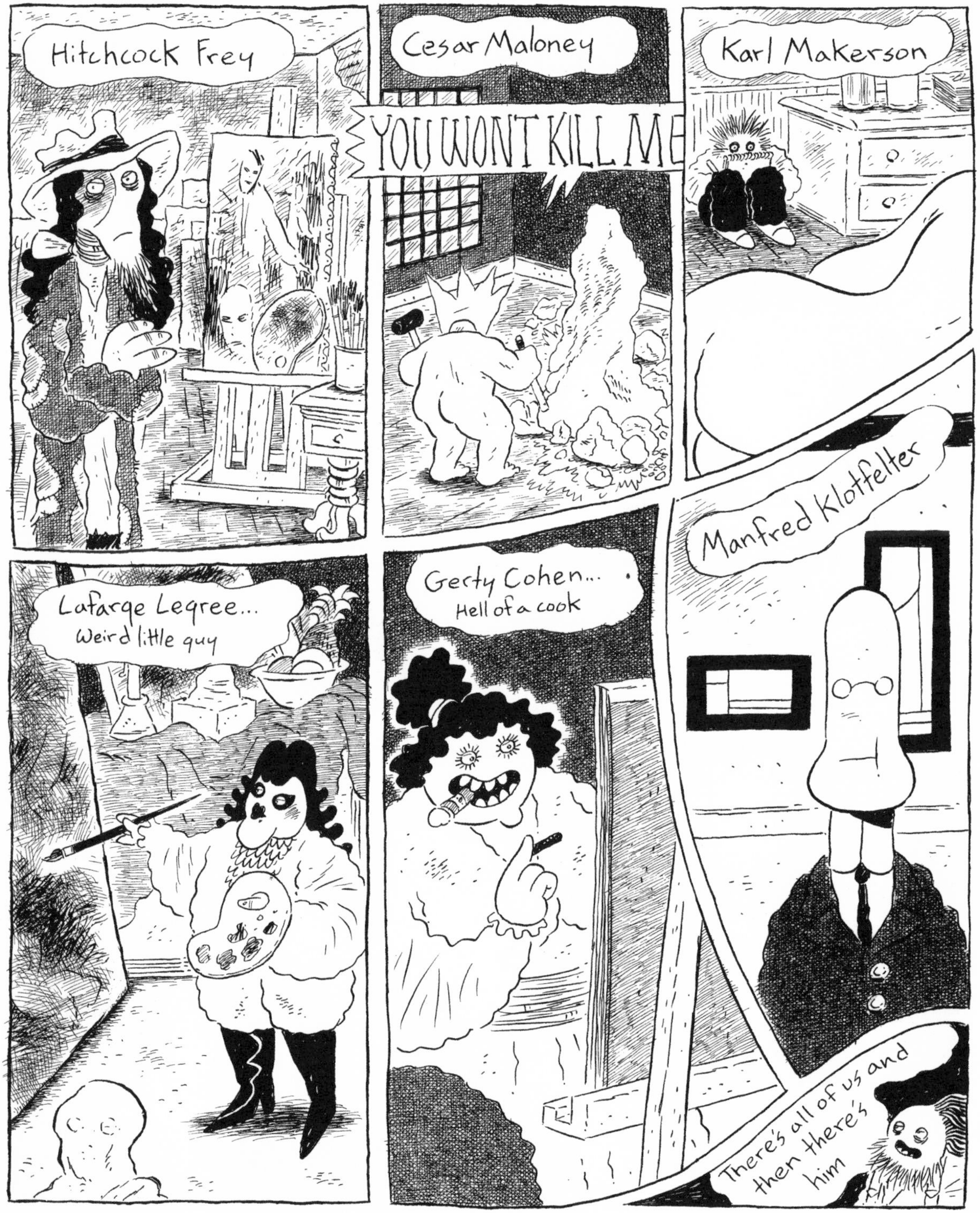
Hitchcock Frey
Cesar Maloney
YOU WONT KILL ME
Karl Makerson
Manfred Klotfelter
Lafarge Legree... Weird little guy
Gerty Cohen... Hell of a cook
There's all of us and then there's him

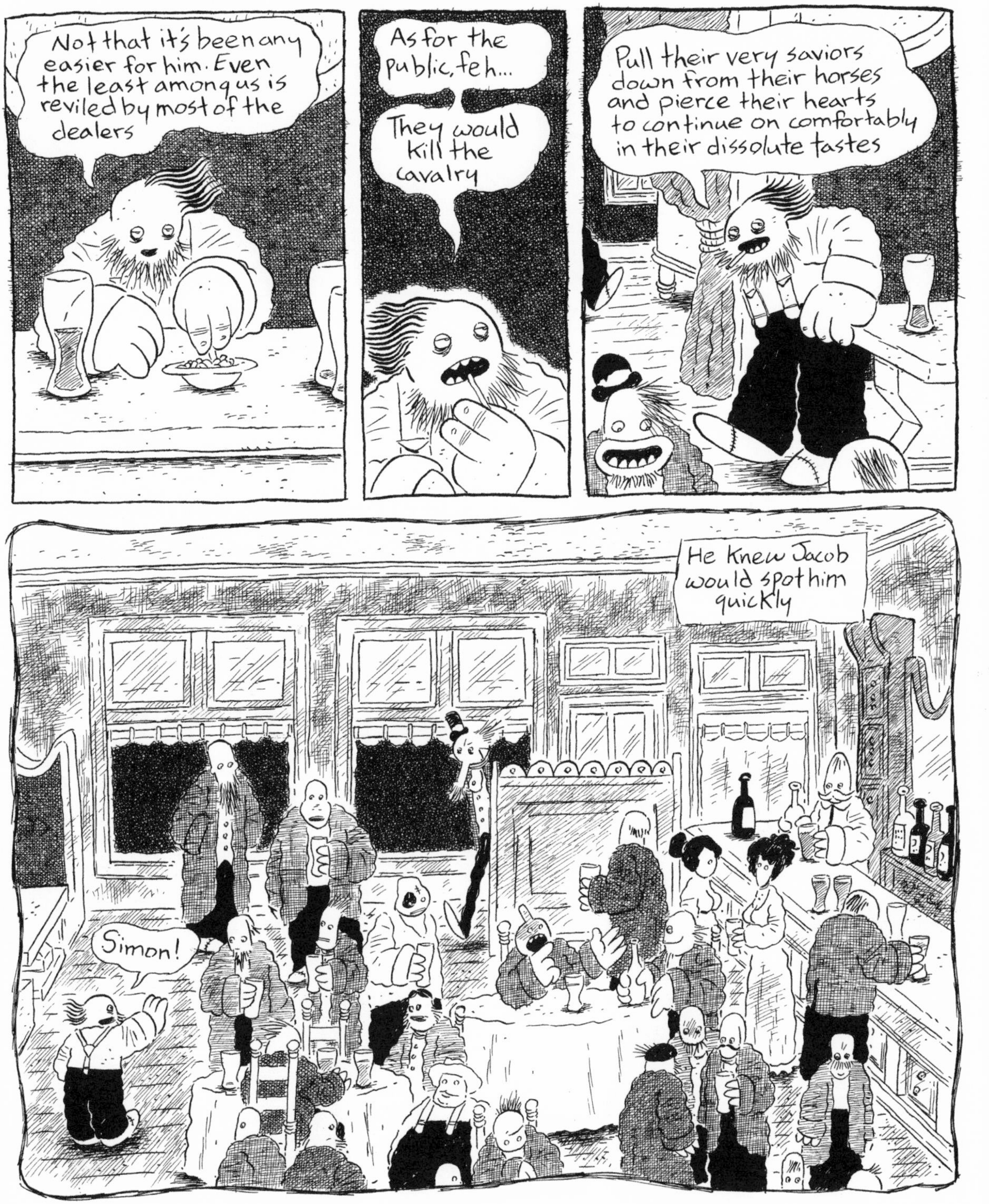
Not that it's been any easier for him. Even the least among us is reviled by most of the dealers
As for the public, feh...
They would kill the cavalry
Pull their very saviors down from their horses and pierce their hearts to continue on comfortably in their dissolute tastes
He knew Jacob would spot him quickly
Simon!

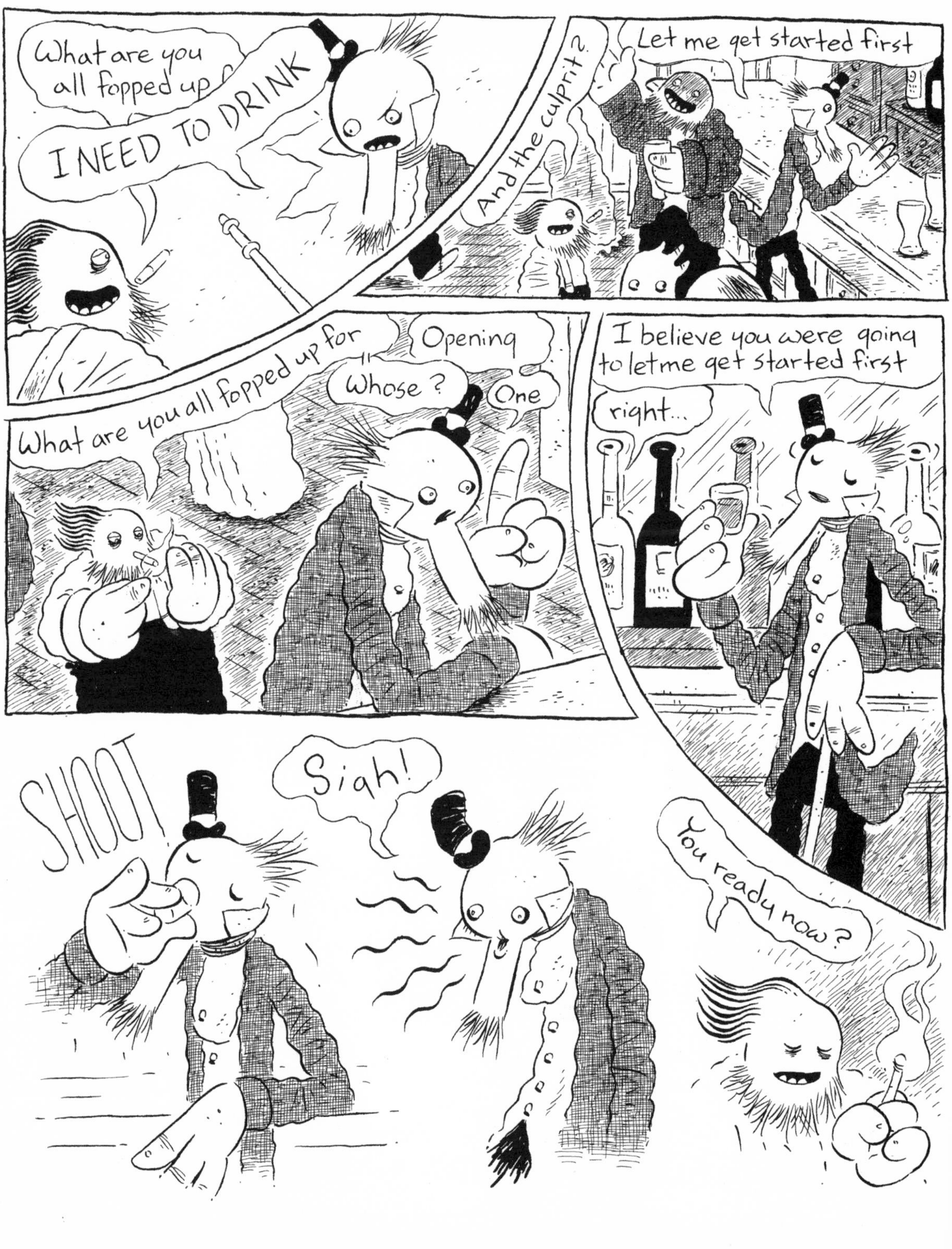
What are you all fopped up
I NEED TO DRINK
And the culprit?
Let me get started first
What are you all fopped up for
Whose?
Opening
One
I believe you were going to letme get started first
right...
SHOOT
Sigh!
You ready now?

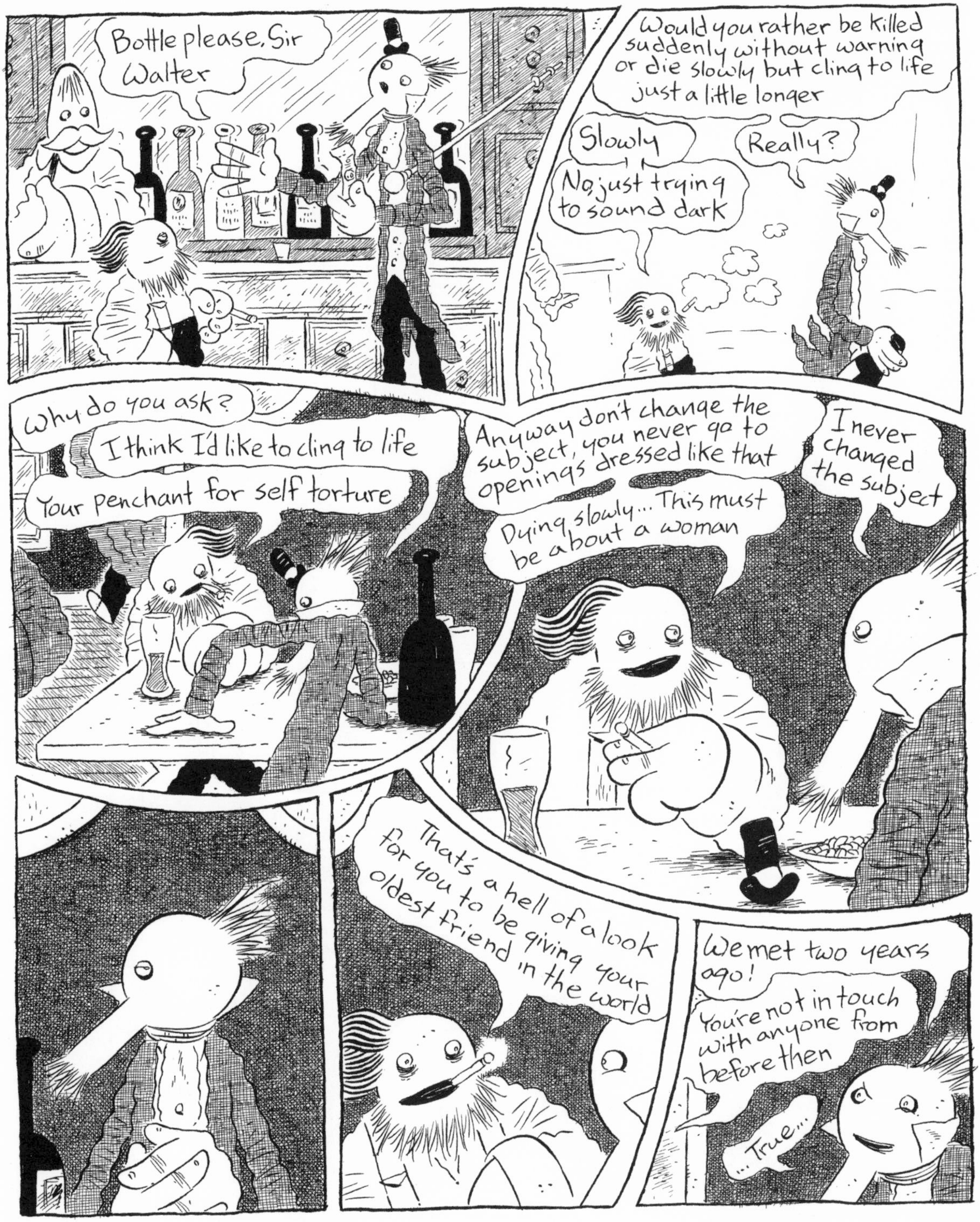

Bottle please, Sir Walter
Would you rather be killed suddenly without warning or die slowly but cling to life just a little longer
Slowly
Really?
No, just trying to sound dark
Why do you ask?
I think I'd like to cling to life
Your penchant for self torture
Anyway don't change the subject, you never go to openings dressed like that
I never changed the subject
Dying slowly... This must be about a woman
That's a hell of a look for you to be giving your oldest friend in the world
We met two years ago!
You're not in touch with anyone from before then
...True...

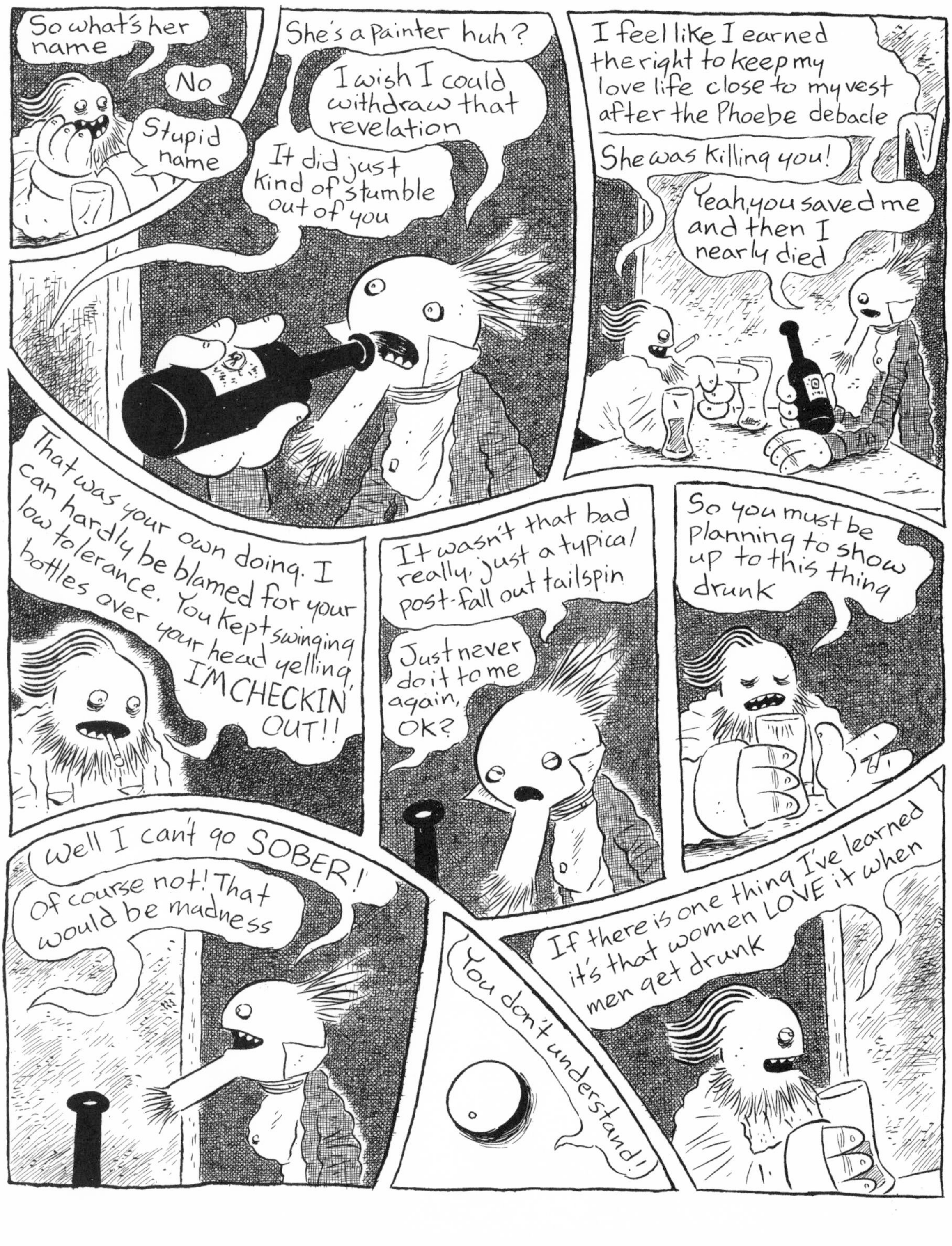
So what's her name
No
Stupid name
She's a painter huh?
I wish I could withdraw that revelation
It did just kind of stumble out of you
I feel like I earned the right to keep my love life close to my vest after the Phoebe debacle
She was killing you!
Yeah, you saved me and then I nearly died
That was your own doing. I can hardly be blamed for your low tolerance. You kept swinging bottles over your head yelling, I'M CHECKIN' OUT!!
It wasn't that bad really, just a typical post-fall out tailspin
Just never do it to me again, OK?
So you must be planning to show up to this thing drunk
Well I can't go SOBER!
Of course not! That would be madness
You don't understand!
If there is one thing I've learned it's that women LOVE it when men get drunk

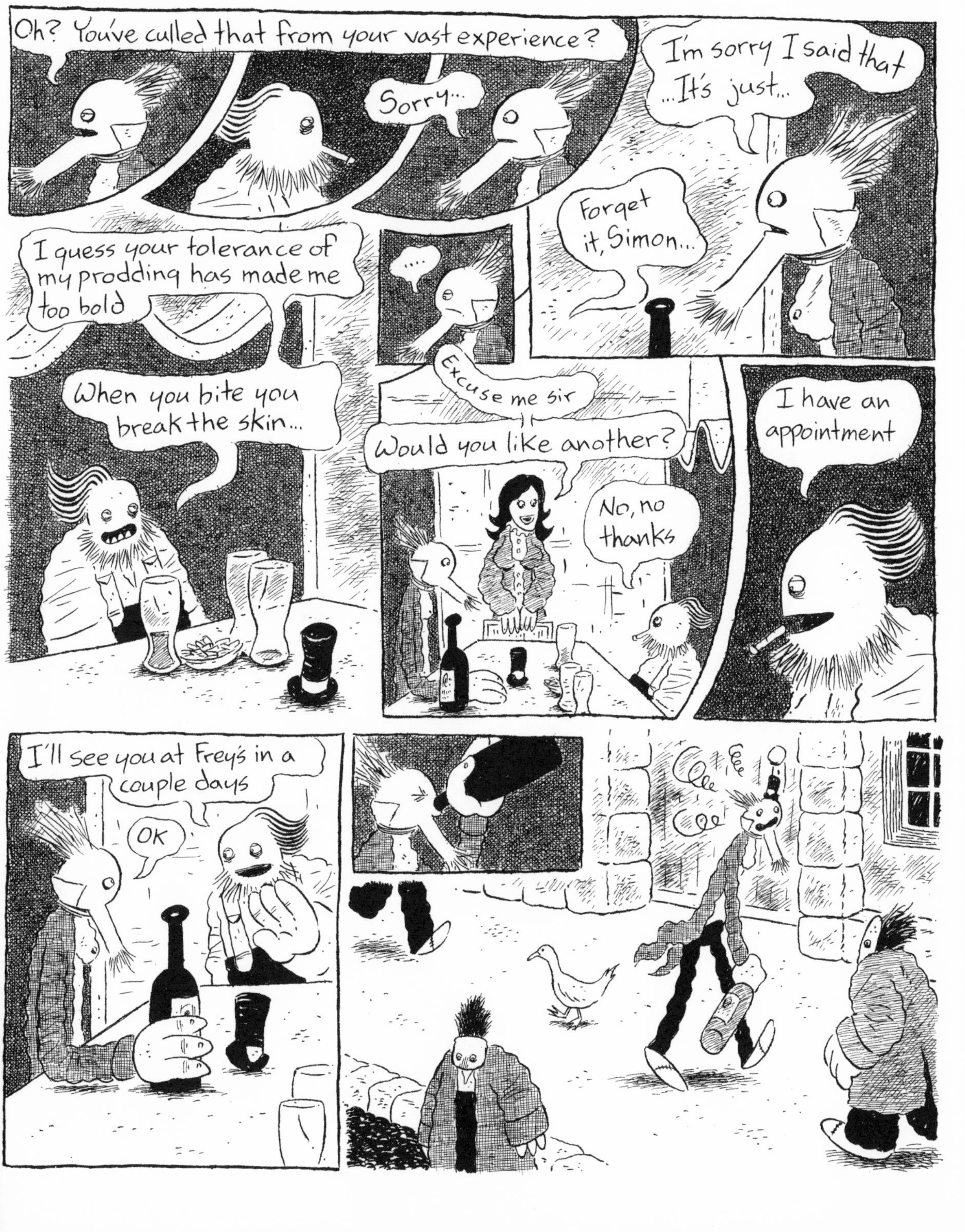
Oh? You've culled that from your vast experience?
Sorry...
I'm sorry I said that ...It's just...
Forget it, Simon...
I guess your tolerance of my prodding has made me too bold
....
When you bite you break the skin...
Excuse me sir
Would you like another?
No, no thanks
I have an appointment
I'll see you at Frey's in a couple days
OK

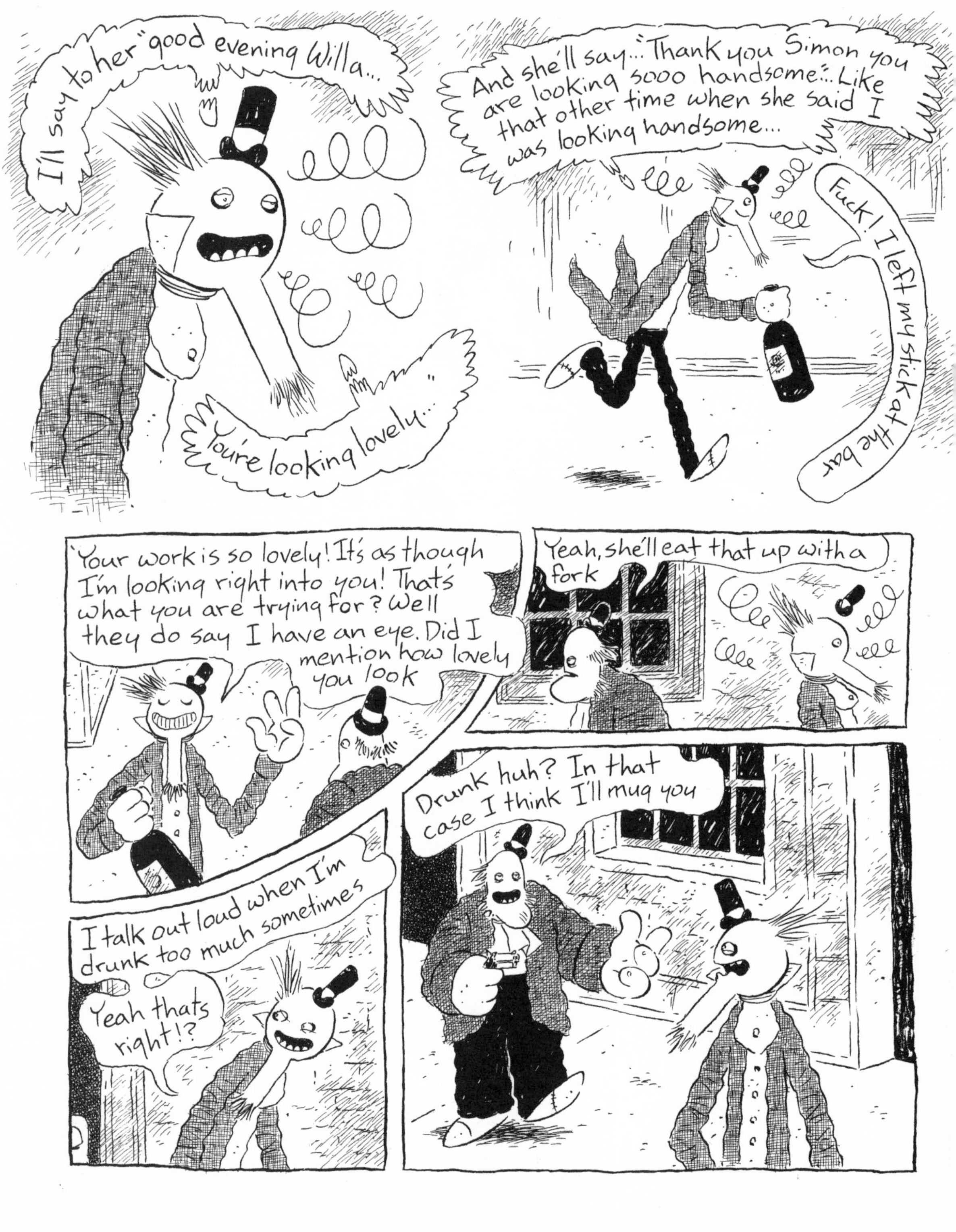
I'll say to her "good evening Willa...
You're looking lovely..."
And she'll say..."Thank you Simon you are looking sooo handsome"...Like that other time when she said I was looking handsome...
Fuck! I left my stick at the bar
"Your work is so lovely! It's as though I'm looking right into you! That's what you are trying for? Well they do say I have an eye. Did I mention how lovely you look
Yeah, she'll eat that up with a fork
I talk out loud when I'm drunk too much sometimes
Yeah thats right!?
Drunk huh? In that case I think I'll mug you

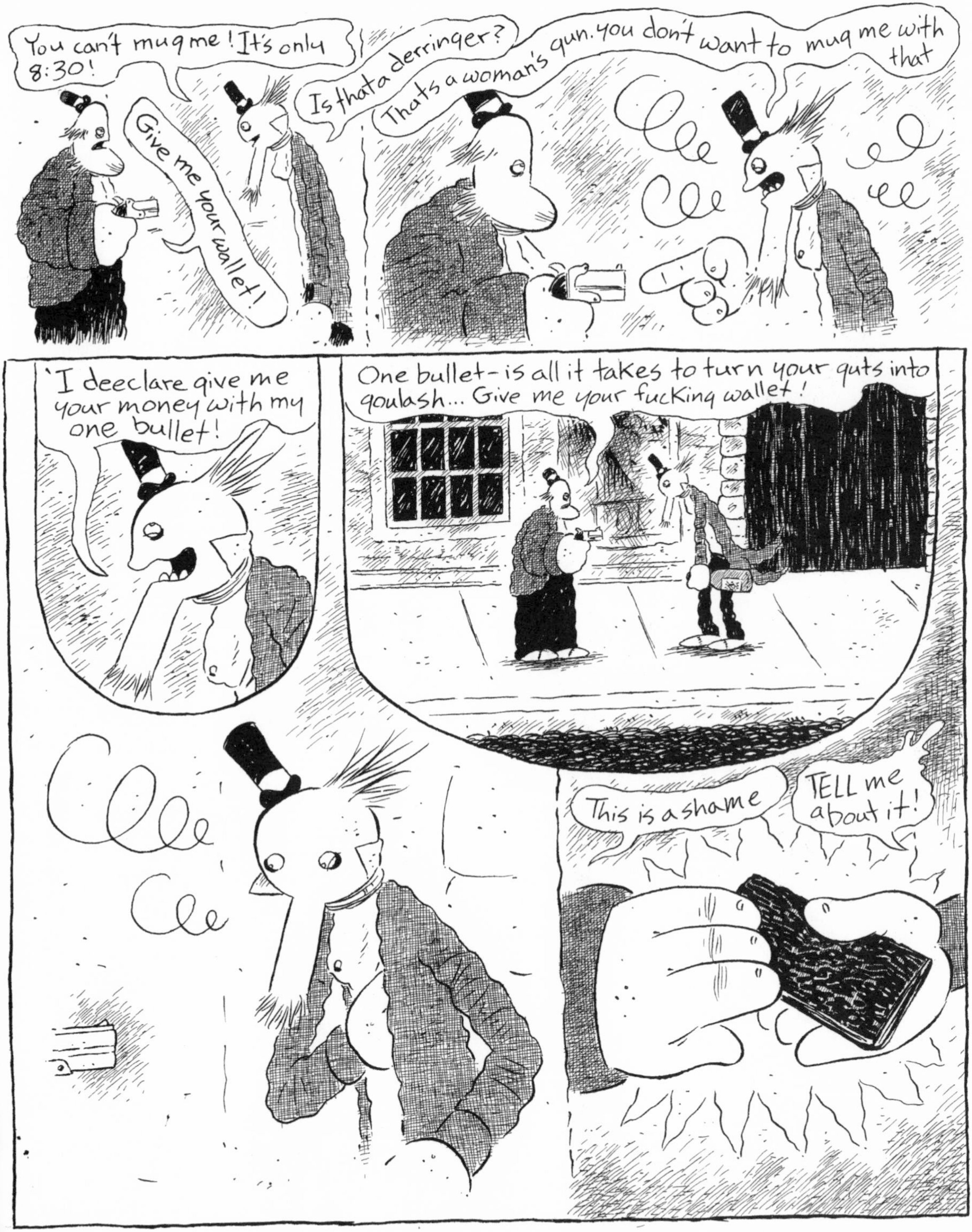

You can't mug me! It's only 8:30!
Give me your wallet!
Is that a derringer?
That's a woman's gun. You don't want to mug me with that
'I deeclare give me your money with my one bullet!
One bullet- is all it takes to turn your guts into goulash... Give me your fucking wallet!
This is a shame
TELL me about it!

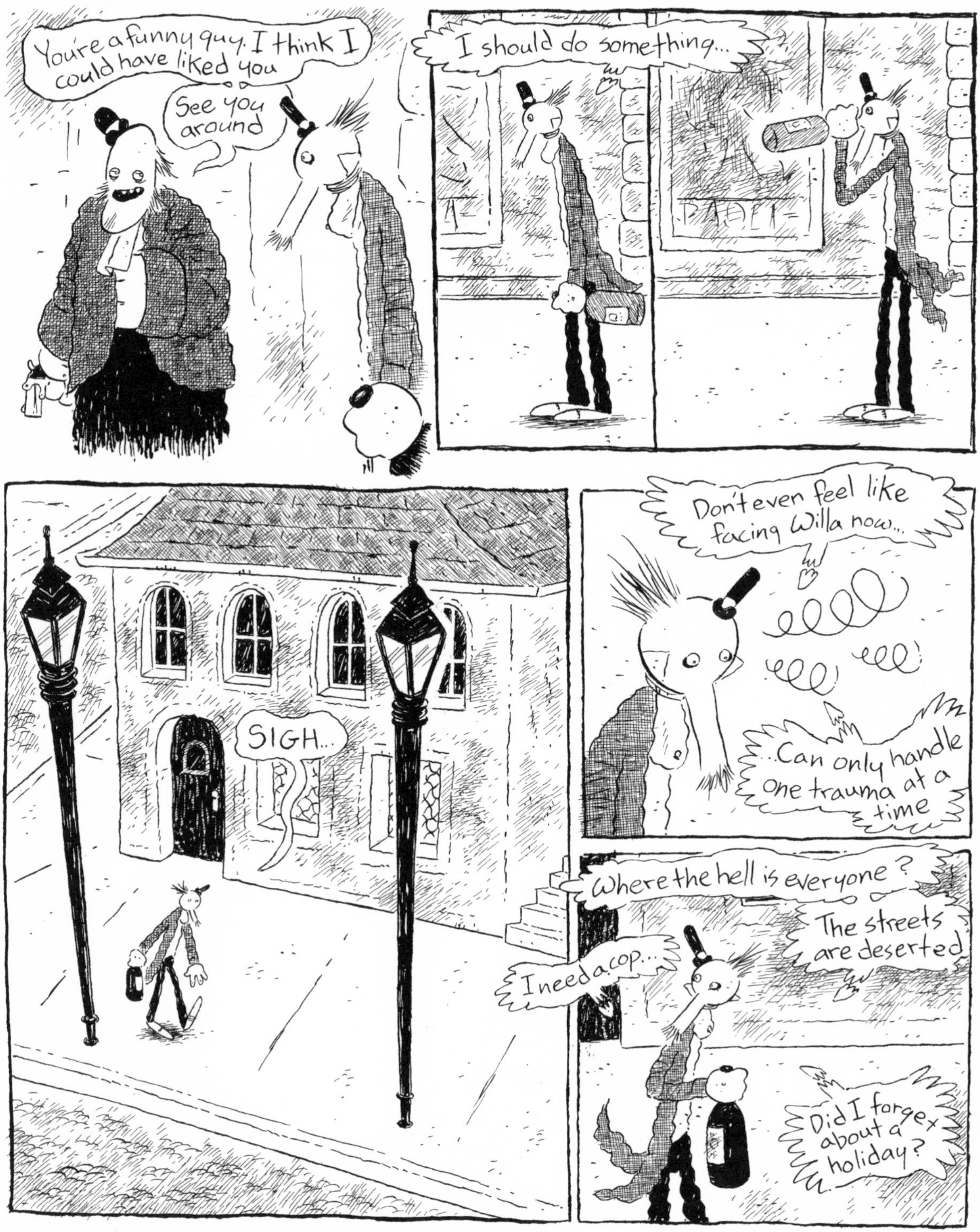
You're a funny guy. I think I could have liked you
See you around
I should do something...
SIGH...
Don't even feel like facing Willa now...
...Can only handle one trauma at a time
Where the hell is everyone?
The streets are deserted
I need a cop...
Did I forget about a holiday?

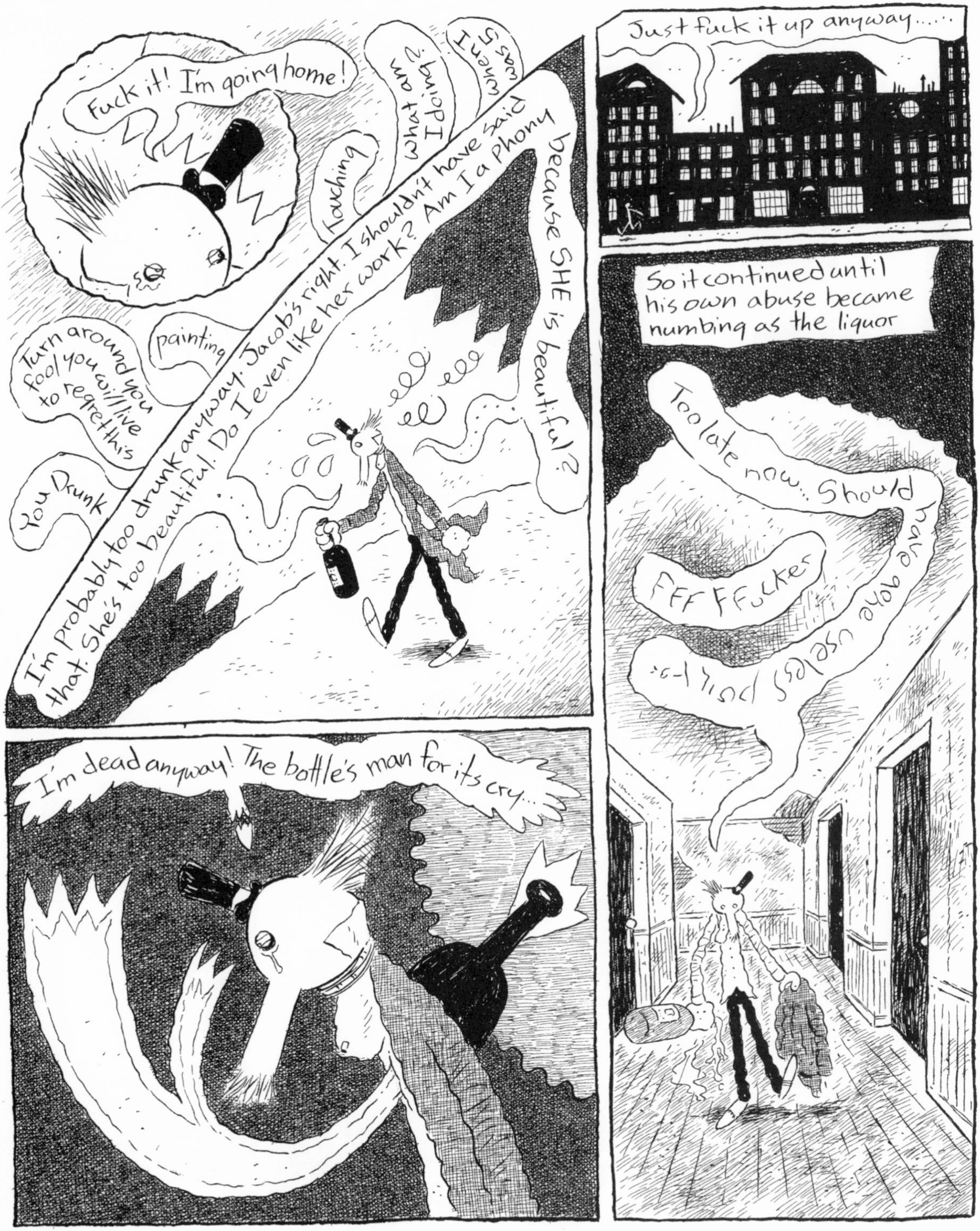

Fuck it! I'm going home!
touching
what am I doing?
when I was 5
painting
Turn around you fool you will live to regret this
You Drunk
I'm probably too drunk anyway. Jacob's right. I shouldn't have said that. She's too beautiful. Do I even like her work? Am I a phony because SHE is beautiful?
Just fuck it up anyway......
So it continued until his own abuse became numbing as the liquor
Too late now... Should have gone useless loser..
FFF FFuckers
I'm dead anyway! The bottle's man for its cry...

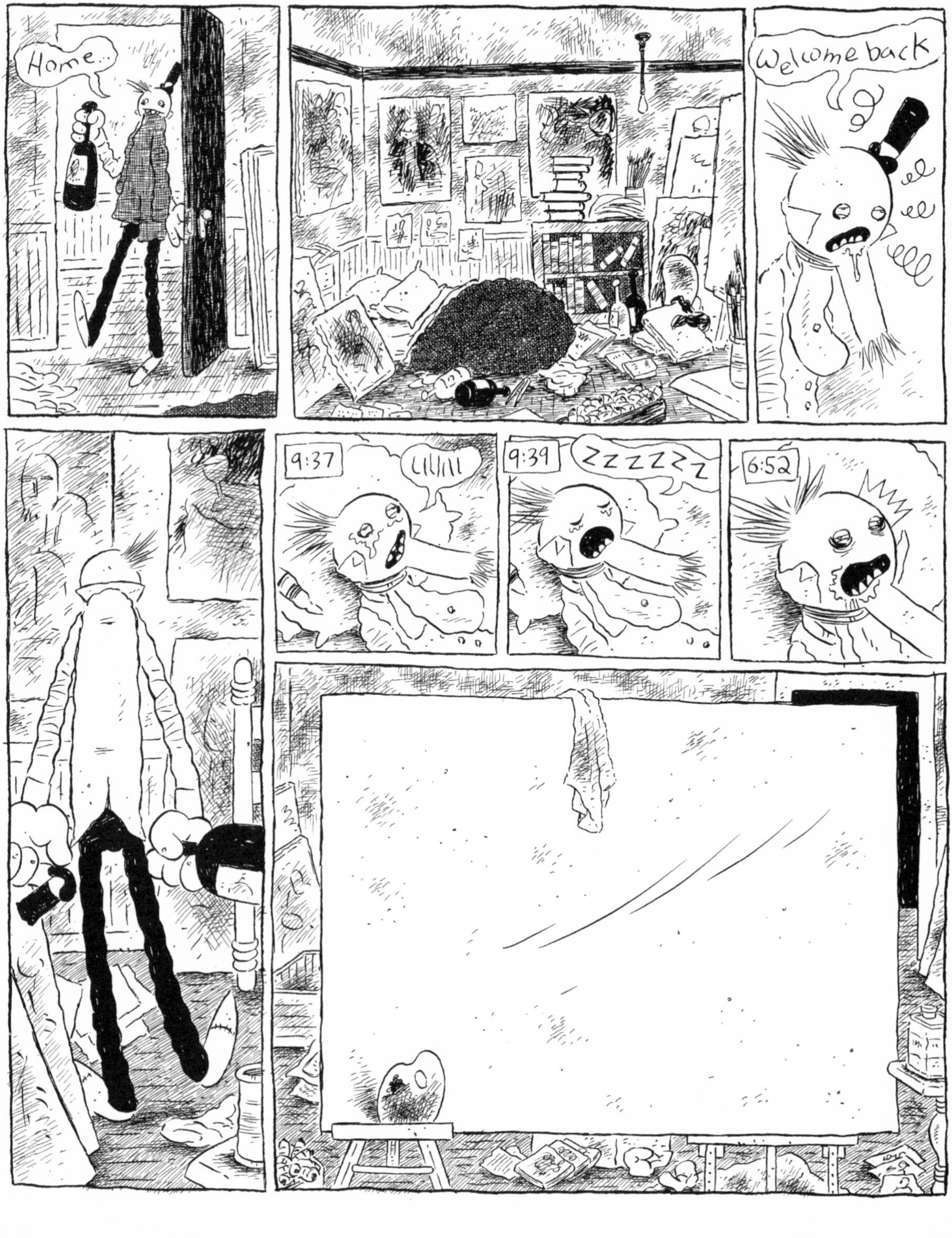
Home...
Welcome back
9:37
UHHH
9:39
ZZZZZZ
6:52

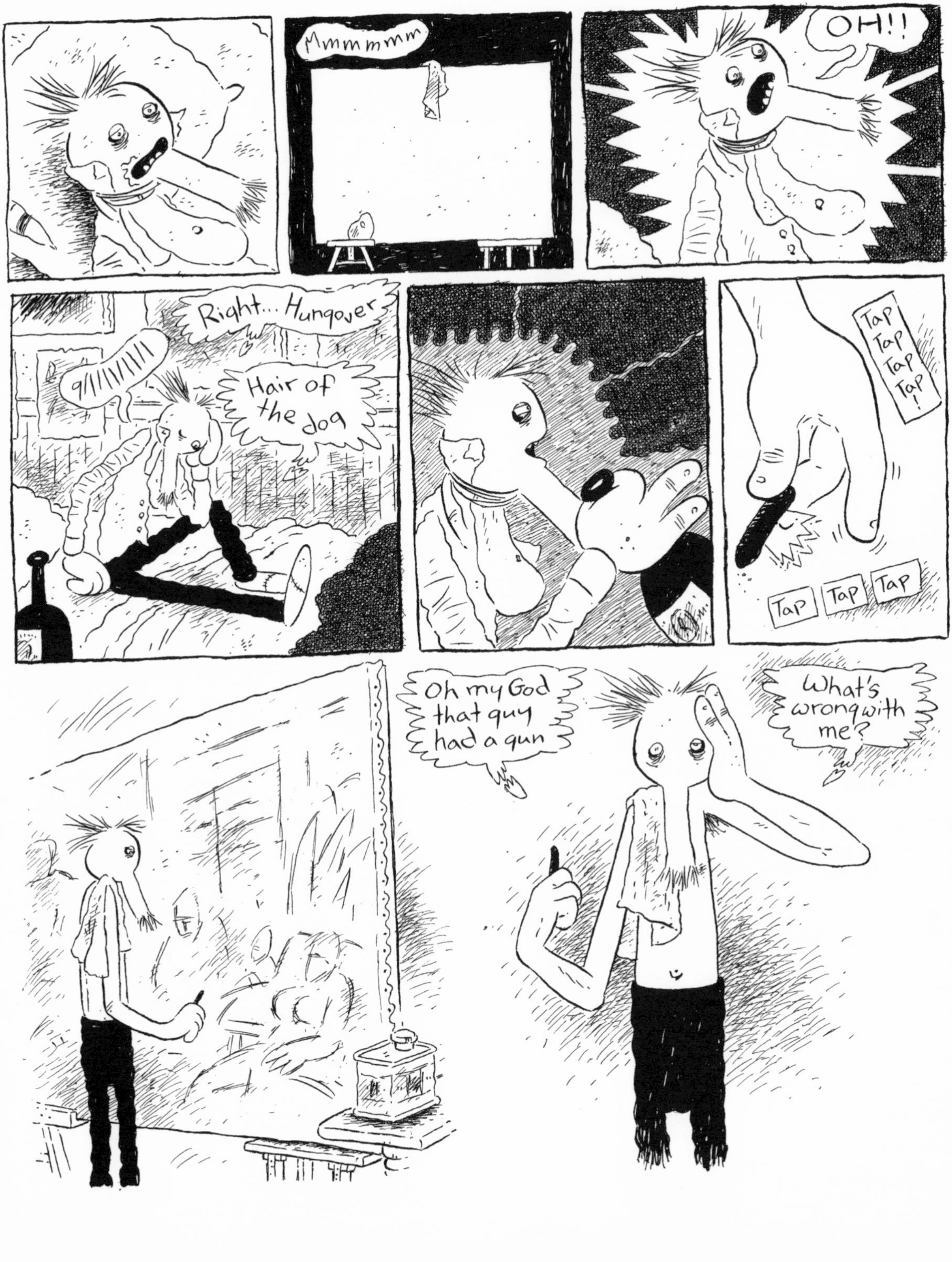
Mmmmmm
OH!!
Right... Hungover
9/11
Hair of the dog
Tap Tap Tap Tap Tap!
Tap
Tap
Tap
Oh my God that guy had a gun
What's wrong with me?

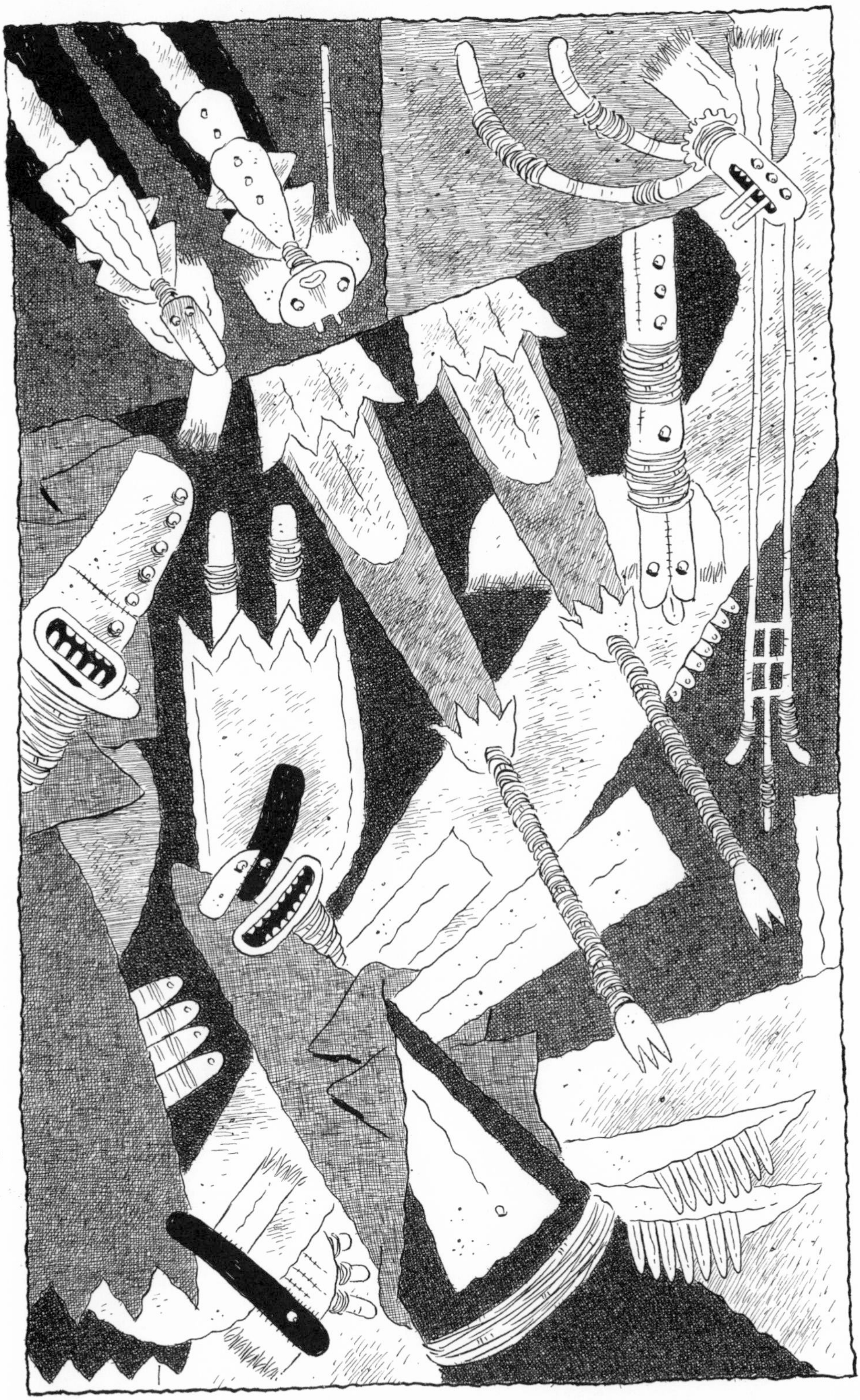

Related Papers

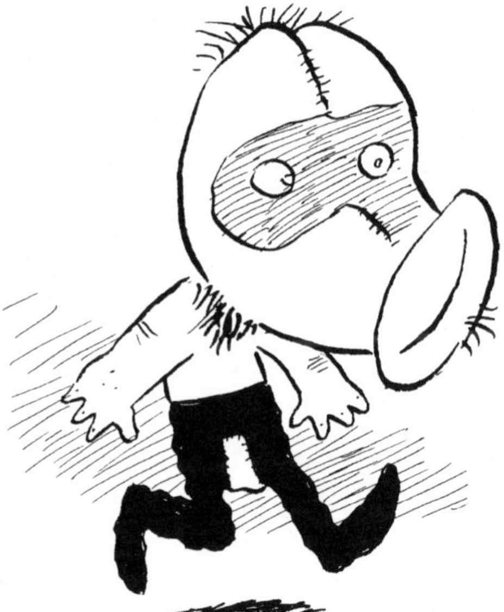

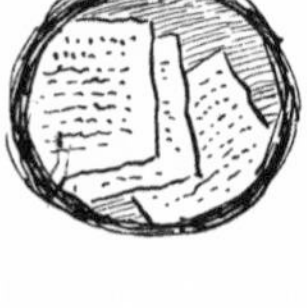

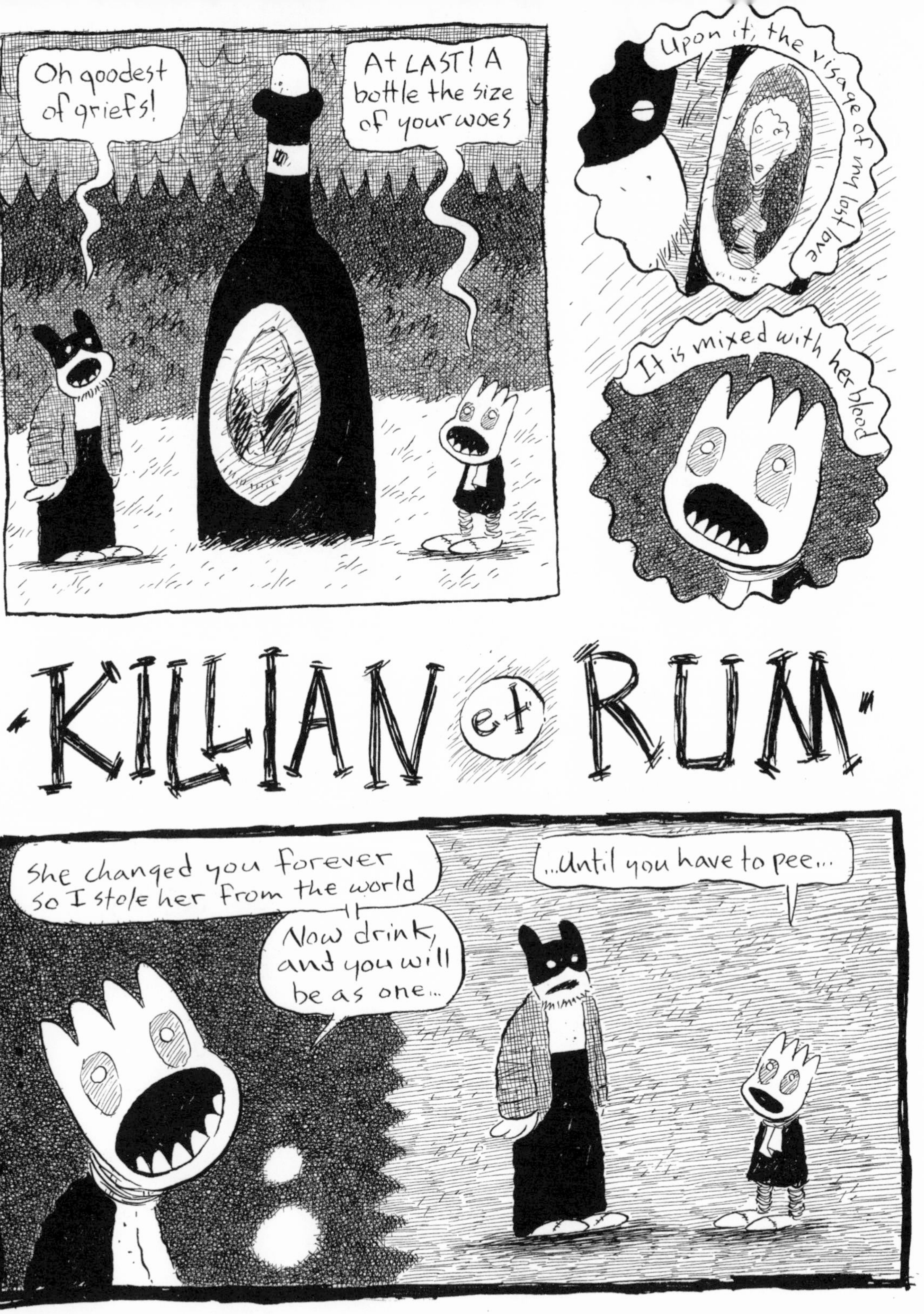
Oh goodest of griefs!
At LAST! A bottle the size of your woes
Upon it, the visage of my lost love
It is mixed with her blood
KILLIAN et RUM
She changed you forever so I stole her from the world
Now drink, and you will be as one...
...Until you have to pee...

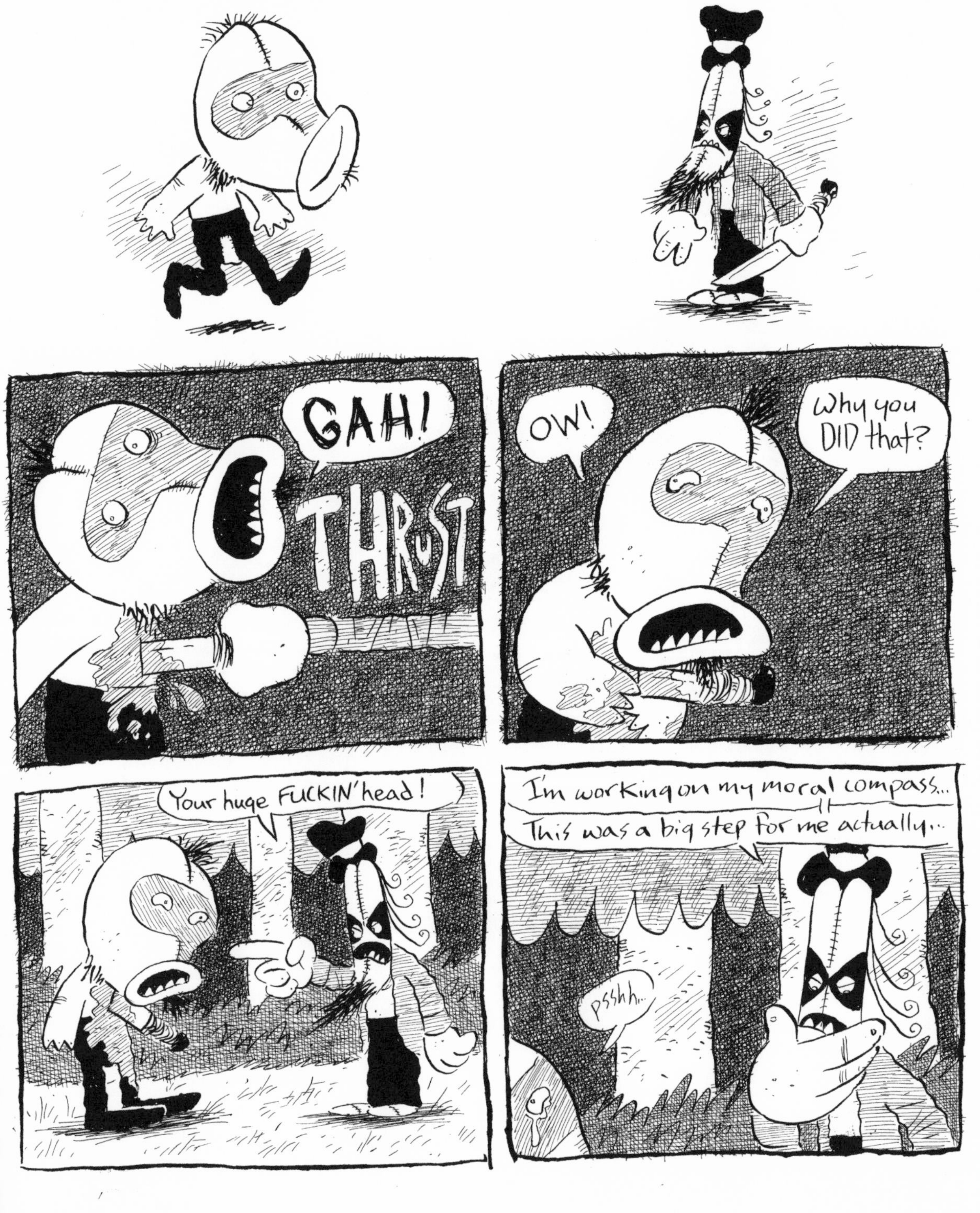
GAH!
THRUST
OW!
Why you DID that?
Your huge FUCKIN' head!
I'm working on my moral compass...
This was a big step for me actually...
psshh...

I have a joy in slavery!

GLUG!

My taskmaster is a wonder! A free pass from responsibility and women!

He even strips away all of my worst rememberings

I could do without his beatings of course

But memory would whip me twice as hard

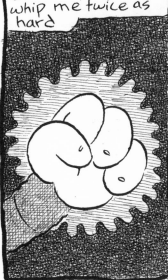

I know that he will eventually tire of me and kill me

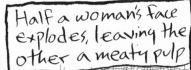 I am plagued by terrible dreams

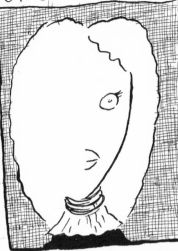 Half a woman's face explodes, leaving the other a meaty pulp

 A dog is stripped away by sound waves in cold cut slices, flesh, bone and all...

 I awake in a deep sweat

 Forced to wonder if I really know my own soul

 Fearing both a return to sleep, and the dawn

 Both come in spite of my apprehension

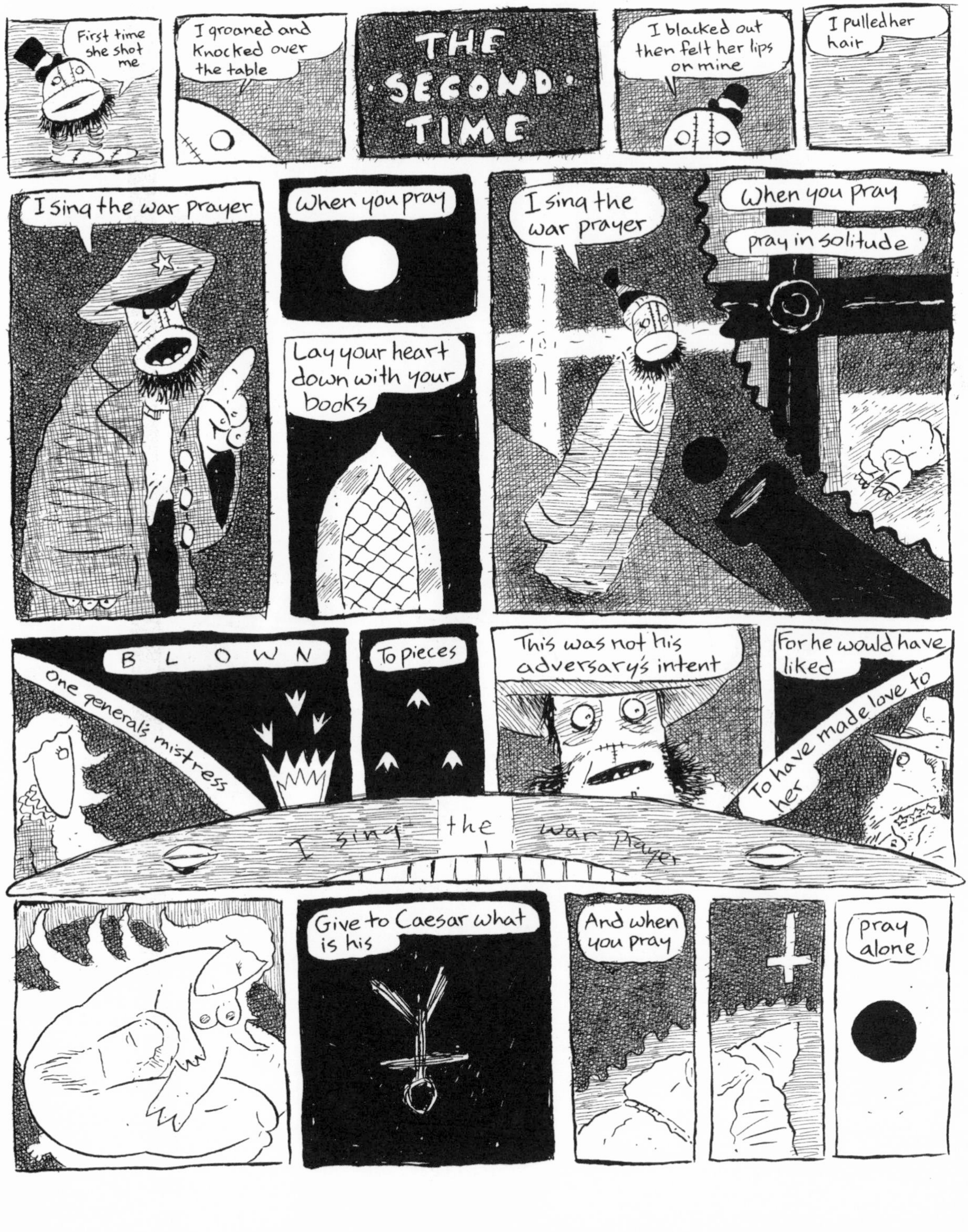

First time she shot me
I groaned and Knocked over the table
THE SECOND TIME
I blacked out then felt her lips on mine
I pulled her hair
I sing the war prayer
When you pray
Lay your heart down with your books
I sing the war prayer
When you pray
pray in solitude
B L O W N
One general's mistress
To pieces
This was not his adversary's intent
For he would have liked
To have made love to her
I sing the war prayer
Give to Caesar what is his
And when you pray
pray alone

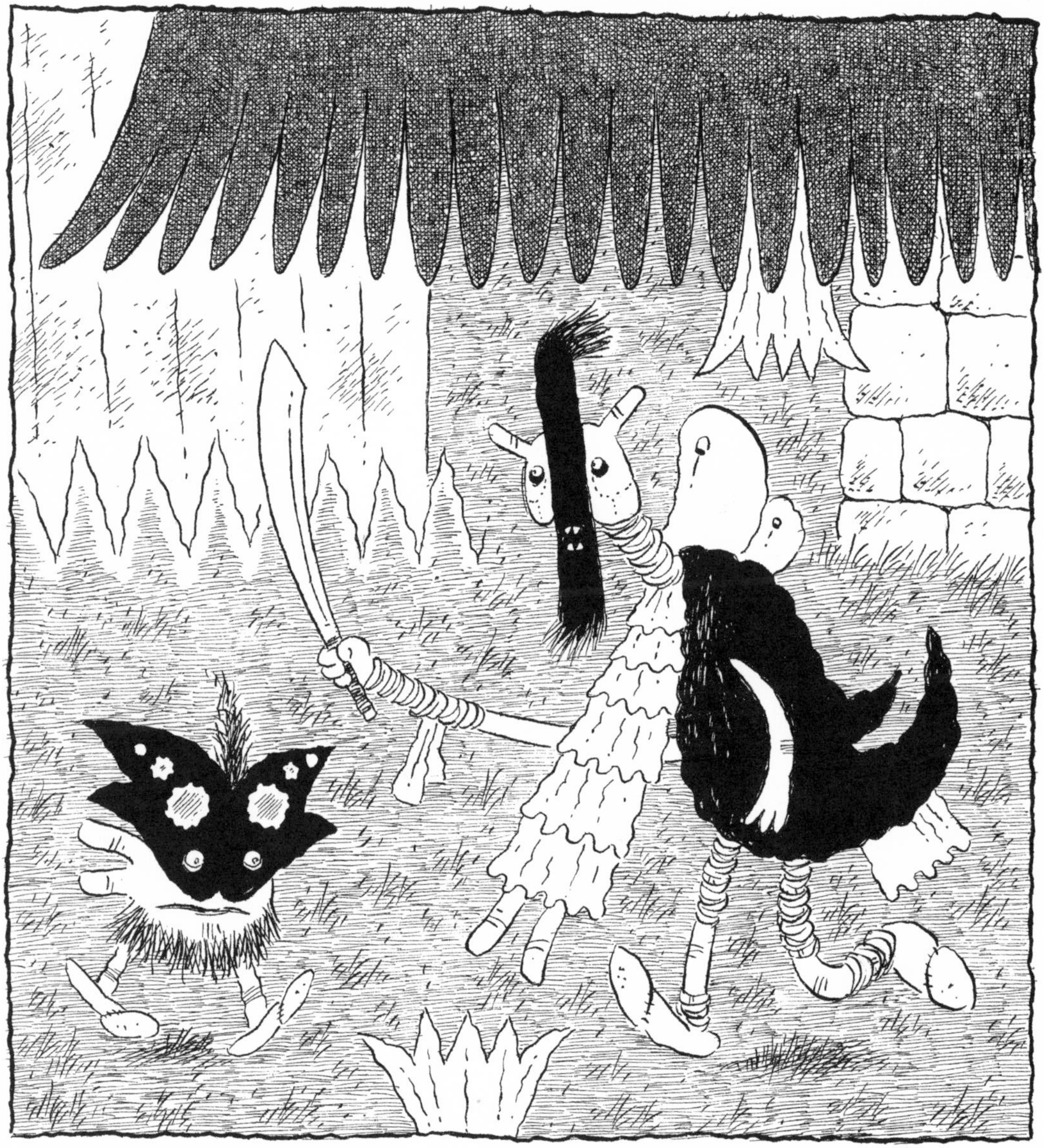

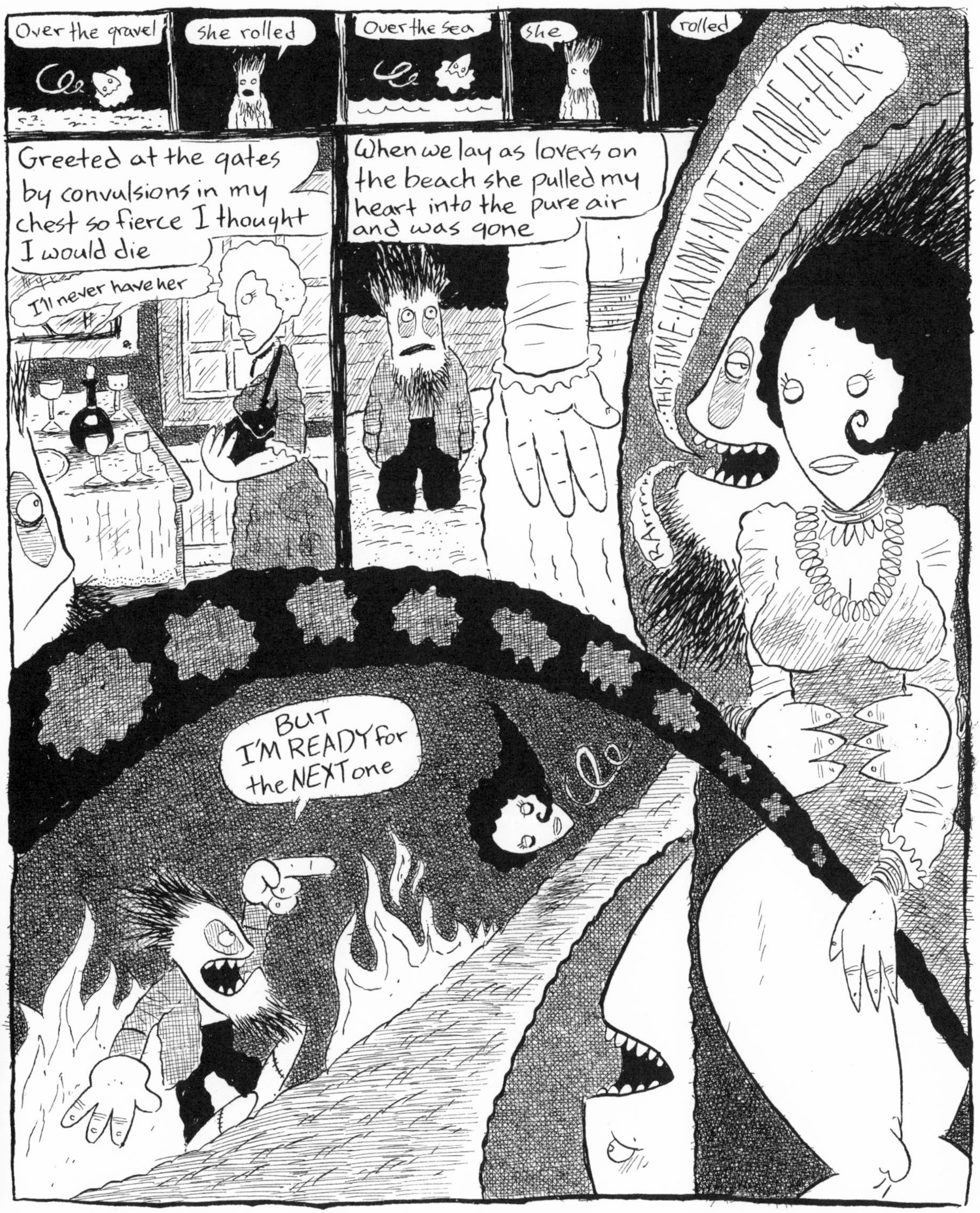

Over the gravel
she rolled
Over the sea
she
rolled
THIS·TIME·I·KNOW·NOT·TO·LOVE·HER...
Greeted at the gates by convulsions in my chest so fierce I thought I would die
I'll never have her
When we lay as lovers on the beach she pulled my heart into the pure air and was gone
RArrrr
BUT I'M READY for the NEXT one

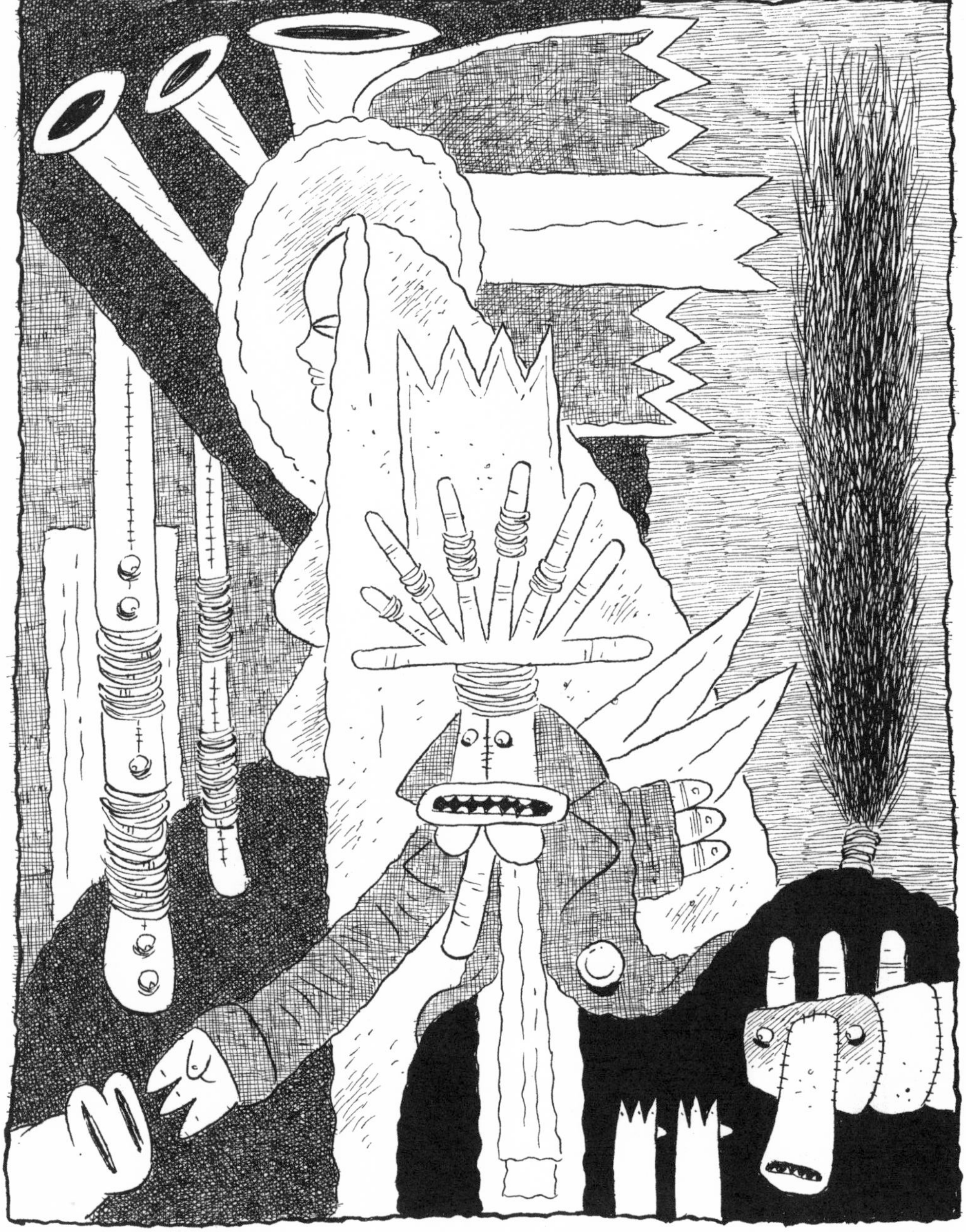

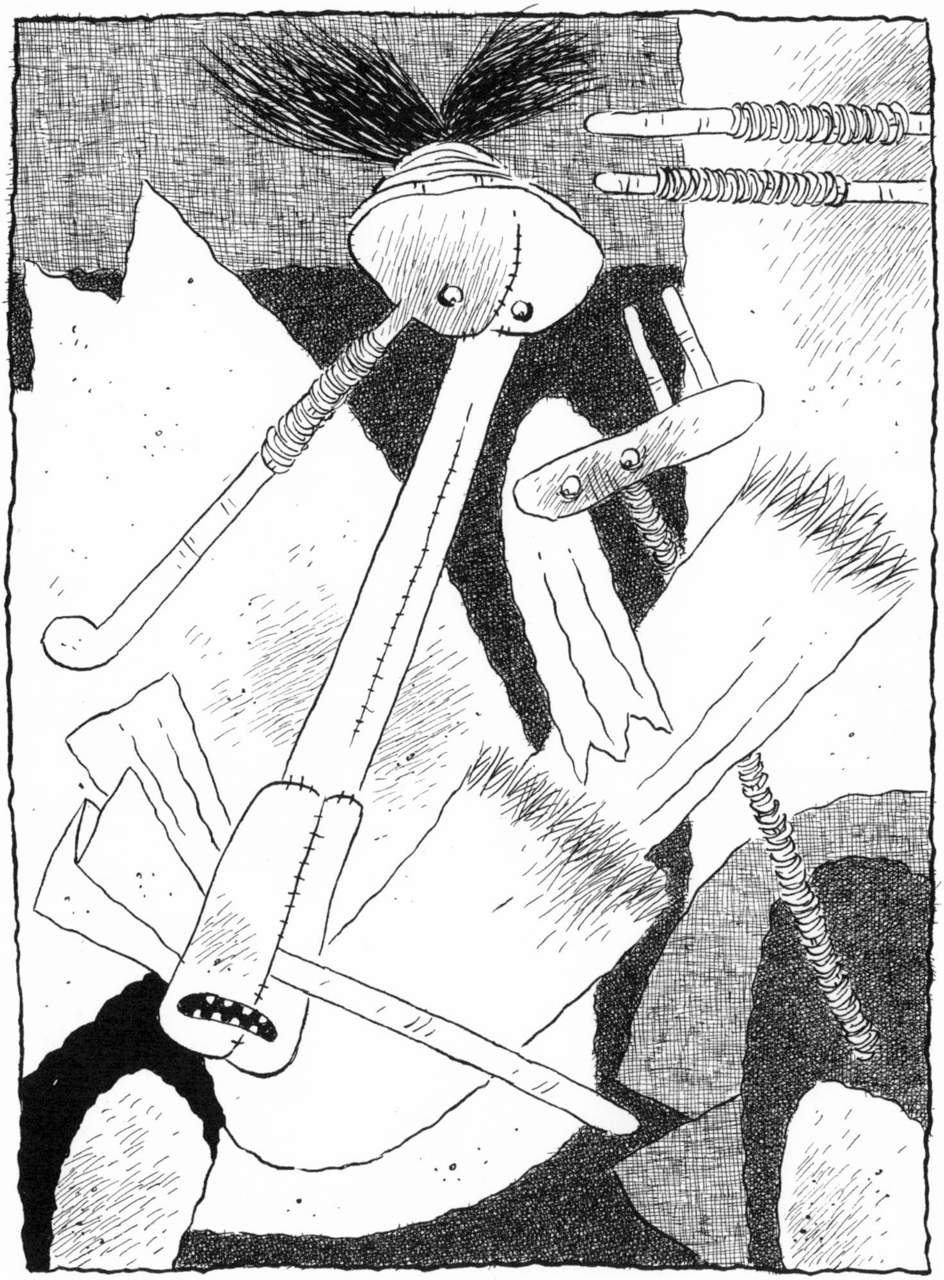

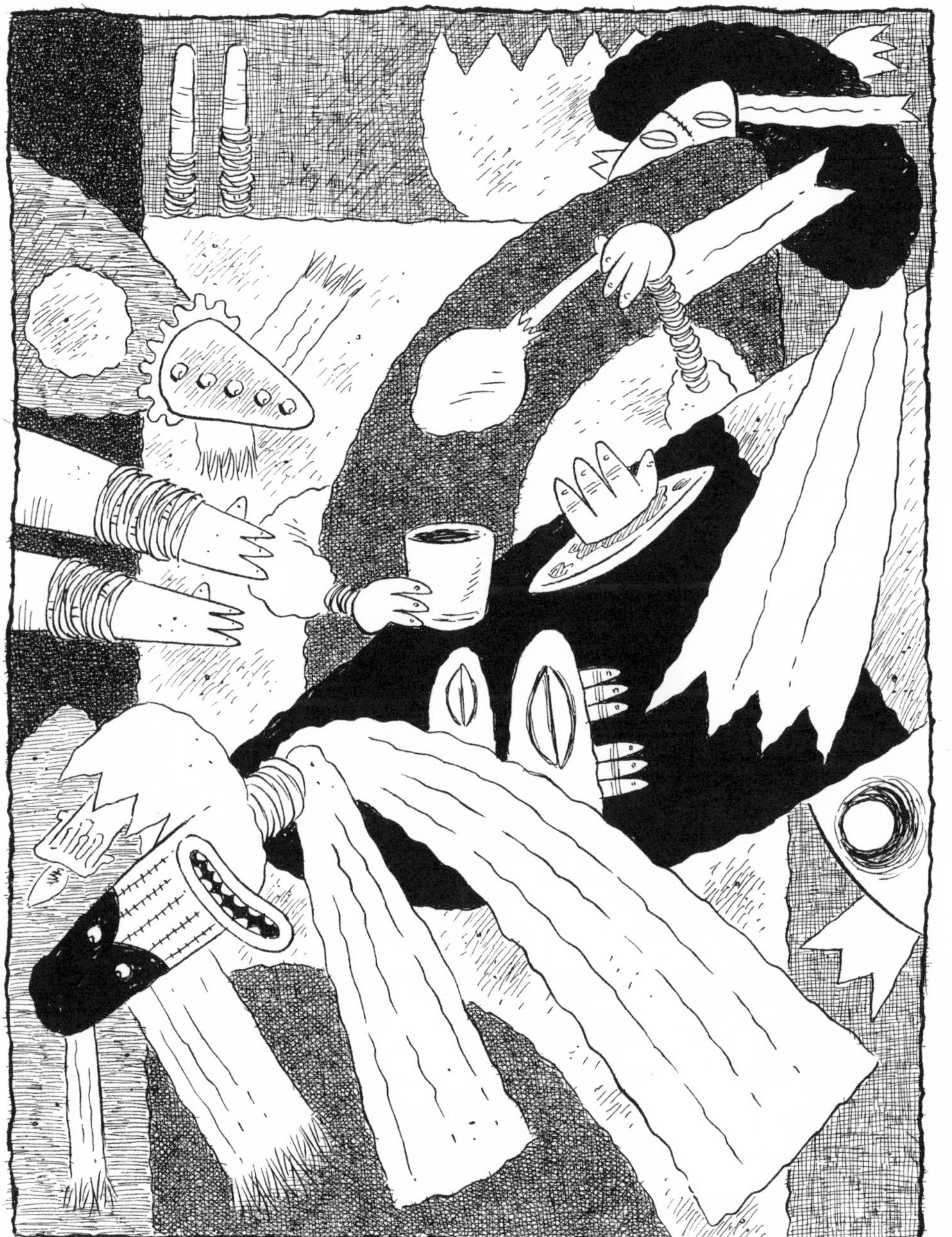

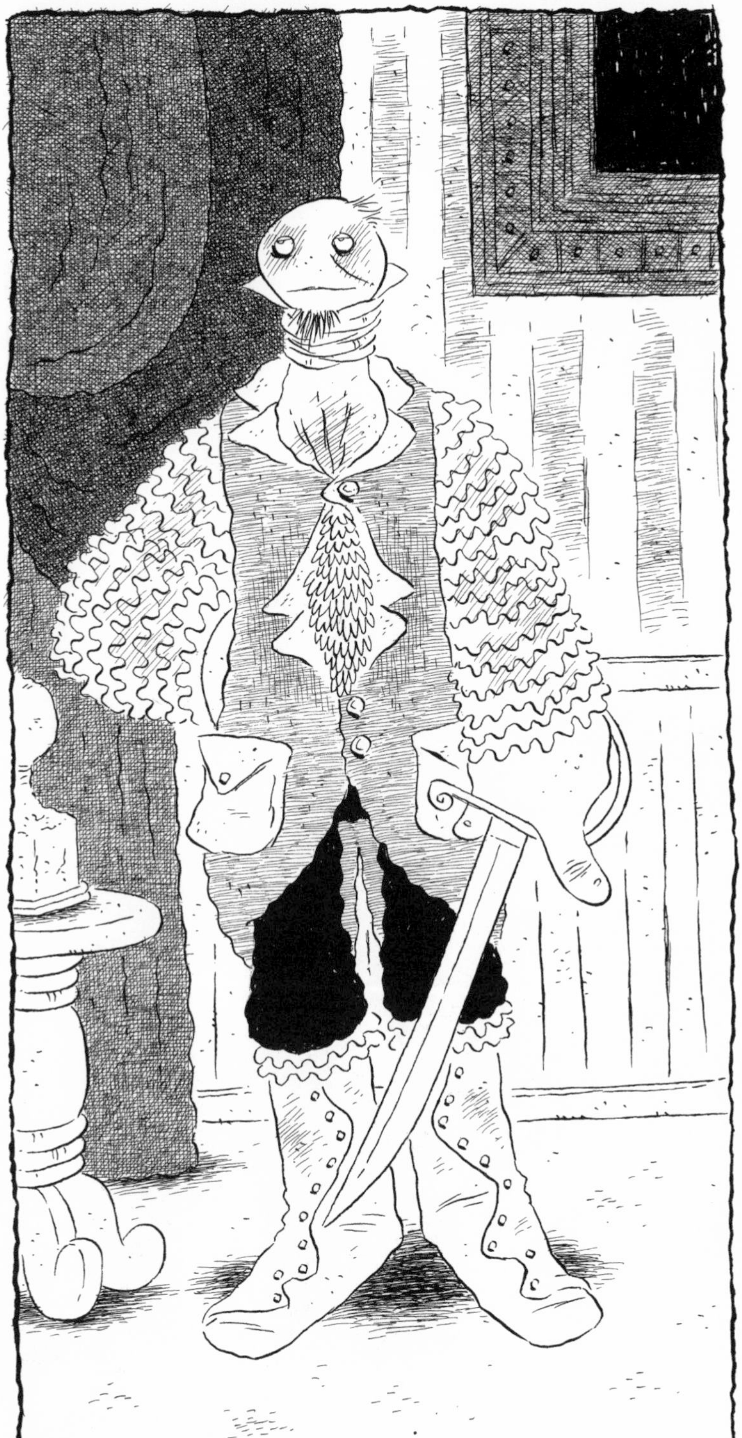

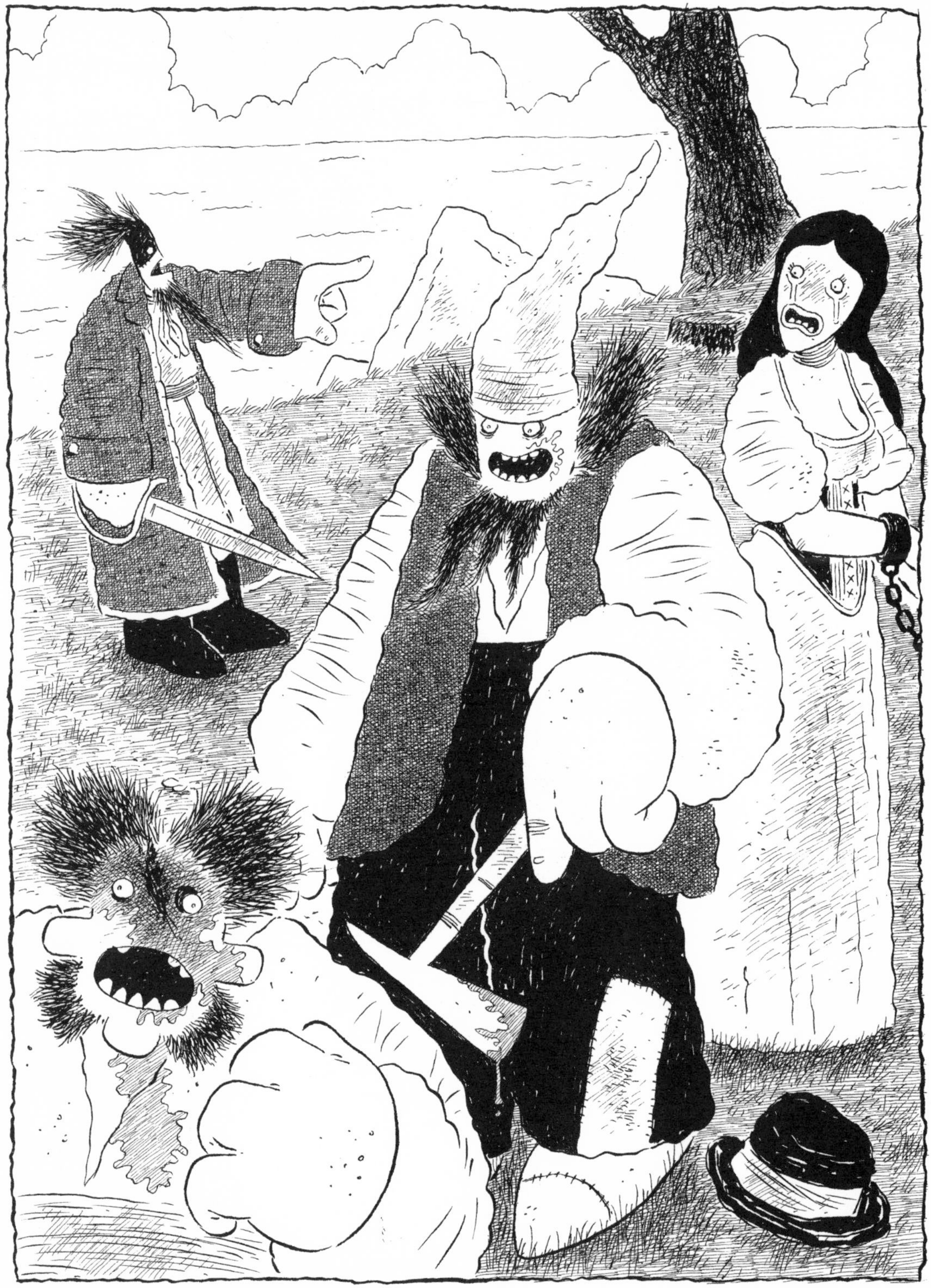

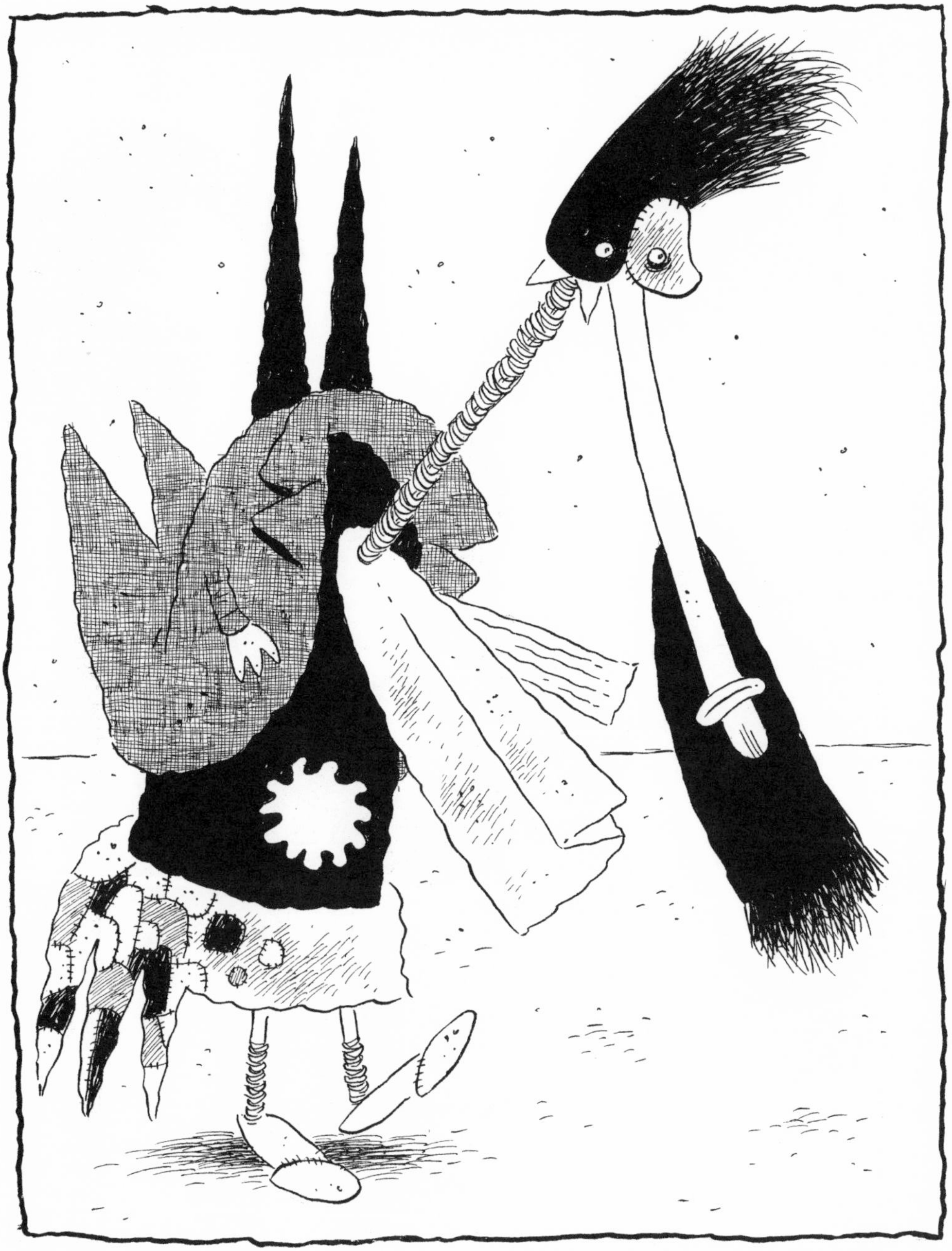

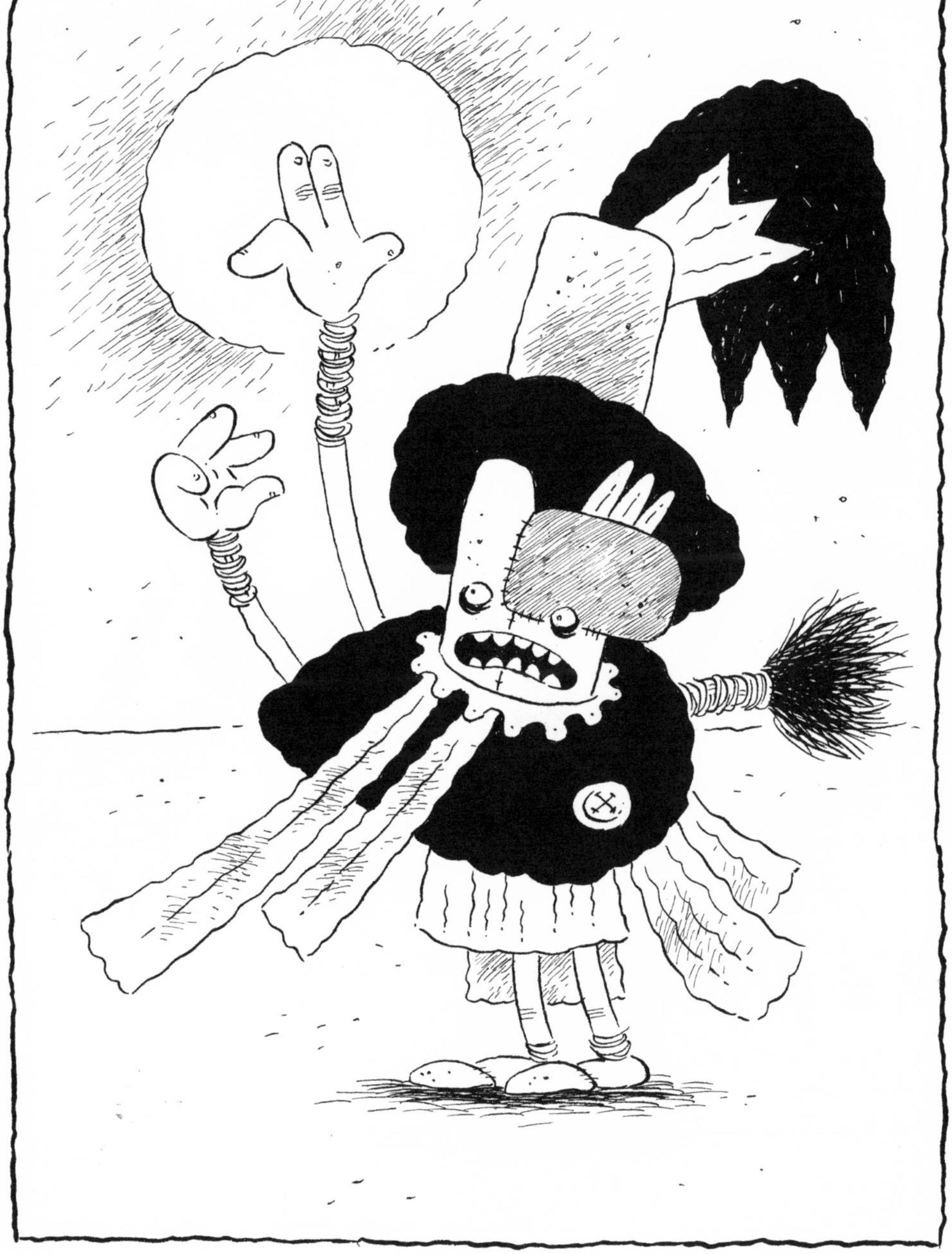

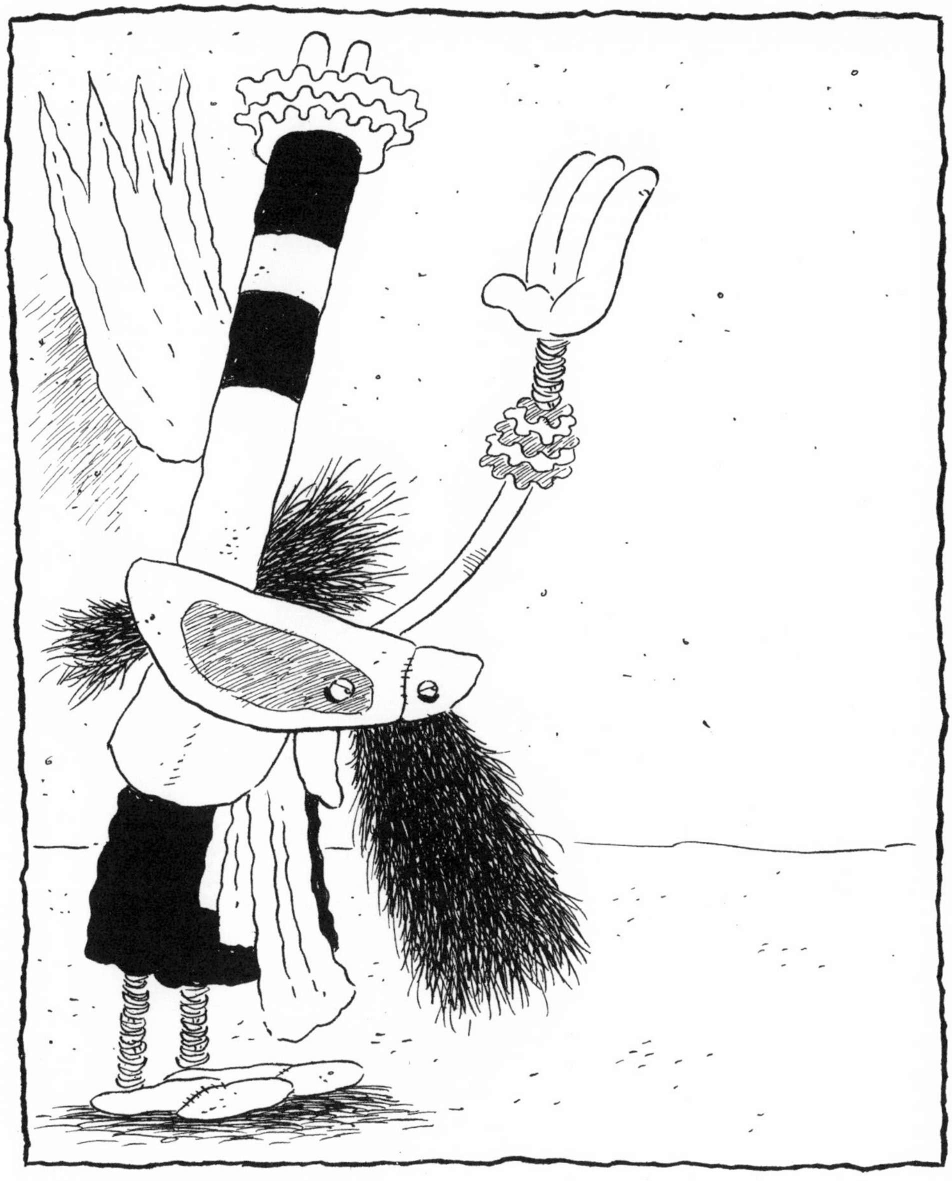

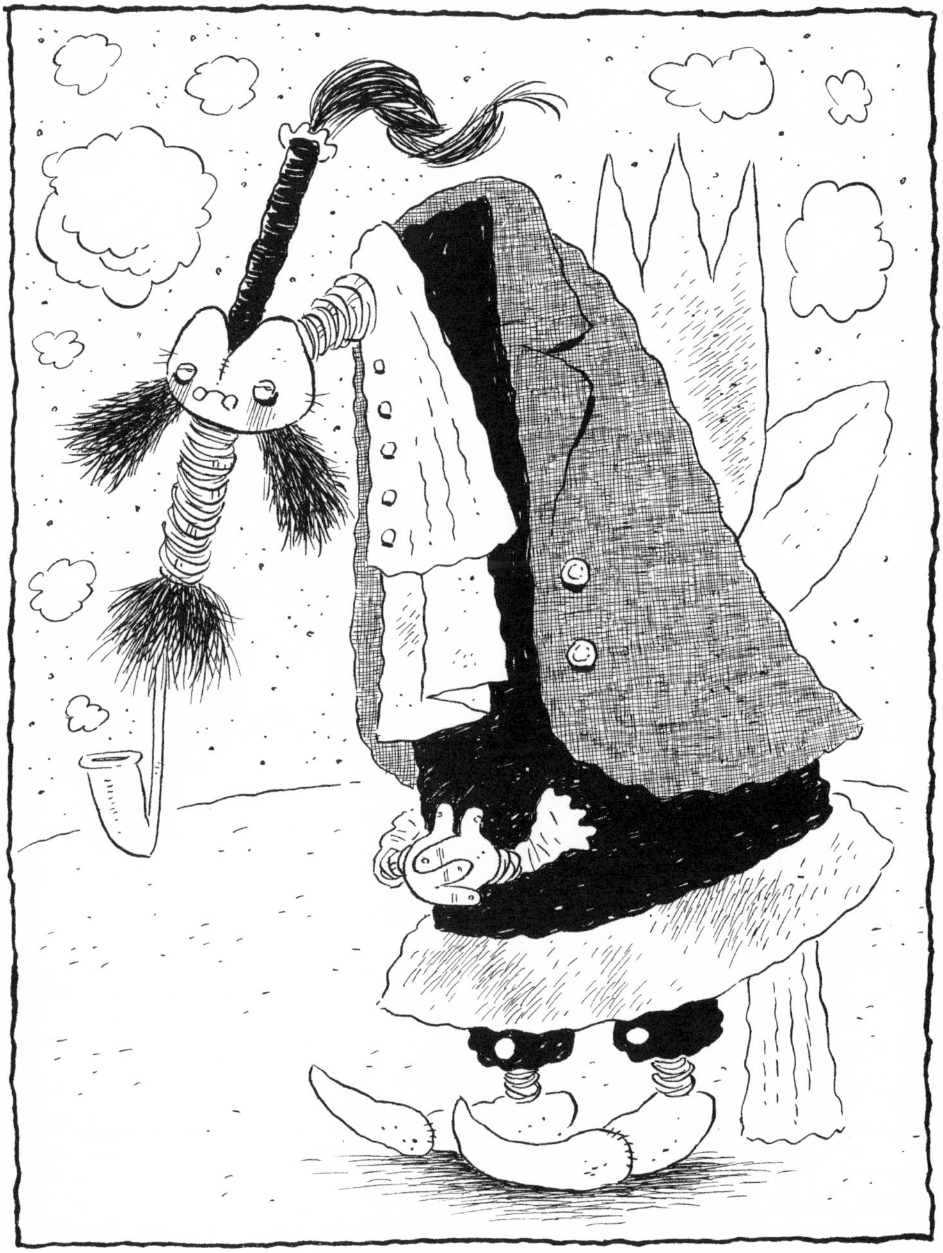

Excerpt From Agamemnon

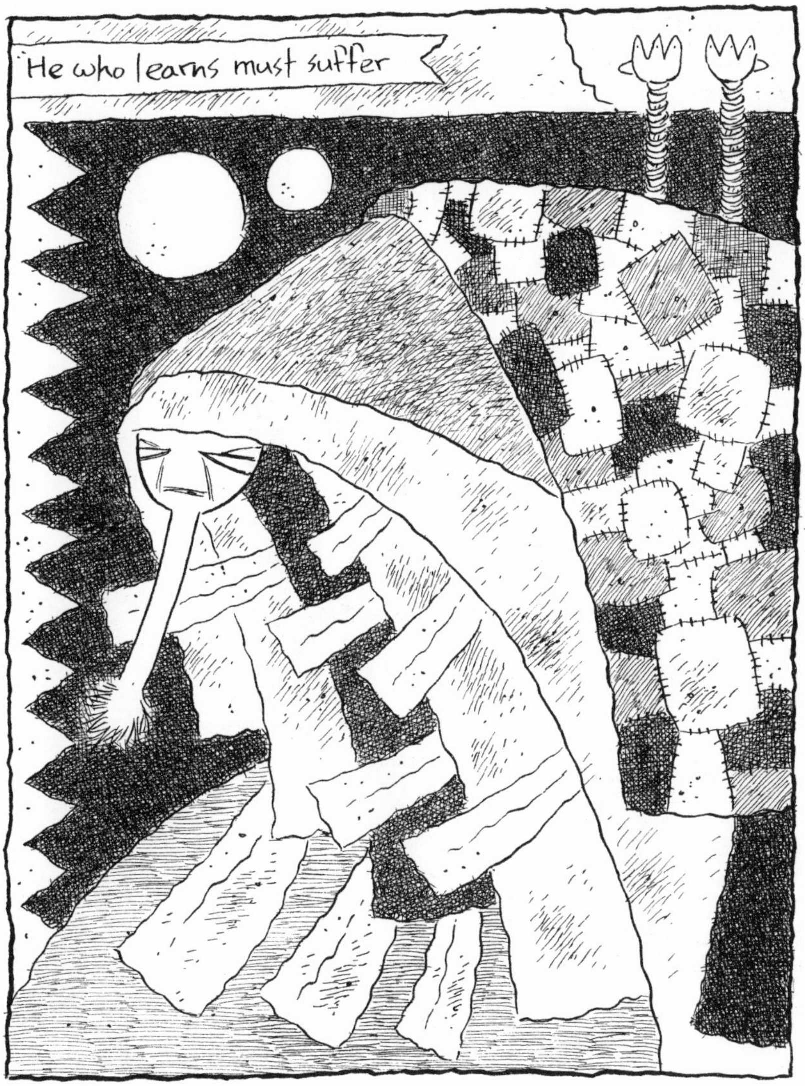
He who learns must suffer

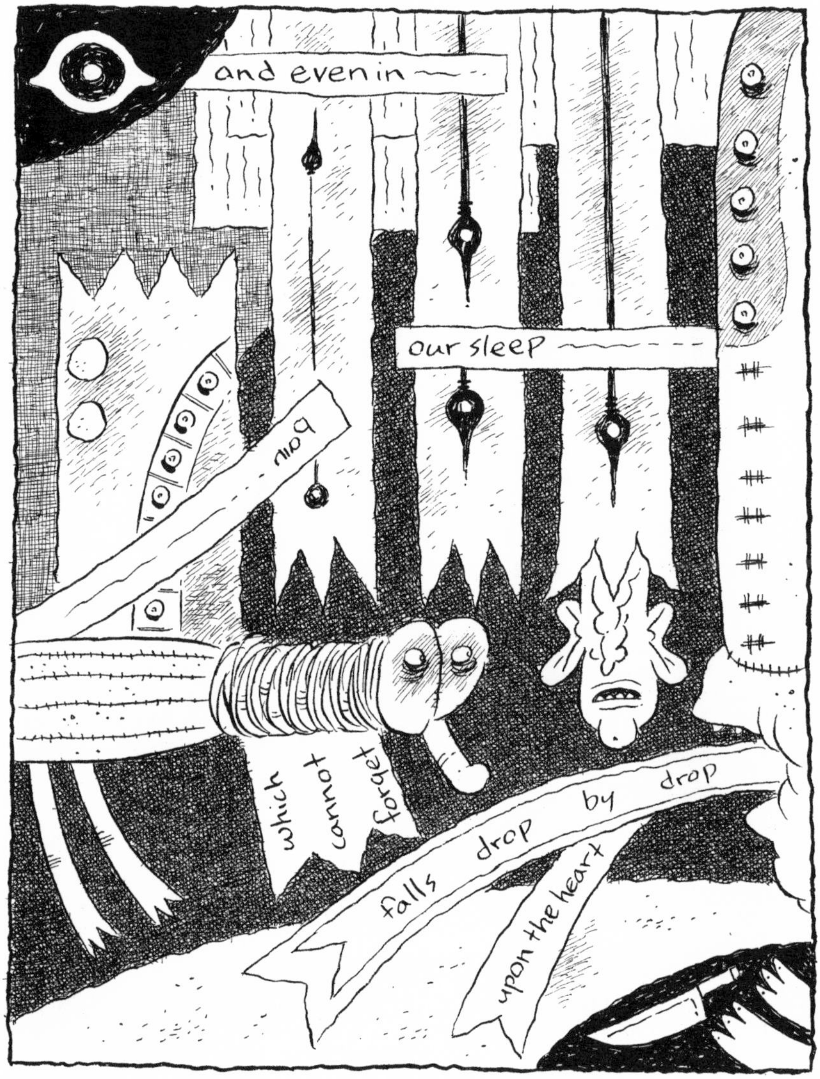
and even in
our sleep
pain
which cannot forget
falls drop by drop
upon the heart

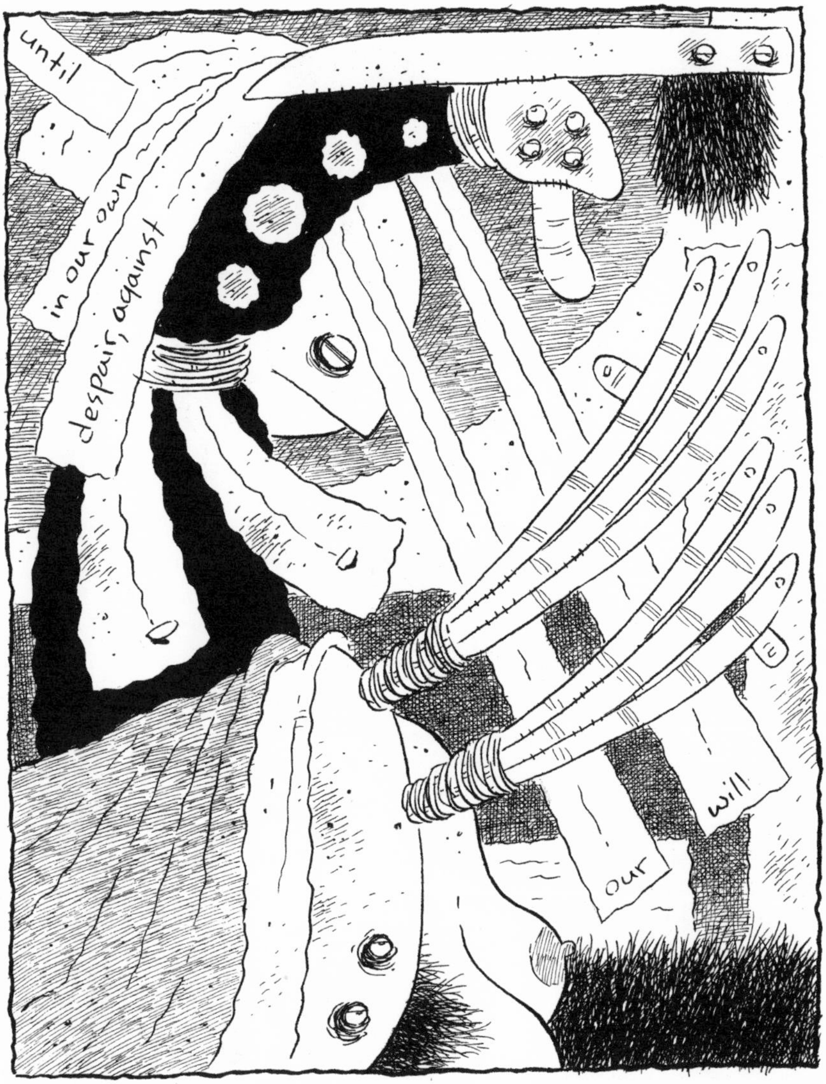
until
in our own
despair, against
our
will

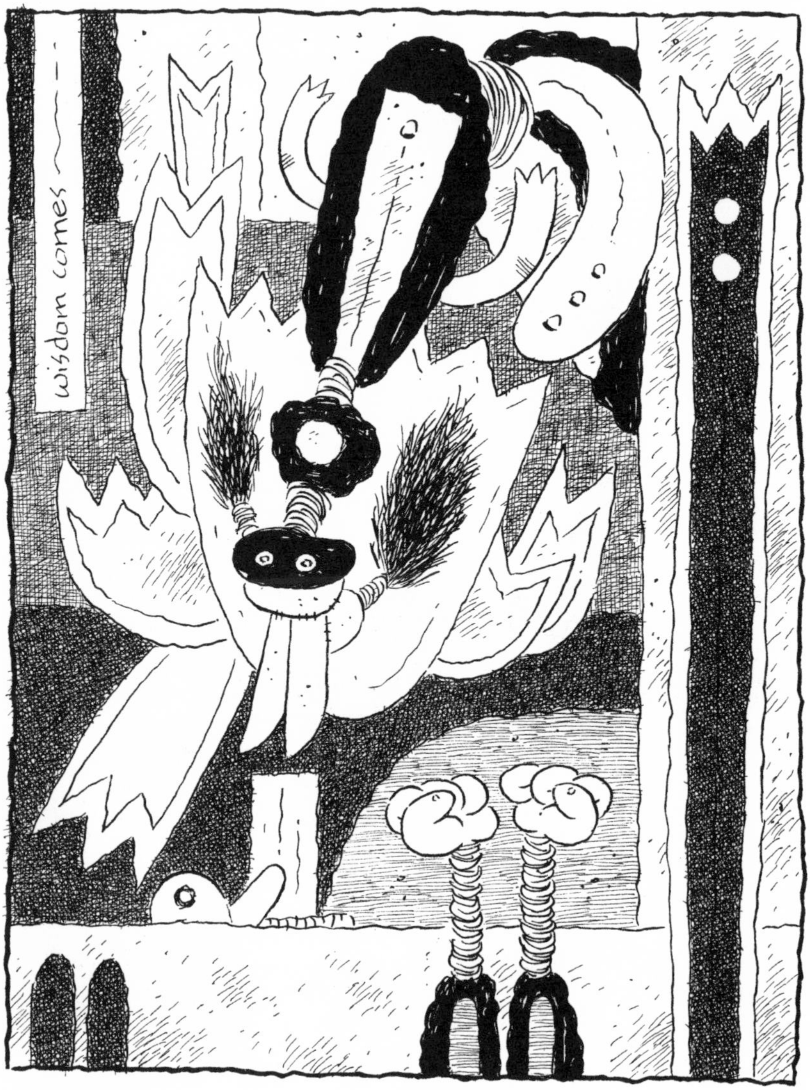
wisdom comes

Through the awful
grace
of
God

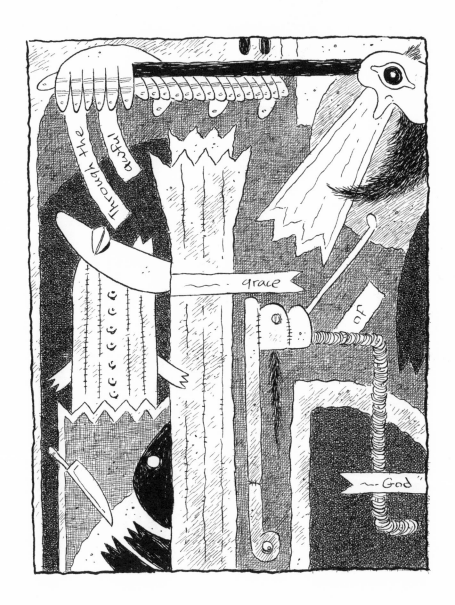

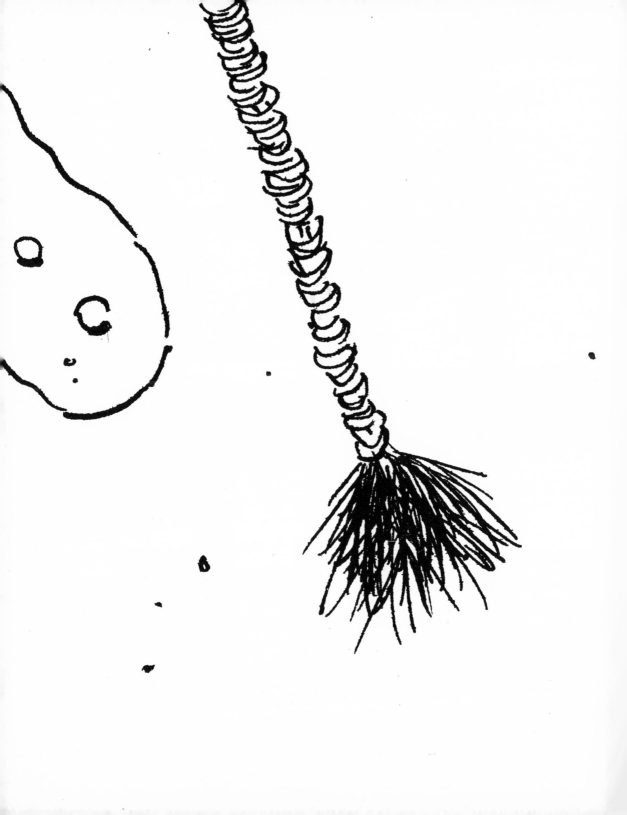